HOME IS SOMEWHERE ELSE

SUNY Series,
Margins of Literature

Mihai Spariosu, Editor

HOME IS SOMEWHERE ELSE

Autobiography in Two Voices

Desider Furst
and
Lilian R. Furst

STATE UNIVERSITY OF NEW YORK PRESS

Production by Ruth Fisher
Marketing by Bernadette LaManna

Published by
State University of New York Press, Albany

For information, address the State University of New York Press,
State University Plaza, Albany, NY 12246

Library of Congress Cataloging-in-Publication Data

Furst, Desider.
  Home is somewhere else:autobiography in two voices/Desider Furst
and Lilian R. Furst.
      p.   cm.—(SUNY series, margins of literature)
    ISBN 0-7914-1969-X (cloth:alk. paper).—ISBN 0-7914-1970-3
(pbk.:alk. paper)
    1, Furst, Desider. 2. Furst, Lilian R. 3. Jews—Austria—Vienna—
Biography. 4. Refugees, Jewish—England—Manchester—Biography.
I. Furst, Lilian R. II. Title. III. Series: SUNY series, the
margins of literature.
DS135.A93F873   1994
943.6'13004924—dc20
[B]   93-31274
                                                                        CIP

To

Stephen M. Ford, M.D.

For sharing this journey of exploration

CONTENTS

LIST OF ILLUSTRATIONS

PREFACE

$(L R_F)$

This is an experiment in dual autobiography with a father and daughter narrating the same set of dramatic experiences. It hinges on their flight from Vienna in 1938 and the stages of their relocation to Manchester, England. This centerpiece is embedded in a retrospective account of the father's life before 1938 and a continuation of the daughter's into adulthood.

The idea of such a dual autobiography was first suggested to me some years ago by a friend, Marilyn Yalom, who specializes in autobiography, biography, and gender. At that time I was not ready to embark on it. But after writing some shorter autobiographical pieces, including a professional life for a volume edited by Lionel Gossman and Mihai Spariosu, the idea gradually grew in my mind. I received encouragement from various friends, and a decisive impetus from the enthusiasm of my former student, Ester Zago.

My father had written his autobiography in the early 1970s after his retirement and our move to the United States. As a dental surgeon in Manchester, before the days of Musak, he would distract his patients from their treatment by story telling. He was a gifted raconteur, had led an eventful life, and also had a fund of anecdotal wisdom. One of his patients, the historian Eric Robinson, urged him to write it all down. That is what he did over the course of several years, eventually producing a 135 page manuscript, laboriously typed with two fingers on his tiny 1930s portable Olivetti.

I was glad he had found so absorbing an occupation while I was out teaching. I didn't read what he had written even after it was finished. Perhaps that seems a curious posture on my part. He never read any of my work either, and I didn't expect it. He would sometimes attend public lectures I gave on scholarly topics and assure me that the audience had been attentive and some of them had looked as if they understood. He didn't question me much about the substance of my work, although he once commented that he had known that one could earn one's living by writing novels, but was amazed that one could also do so by *reading* novels. We each had our separate spheres of interest: his were more in history, the world situation, and mechanics, mine primarily in literature and aesthetics. Respecting the differences, we lived quite happily as a joint household for the sixteen years between my mother's death in 1969 and his in 1985.

My ulterior reason for not reading his autobiography was my fear of disappointment and of hurting him by somehow betraying that response. Though an avid reader throughout his life and with a large vocabulary in English, his third language (Hungarian and German were his first and second), he had no experience of writing. His weekly letters to me during the fourteen years I was away from home were markedly laconic and lapidary, and led me not to have much faith in his literary abilities.

I was totally mistaken, as I found out when I finally did read his draft. In 1983, while we were at Harvard, a friend of his, Dante della Terza, wanted to read it, and I didn't like to let it out of the house without first taking a little look. I was astonished and fascinated. The narrative was organized into chapters under the names of the places where we had been. It was vivid, gripping, and moving in its directness, psychological perspicacity, and flashes of humor and irony. Its somewhat strange English did not detract from a certain poetic quality. A close friend in Dallas, the late Sally Ramsey, and her mother also read it and were equally impressed. In many ways a remarkable document of its time, it was deposited in a social history archive at London University. My father had some thoughts about publishing it, but didn't pursue the matter.

The immediate impetus to my own writing was the publication in July 1991 of *Between Two Worlds*, the autobiography of another friend, Susan Groag Bell, who had gone from Czechoslovakia to England and on to the United States. Her account of her experience of English boarding schools reminded me of my own in Chertsey, and in the few remaining days of that summer at Stanford I found myself writing about that episode in my life. Because the title was a place name, as in my father's manuscript, I suddenly saw the possibility of a dual autobiography in which the chapters interfaced by alternation: the child's impressions complemented by the adult's broader vision and fuller understanding. I wrote my sections on Vienna, Cologne, Brussels, London, Bedford, and Manchester without rereading my father's, of which I had, after an interval of eight years, only a vague recollection. When I then went back to his draft, I was struck by the emergent pattern of disparity within similarity. We were writing about the same happenings but from different points of view: mine largely the reactions of a child, limited in horizon, and torn between fear and hope; his the historically oriented perspective of a well informed adult with a sense of responsibility toward his family.

Both of us have written, to use his words, "as accurately and honestly as possible" from memory without having kept notes or a diary. I have not attempted to eliminate discrepancies between the two versions. For instance, in my account of our crossing the railroad bridge into Belgium I mention the presence of a dog, whereas my father doesn't. This puzzled me until I realized that the dog was there in my mind because I had heard that the

German border patrols used dogs to catch escapees.
I should add that since earliest childhood I have been
terrified of dogs. I left that detail because I am intent on
recording what was in my mind, and the dog was surely
an element of my fear. The discrepancies, differences of
perception, emphasis, and mood serve a central function
of diversifying, and thereby neutralizing the
repetitiveness that is the essence—and the potential
pitfall—of the dual voice method.

I have acted as a discreet editor to my father,
correcting occasional spelling mistakes and amplifying
slightly by adding footnotes at certain points for the sake
of clarity. I have also taken the liberty of making a few
cuts and of doing some rearrangement to ensure
continuity. But I have wanted to let his distinctive voice
come through, including his sometimes idiosyncratic turn
of phrase.

Just as his writing was a memorial to my mother,
mine is a tribute to him and to her for bringing me
through to safety. It is also, inevitably, in memoriam of all
those who perished. I am very aware, each time I teach
my course on the literary portrayal of adolescence in
twentieth century literature, just how close I came to the
fate of Anne Frank. My father's life story and mine, as
well as my mother's, which I sketch in outline in the
section, "The Silent Third Person," are particular to us in
specific details, yet at the same time typical of a certain
category of persons who happened to be in a certain part
of the world at a certain time. The often bizarre
intersection of historical configuration and personal fate is
the subtext of this narrative, which shows how individual
lives were reshaped into wholly unexpected directions by
the incursion of political turmoil.

My thanks to all who helped and encouraged me in
this endeavor by reading and responding to various
segments: Mechthild Cranston, Sheila and Terry Meyers,
the late Raymond Prier, Barbara Röder, Philip Winsor, as
well as Susan Dambrau and Alice Kuzniar. Madeline
Levine was an ideal reader, full of understanding and of
constructive suggestions. I am much indebted to Mihai

Spariosu for both his enthusiasm for the project and his meticulous editing in the final stages, and to my editor, Carola Sautter, for supporting this rather unusual endeavor. My deepest gratitude is to Stephen M. Ford, M.D. to whom this book is dedicated. He has gently and patiently nurtured and reinforced me so that I was able to face this scar tissue on my soul. If our escape from Austria in 1938 gave me a second lease on life, he has surely given me a third.

Chapel Hill,
Lilian R. Furst.

Introduction

There is an audience for autobiographies of famous people, curious to learn the motives for their actions and often interested in their personal lives. Politicians disclose the background of events; generals and admirals explain their battles; writers, explorers, actors and actresses. want to satisfy the curiosity of their admirers. The public waits eagerly for the disclosure of previously unknown facts and the background of past events. Such books are discussed in the press, find a ready readership, and then are quickly forgotten. It is a short harvest.

I don't belong to any of the above categories. I am an unknown man, a speck of dust in the universe, whose only ambition was to live a quiet, normal life among my friends and relatives. I represent ordinary people like myself, with one difference: nearly all of them perished. They were murdered. For historians they are merely numbers, not persons. I still see them as if they were alive.

This autobiography covers only part of the Holocaust, its beginnings, when not even the worst pessimists could imagine what would happen later. We lived only nine months in Nazi occupied Vienna before we managed to escape. We succeeded despite all the odds against us.

1

Who were we? A couple in their mid-thirties with a six-year old daughter, an inconspicuous family with a circle of friends and relatives. We had both qualified as doctors of medicine at the University of Vienna and specialized in dental surgery. We were not interested in politics and were not members of any political party. Our story is in fact not a unique one; it is that of a fairly large group of similar people. Sometimes it seems to me as if Destiny were running a lottery and we were winners. Why we? God only knows. Many better and more valuable people perished. We were all victims of an unprecedented upheaval, a gigantic hurricane that lifted us out of our homes and dropped us indiscriminately all over the world. We were nobody's responsibility, and where we landed was a matter of luck.

My wife and I had not had an easy task of establishing ourselves in Vienna, and we were looking forward to spending the rest of our lives there. We had a lovely home; we could earn our living and our future looked promising despite the troubled political and economic conditions in Austria. The great catastrophe occurred after the occupation of Austria by the Nazis.

We were unprepared and unfit to fight for our survival. We were no match to the task and had practically no chance to win. We were candidates for failure, and we were aware of it. Many single, strong, and determined persons came to grief. Still, we felt that we had at least to try to get out and away. Our situation was desperate.

The unfailing faith of my wife gave us the strength to carry on and try again and again after frustrations and setbacks. It was a miracle that we three somehow muddled through. Providence led us to helpful people when we were most in need of help. There are good people everywhere; one has to have the instinct to find them. My wife had that instinct.

This is a memorial to her.

Coming To Vienna

In September 1919 about twenty students traveled from the small Hungarian town of Sopron, where I had been born in 1900, to Vienna to begin their higher education. Most of them intended to study medicine. I was undecided. Scientific subjects were my favorites, and I was rather inclined to take up engineering as my profession. I changed my mind. Medicine would be interesting too, and I would be freer, my own master, not an employee. For a Jew this was an important consideration. I soon found that my technical ability and dexterity were indispensable requirements for a good physician—contrary to popular belief, it did not suffice merely to have bad handwriting in which to make out prescriptions. Since I had attended a technical school, I had to make up an exam in Latin by the end of my first year at the university. At that time I regarded it as a nuisance, but later in life I was glad that I had had to learn it. A lack of acquaintance with Latin would have been a serious gap in my education. My knowledge of German was none too satisfactory, either. However, my biggest handicap was my poverty.

For many years afterwards, when I remembered or talked about my student days, I would feel intense pangs of hunger, like a conditioned reflex. Our group of students, mainly from Hungary but with some from Poland, was, with a few exceptions, always hungry. It was a time of near famine in Vienna immediately after World War I, and the official food rations were insufficient to keep body and soul together. If I exercised the utmost restraint and self-control, my weekly bread ration lasted barely three days. We didn't have the means to buy food on the black market. The partly rotting apples that were sold from barges on the Danube canal were manna from heaven. The Mensa Academica Judaica (Jewish Academic Cafeteria), financed primarily by the American Joint Distribution Committee, fed us herring, dried beans, peas, and some sort of porridge. It was a blessing, though not enough in quantity, not to mention its quality. We often had to line up for an hour for this meager fare. There were just too many poor students who took their meals at the Mensa, which was in a cellar in the Alserstrasse. On those days when I had to do without breakfast, a cup of cocoa and a slice of cake was served, under a staircase, another generous gift of the American donors. For a while, Hitler's sister was one of our cooks.

Once the Mensa was completely wrecked by anti-Semitic students. The attack came unexpectedly, at a time when only the cooks and a few students were there. They fought back with herring missiles. Anti-Semitic students often prevented us from entering the main university building. They beat up those whom they caught inside and ejected them roughly. The building was under university jurisdiction, so that the police were not allowed to enter. Sometimes the police arrested those who had been thrown and kicked out.

Several times clothing and shoes came from the United States too. They lay in heaps in a room, and whatever we pulled out was potluck. There were lots of cutaways — just the right clothes for us! With the shoes it was even worse. There were odd shoes, and if one found a shoe that fitted, it was a hopeless task to dig out the other of the pair. A friend of mine attempted it. He took off one of his own shoes to try on others, and when he gave up, he had an unpleasant surprise—someone had mixed his shoe into the pile, and he was unable ever to spot it again.

We shivered in the unheated lecture rooms and in our "digs" (lodgings). I didn't have any heating facilities. One Jewish professor, M. Hajek, set up an arrangement in his hospital: we could use some cellars and passages there for study. It was a blessing, especially on weekends when all the libraries were closed. Those few of us who had some money studied in the coffeehouses.

We were about six hundred freshmen in medicine, and less than half qualified as doctors.[1] A number dropped out soon after they realized that the courses were too difficult for them; others were compelled to give up for financial reasons. They came from middle-class families who had become impoverished during and after the war [World War I]. Many were lured away by the prospect of making money quickly and easily. There was a kind of financial—but not economic—boom. Coffeehouses and inns were converted into private banks and currrency exchange offices. Some people made fortunes through financial speculation and manipulation. The paper money of the old Habsburg Monarchy could not be speedily replaced by the newly created states. The Austrians printed a complicated stamp over it and kept the value as it had been. Other states each valued and devalued the currency differently. There was a lot of smuggling from country to country according to the changed valuation. The Hungarians, for instance, put a primitive stamp over the money and devalued it by 50 percent: the banks gave fifty stamped Kronen (crowns) for every hundred unstamped ones. The stamp was soon forged, so that people could get their money stamped privately at a discount of 10 percent. Bonds and shares were more complicated but very profitable for those who knew the ins and outs and were willing to take risks. It was a time of bliss for financial jugglers and swindlers. Some of my colleagues lost their money, repented, and returned to medical school.

I remember the financial adventure of one of my colleagues who bought a kilo (two pounds) of saccharin from a stranger. This was a rare commodity. In a doorway he tasted a small sample and paid a large sum for it. When he opened the parcel at home, it turned out to be some tasteless white powder. He told us what had happened, expecting some sympathy, but he became a laughingstock instead. We poor ones were spared this sort of temptation. It took a few years for the financial and economic conditions to settle. The private banks were changed back into coffeehouses, and the trading firms melted away. Many of the prospective doctors lost their wealth, and ended up with neither money nor a diploma.

It still puzzles me how I stuck it out and carried on with my studies. I was young and determined to make a success of what I had started. Was I waiting for a miracle to improve my situation? I don't know and can't explain it. TB scars on my chest X-rays are the hidden evidence of those grim years.

I would never have dared to embark on such a long course of study at the University of Vienna without the encouragement of the father of a fellow student from Sopron. I coached the son for several years, and we were close friends, too. He was a likeable and gifted boy from a wealthy family. His parents had lived in Vienna before moving to Sopron, where they owned a factory. They wanted their son to study medicine in Vienna. The father asked me to keep an eye on him, and arranged a private scholarship for me among his affluent business partners. A moderate sum, it was a fortune to me. Alas, it lasted only through the first year. The son let us down. He enjoyed his unrestricted freedom and was introduced by some new friends to the social life of Vienna. I rarely saw him at the university, and my warnings fell on deaf ears. He got involved in a love affair with a girl, and after a sham suicide attempt he dropped out. That was the end of my financial support.

I spent the summer vacation at home in Sopron, earning some money by teaching and studying for my impending exams. During that time I escaped by a hair's

breadth being drafted into the Hungarian army. A number
of my friends and I had received invitations to meet the
mayor of our town. What an honor, we thought. At the
town hall we were herded into a room and ordered to strip
for a physical examination. There was a recruiting
committee, and those who were deemed fit—nearly all of
us—had to sign a form that we were volunteering for the
army. I protested, showed my university card, and was
exempted. All the others had to serve in the army for at
least a year—an army made up solely of volunteers, in
accordance with the Versailles peace treaty!

The connections I had made during my first year
were very helpful when I returned to Vienna for the
second year. I managed to find cheap "digs" in Hernals, a
working class suburb, and free meal tickets from the
American Joint Distribution Committee. I was kept going
by coaching my fellow students and by translating from
French into Hungarian and German such things as the
instructions for the then-new permanent waving
procedures. As neither my French nor my German was
very good, I sometimes wonder how those permanents
turned out!

I was recommended to be the tutor and mentor to a
ten-year-old boy from a wealthy family. I spent the
weekends at their home, and in addition to some payment,
I got my meals. It was a happy family and he was a bright
boy. Unfortunately, half a year later his father died after
an appendectomy.

Quite a number of my friends were in an equally
miserable position. We decided to form an "Association of
Hungarian Students" with the subtitle "Victims of the
numerus clausus.² Some well-known personalities in
Budapest, including a member of parliament, took up our
cause and agreed to support us. Soon Jewish
congregations throughout Hungary were raising funds for
us. I was on the executive committee and we distributed
the money as fairly as possible. These sums, though
modest, were a godsend.

My people helped me as much as they could, but they
had to struggle to make ends meet. When I was sixteen,

my father died at an early age after a long illness. My two elder brothers were penniless emigrants to Brazil, my two sisters worked as office clerks, and my youngest brother, a highly intelligent fellow, became a carpenter and furniture maker after finishing high school. He deserved a higher education, but we couldn't afford it.

Several times I was on the verge of giving up my studies and taking an office job, it would have solved all my problems. Still, I passed the exams without any difficulty, I made a number of friends, and despite all the misery, I came to love Vienna. Being poor as a church mouse, I was of no interest to the sweet Viennese girls, and having so many worries, I didn't miss them either. There were however, some very clever girls among my fellow students, and I enjoyed their company at the university and the libraries. My depressive moods disappeared and I carried on.

My hardest time was in September 1922, when I could barely scrape together the small sum necessary to return to Vienna. Then I struck oil! By chance I met a friend who was a student of commerce and business administration. He had a part-time job with a Hungarian transport firm which he wanted to give up, and was looking for a successor. I gladly accepted his offer, and this solved my problems nicely for the next two years, until the firm closed down. I never actually met my bosses, Messrs. Gyenes and Markovics. I had an office at 5 Rotenturmstrasse near St. Stephen's cathedral, where I went several times a week to collect my instructions and the firm's mail. Once or twice a month I had to travel to Gänsersdorf, on the Vienna–Budapest railroad line, to a yarn factory that was located nearby. I had to take over some fifteen or twenty crates destined for the Textile Manufacturing Company in Vacz near Budapest. Under my supervision they were transported to the railroad station and loaded into a wagon. I had to note the wagon's number and send telegrams to a Mr. Kósa in Hegyeshalom (the first station over the border in Hungary) and also to the customs office. I had to inform them that wagon no. X was on the way to Hungary. Then I would return to

Vienna and send a report to the firm's headquarters in Budapest. Each time it took me the better part of a day. My commission depended on the number of crates, and my payments arrived promptly. I earned just enough to exist without neglecting my studies—it wasn't difficult to get away from the university for the odd day. There was something mysterious about the firm, but it wasn't my business to be nosy. My guess is that the firm had special connections with the Hungarian customs office.

My next problem was to pass the twelve final exams. It took nine months, from September, 1925 to June, 1926, and during that time I had scant savings and no earnings. Without the help of my younger brother, who had a good job by then, I could hardly have managed it. We were a close family, ready to help each other if one of us was in trouble.

I considered myself extremely fortunate. Some of my colleagues contracted tuberculosis, others went insane or committed suicide. One of the saddest cases was that of a fine young man who jumped out of a hospital window. He broke some limbs, but his life was saved. It was heartbreaking to see him dragging about on crutches. Another one, Dr. Hajnal, studied under appalling conditions, and when he finished, drowned himself in the Danube. Most of my close friends struggled through, and some went on to remarkable careers in various parts of the world.

I was now nearly twenty-five years old, a qualified M.D. from the University of Vienna, and without any means whatsoever. I couldn't practice in Austria, Hungary, or any other part of the world.[3] The future looked very bleak indeed. When I spoke of my predicament to the head of the Rothschild Hospital in Vienna, where I was working as an unpaid volunteer in the department of internal medicine, he replied: "You are a superfluous man."[4] That hurt me badly. I was determined to fight for a place in the sun.

That was when, with borrowed money, I started my training as a dental surgeon.[5] Dentistry appealed to me as a mixture of medicine and engineering, with a lot of scope for my instincts as a "fixer." It was hard to get into the Dental School, but I received a personal invitation from two professors who had evidently recognized my potential. Besides, they too had come from Hungary. While still in training myself, I gave theoretical instruction to two colleagues who had not yet gained admission. They got their practical training with a dental surgeon and set up practices in the suburbs. Both made a good living.[6]

I was determined to stay in Vienna and pursue my naturalization as an Austrian citizen, which I eventually got in 1928 through a friend of my father's who had the right political contacts. One day I read an advertisement that a dentist urgently needed an assistant. He interviewed me the next day and offered me the job. When I confessed to him that, as an alien I was not entitled to practice, his answer was that his only interest was in my competence as a dentist. I worked in that practice for nearly a year. It was a mass practice, and I learned there how not to practice dentistry. I needed the money badly. The head of the group would let us juniors do the hard part of preparing the fillings by excavating the decayed areas, and then would come in and tell the patient: "I can personally put the filling in for you—for a small extra charge."

My future wife was working as a volunteer at the dental hospital. She had come to Vienna in 1914 from her hometown of Buczacz in the province of Galicia not far from the Russian frontier. As the defeated Austro-Hungarian army retreated, starved, exhausted, with blood seeping through their bandages, panic spread among the population at the prospect of a Russian occupation. My wife's family fled with six children, ranging in age from four to twenty. It happened so suddenly and unexpectedly that they had to leave everything they couldn't carry. It took an adventurous journey of two weeks before they reached Vienna. This experience had made such an impression on the young, meticulously clean girl that she swore never to become a refugee again. The refugees were disliked by the Viennese authorities and the general population. Still, her family somehow managed to settle in.

My wife had long dreamed of studying medicine, but her parents did not favor this goal. A girl from an Orthodox Jewish family should get married at the first reasonable opportunity; that was the tradition. Since they couldn't make her change her mind, they reluctantly agreed. We met in medical school, but I, in my charity cut-down cutaway[7] and shabby leather leggings, was far too poor and provincial to dare approach her. Once, at a student outing, I danced with her.

After my Austrian citizenship was granted, we decided to get married. This was in September 1928. The following ten years were the happiest of our lives, despite Austria's economic and political problems. Then the Nazis occupied the country.

Vienna

(LRF)

My first distinct independent memory is of the day the Nazis marched into Vienna in March 1938. March in Vienna is usually rather cold, gray, and inhospitable, but on that day the sun was shining and the sky was of the deep blue I now associate with North Carolina or California. I remember so well leaning out of the window of our apartment on the Maria-Theresienstrasse trying to see what was going on on the Schottenring, part of Vienna's inner circular road, at the end of our street. Around the corner was the Berggasse, where Freud lived. Because of the freak warmth the windows were wide open, double windows with special padded cushions like tiny mattresses between them to keep out the cold. It was already unusual that I, a small six-year old, should have been allowed to lean out of the fifth-floor window alone. Normally my nanny or some other adult was there to make sure I didn't fall out. But nothing was normal that day; everyone was so preoccupied that I was left to my own devices. Both the maids had gone out to join the crowds, while my parents huddled in their office, conferring in whispers.

I had no understanding whatsoever of the scene being enacted before my eyes. I had heard politics discussed, and I knew that my nanny held such strong views (for or against whom or what?) that my parents feared for our safety, lest she express them too loudly to the other nannies and their charges, whom we met in the park every day. I had picked up slogans from her which I proclaimed like a parrot. But that had all been mere talk, and now here there was action: soldiers marching in formation, dignitaries in motorcades waving to the cheering bystanders, bands playing military music, and chants of "Heil Hitler!" The public jubilation outside was in stark contrast with the silence within. The daily round of life had ceased in the face of this event that I was witnessing. The pervasive atmosphere of mourning in our home was eerie and ominous. I felt uneasy, not knowing what would come next. The security of my childhood had been violated once and for all, although it is only in retrospect that I have come to realize that from that day on things would never be the same. It is a landmark in European history and in the lives of all who experienced it.

I had often before hung out of that same window early on summer mornings. That I remember clearly. My father would hold me as we looked out together and explain that it would be a fine day because the swallows were flying high. Then we would go out before breakfast, across the road to a little tobacco store to buy the newspaper. My father was always an avid newspaper reader; when asked what he did, I used to say "A,B,C." In the evenings at the coffeehouse he would read the *Frankfurter Allgemeine*, the *Neue Zürcher Zeitung*, and the *Manchester Guardian*, the reassuring liberal papers. He later commented ruefully that he should have been perusing the *Völkischer Beobachter*, the Nazi organ, to find out what was going on. It's strange that newspapers were not delivered in Vienna, while fresh rolls were brought to the door at dawn. I loved that little morning walk; it felt good to be out in the fresh air and to have my hand held tightly in my father's secure grip.

With many other experiences I can't distinguish what I remember from what I was subsequently told. I still have an album with photographs of myself from about ten days of age on up. I was an only child and my father was an enthusiastic photographer, so there are pictures galore of me: lying on the dining room table when I could just hold my head up; standing up flat-footed and knock-kneed; in a bathing robe in Baden, a resort near Vienna; in an Indian feathered headdress; in a Red Riding Hood costume; on a tricycle; with my mother and my aunt; with my nanny; with my grandfather holding his prayerbook above my head; on a toboggan with my father on the Semmering, a mountain resort where we would go in winter. There are many pictures that record my childhood, each with its own story, but none in my own memory except such flashes as the morning walk.

By all accounts it was an enchanted, almost fairy-tale childhood as long as I remained unaware of the world beyond my family and friends. I had immediately been named *die kleine Fürstin* (the little princess) by the nurses in the exclusive Sanatorium Löw where I had been born. The names I was given by my parents, Lilian Renée, are an equivalent of my Hebrew name, Rachelea. My mother was Sarah, my aunt, Rebecca, and so my grandfather wanted the third of the Biblical matriarchy for his first grandchild, to which Lea was added in memory of my great-grandmother. The translation into Lilian Renée, an English and a French name to complement my German family name, reflects a certain international consciousness. My names, through slightly unusual in Austria, would stand me in good stead worldwide. Indeed, I believe that I was born into what was to become my profession, Comparative Literature.[1]

Cosmopolitanism was ingrained in my parents, who had both come to Vienna from other parts of the pre-1914 Habsburg Monarchy (our laundry in the 1930s continued, incongruously, to be called the Habsburg laundry!). By the time I was born in June 1931, all their struggles seemed to be over; my parents had established a dental practice after their marriage in 1928 in the large apartment that my mother's eldest brother Robert had acquired and furnished for her as she was completing her medical studies. When they were listed in the Viennese telephone book, they later told me, they believed they had made it for life—provided they could drum up enough patients in such a highly competitive medical market.

Their future seemed as assured as it could be in the Europe of the 1930s, still under the shadow of the devastating German inflation from the previous decade, not to mention the first stirrings of the Nazi movement. My parents were delighted that I was a native Viennese. While they had grown to love the city for its rich cultural offerings, its graceful beauty, and its pleasant climate, they would always remain, at some level, outsiders. In contrast to the American tradition of welcoming newcomers to the melting-pot, the Viennese were skeptical of "Zugeraste," the derogatory distortion of *Zugereiste* (new arrivals). They would make bitter jokes that Vienna was populated by *Herzogowiener* and *Buckowiener* (people from the provinces of the Hapsburg Monarchy) rather than genuine *Wiener* (Viennese). The prejudice against Eastern Jews was particularly strong despite their signal contribution to the city's artistic and intellectual life. Yet these prejudices were taken as the price one had to pay for the privilege of living in this wonderful city, a disagreeable facet of the Austrian tradition, which did not, however, seem immediately menacing.

I had a nanny to look after me because my mother quite naturally wanted to continue in her profession. My nanny was hired several months before I was born, and arrived when I was brought home at ten days of age. It was a big step for her to come to Vienna from the small town where her father was mayor. She had had formal training in infant care, and was proud to wear her grey uniform with its white starched apron and a long blue headcovering, rather like a nun's. Since I was her first charge, she tried to bring me up by the book. This led to a number of confrontations with my father, who thought her to be of limited intelligence, and would have liked to get rid of her. One hot summer's day I came back from the park very thirsty, and nanny wouldn't let me drink more than two glasses of water. When she herself wanted to drink more at lunch, my father stopped her. I think she got the message. She certainly stood in some awe of him, and he made it clear that he and my mother would have the last word on my upbringing. Nanny slept in the nursery with me, cooked and washed for me, even carried my handkerchief so that I would have to run to her to have my nose blown! I both loved and feared her. She was tall and gaunt, but I thought her beautiful. I could say her name, "Teta" (and "Papa") before I managed "Mama," which caused a good deal of jealousy. In a way I had two mothers: strict, plain Teta for everyday, and gentle, elegant Mama, hovering in the background, sometimes occupied by her patients, but always there at bedtime and weekends. Because it was such a treat and a privilege for us to be together, we developed a very fine relationship, really a friendship that persisted into my adulthood. My nanny's impact, on the other hand, was mixed—in the long run my father was right. For sure, my early battles with her turned me into the strong-willed person I am. She also inculcated the value of discipline and self-discipline. "A little girl who wants to look nice must put up with a certain amount of discomfort," she would tell me as she curled my fine straggly hair with heated tongs. But she harmed me by threatening that a big black dog—or a man—would come if I didn't go to sleep quickly. Fortunately, I ended up fearing dogs, and not men.

Teta stayed until I was five, although by then I was going to a Montessori kindergarten in the mornings. I loved playing with the other children and the splendid messes we made with paint and plasticine. When I came home at lunchtime, Teta would strip me to the skin and put a whole set of fresh clothes on me. She was opposed to the kindergarten, believing that I would only pick up germs and bad habits. My mother took no notice of her grumpiness or her insistence on changing my clothes: if she wanted to do all that extra washing, let her!

When she left, she went to an Indian family in England, and eventually moved with them to Ceylon, where she married a German engineer and had three children of her own.

She was succeeded by a nursemaid. The first one didn't last long. She complained how lazy and whining I was, dragging my feet on the way back from the park. It turned out that she had put the wrong shoe on the wrong foot. She was peremptorily dismissed, and followed by Ridi, a smiling young woman, who got the shoes right, but later married a vehement Nazi. After the war, in which her brother lost a leg at Stalingrad, she thought less well of the glorious life she had led for a while.

I recall the daily, weekly, and annual rhythm of our lives during my childhood. My father saw his patients in the office in our home in the mornings, and in the afternoons worked in a clinic for bank employees. My mother would supervise the household, go to the dressmaker or milliner in the mornings, and see her patients in the afternoons. All our clothes were made for us. Besides a tailor and a shoemaker for my father, we patronized no fewer than three dressmakers: a seamstress who came every couple of weeks to sew my clothes, lingerie, and household linens; a moderately-priced dressmaker who made most of my mother's wardrobe; and a fancy one who went to see the Paris fashion collections, and who would provide one or two special outfits each season. Far from being snobbery, this represented thrift, for ready-made garments were considered expensive and ill-fitting. My days were spent with my nanny in the park, where I played with my regular friends, escorted by their nannies. Sometimes I would meet patients on their way in or out. I had my favorites among them and my dislikes, especially an obstetrician who would leave a trail of sickly sweet scent. Following European etiquette, they would want to shake hands with me, but I often held mine behind my back and explained that they were already washed for eating and so I mustn't touch anything. In the evenings, after a hasty supper and good night to me, my parents almost invariably would go to one of the coffeehouses to meet friends. The coffeehouse was, of course, a great Viennese institution, where one could sit for hours for the price of a cup of coffee, play chess, read the newspapers, or just chat. Many people had their *Stammlokal* (habitual haunt); my parents generally went to the Hotel Sacher. There were literary, artistic, and political coffeehouses, and in summer, open-air ones. The habit of going to coffeehouses was fostered by the city's relatively small size, safe streets, good public transportation, and moderate climate. To entertain at home was a rarity. Some evenings my parents would go to the opera, the theater, or the cinema before the coffee-house.

Once I too was taken to the theater, to see a matinée of *Peter Pan*. For this special occasion I wore the most elegant clothes of my childhood: a navy blue velvet skirt and bolero with a white blouse that had red smocking on the front. There was also a matching navy blue velvet coat and a hat with ribbons hanging down the back. I was so excited that I took in little of the play itself, but the Viennese theater and all the ceremony attendant on the performance made a great impression on me. During the intermission we walked in a gallery hung with portraits of dramatists and famous actors and actresses who had appeared there. In another area of the foyer, tiny, dainty sandwiches and desserts were being served with all sorts of beverages. This was the world I, a native Viennese, was to inherit. I would skip up and down the steps at the front of the university, declaring that Papamama had gone there and so would I. Naturally, I would study medicine (what else?) and most probably marry one of my park companions, settling down to a life that was a continuation of my parents'. That was my expectation.

On Friday evenings my mother's entire family congegrated at my grandparents' apartment for dinner. I would meet my two cousins there, both somewhat younger than I, and we would romp between a pair of sofas, jumping on and off with great glee, while the adults sat around an oval table. Candles were lit, and there was a festive atmosphere. Both sides of my family were fairly orthodox in their observance of Judaism; our household was kosher, with strict separation of milk and meat and with different sets of dishes and cooking utensils, as well as extra sets for Passover. The maids were trained in these practices, which become second nature once one grows accustomed to them. My grandmother often sent over delicacies, but on the whole we ate modestly and abstemiously because of my father's recurrent gallstones. Indeed, the maids would complain now and then that the gentry's diet was inadequate for them and would bring in extras, which couldn't be put onto our plates if they were such a non-kosher item as ham.

On Saturday afternoons my mother and grandmother and I would go to Gerstner's, a famous pastry shop on the Kärtnerstrasse, the central, elegant shopping street. My father, a soccer fan, would go to the game. On Sundays my uncle Robert would often take us in his car for a day in the mountains or at some nearby scenic spot. Sometimes he took us out to lunch in a hotel, although I preferred a picnic in a meadow. That was about as much contact as I had with the "country" as a child; we didn't keep any pets either. In late spring we would visit my father's family in Sopron for a few days. Once a year we went to Karlsbad, in Czechoslovakia, for my father to take the waters to keep the gallstones at bay. In summer we would take a vacation for a week or two, gradually going further afield as I grew older. Our last vacation, in 1937, was in Italy, where I learned to swim. Christmas was time for the Semmering, where we stayed at a hotel owned by the bank employees' clinic for which my father worked. There were Christmas festivities with delicious cookies and a big tree. I knew it wasn't our holiday; I would rewrap my Hanukah gifts, have them put under the tree, and pretend they were a surprise.

Once, when I was two and a half, I was asked by a little boy in the park whether we had a Christmas tree, and I answered no. At that he shouted, "Then you must be a Jew!" I had no idea what the word meant, but it sounded so dreadful, like being a leper, that I wept for a week. It was no consolation to be told that Papamama (as I called my parents in a collective noun), my grandparents, all our family, and most of our friends were also Jews. Only when nanny said she was Jewish (which she wasn't) did I begin to become reconciled to my fate. That was my introduction to the most basic fact of my life.

Everything changed after that day in March 1938 when I watched the parade. I don't recall the exact sequence of the changes; they started slowly, yet within a few months had accelerated alarmingly. No more outings to Gerstner or the coffeehouse or the theater for my parents. German Jews we had met in Karlsbad in the mid-1930s had assured us that things were not so bad, that the Nazis' bark was worse than their bite, that one should lie low until this blew over, for the regime was so extreme that it could not possibly last in a rational, civilized nation. The maids had to leave, forbidden to work for Jews; they were tearful and aggrieved at losing good jobs. I was forced to transfer from the local elementary school, where I had started the previous autumn, to a school solely for Jews. It was down the hill from my first school; my former classmates would run at us as we came out, throwing stones and shouting invectives. My new first grade teacher was an elderly professor of zoology, dismissed from his university post on account of his racial impurity. He had no idea how to handle six-year-olds; he would read us stories, play his violin, and beg us to be good. We soon understood that we had to make the best of a bad situation. The class grew smaller and smaller as children disappeared mysteriously: into emigration or concentration camps?

"Concentration camp" was one of the terms in a whole new vocabulary I acquired. Exit permit, visa, arrest, disappearances, half-Jew, quarter-Jew, foreign currency— not the usual concerns of seven-year-olds, nor did I understand it all. But I sensed that we were very unwelcome, in danger, groping frantically for a way out but to where? to what? The stable routine of my life was replaced by a constant improvisation that brought an aching sense of uncertainty. Once law-abiding, tax-paying Austrian citizens, we had suddenly become undesirables, enemies of the state because of the religion into which we

had been born. The mood in our home was muted, with
conspiratorial telephone conversations and many rumors
flying. I knew that I had to keep quiet, literally and
metaphorically. We listened in fear for the steps of the
storm troopers along the corridor, and opened the door
only to the agreed family signal, three staccato rings of
the bell.

One scene from those days sticks in my mind as
particularly bizarre: I saw my parents burning books. We
had a huge, tiled slow-combustion stove in the hall, which
burned all winter and heated the entire apartment. Into
its mouth my parents were feeding stacks of books. It was
an almost uncanny sight for me, an emblem of the
overthrow of the normal order of things. Books had always
been treated with a loving respect in our home as the most
faithful friends. This riddance of books banned by the
Nazis struck me like some horrible sacrificial act, as
indeed it was.

Two events made clear the seriousness of our
situation, marking the point of no return, when we
realized that we would have to leave the country. One was
the promulgation of a law in September 1938 that barred
Jews from practicing any profession, so that we lost our
livelihood. The wealthy, who had foreign accounts, had left
early without much ado, to wait and see how things
developed from the safety of neutral ground. Similarly,
those who had neither money nor a trade could move on
more readily than doctors, dentists, and lawyers, whose
qualifications were worthless elsewhere. So the middle
class was the most reluctant to leave. Nor was it easy.
Paradoxically, the Nazis wanted to be rid of the Jews, yet
invented innumerable obstacles to emigration. You had to
have not only a current passport, but also certificates that
your rent, gas, electricity, telephone, and taxes were fully
paid, that you were not abandoning any property, and that
you didn't have a relative in an insane asylum as a burden
to the state. Each of these certificates was valid for only
one month, so that it was virtually impossible to get them
all together at the same time. Hardest of all to obtain was
a visa to another country; no one wanted us.

Besides the forced closing of the practice, the strongest impetus for us to emigrate came from the arrest of my two eldest uncles. Highly respected members of the Chamber of Commerce who were often asked to adjudicate disputes between businesses, my uncles were all of a sudden clapped into jail without charge. I cannot find words to describe the reaction of the rest of the family—consternation? panic?—every term seems too weak for the terror that hit us. If they were deported from the local jail to a concentration camp, as they likely would be within a few days, they were lost. I know nothing of the negotiations for their release, except that the Nazis were short of money and these two uncles were wealthy. In return for a sizable donation to the Nazi Party, they were not only released from jail, but also allowed to leave Austria. They flew to London the same day. My grandparents and aunt took a trip to Paris, and from there went on to London, too. My two younger uncles, one with his family, left by using false Czech passports, posing as tourists to England.

By mid-autumn of 1938 only we were still stranded in Vienna. My father had hopes of a visa to Australia, where able-bodied, educated men were needed. I was registered for a "children's transport" which would take me to a family in Norwich, England, that was willing to bring me up alongside their own daughter, a girl of my age. They sent us a picture of themselves, which I viewed with a singular lack of enthusiasm, despite the kindness of their letter. And where was my mother to go? It was decided that we had to stick together, come what might. This was a crucial and, as it turned out, wise decision, for so many families who split up were never reunited, and the survivors felt unending guilt. But psychological damage of one kind or another seems to have been inescapable. I came to regard my parents as the sole sure protection from a hostile world. Even now, an American citizen, tenured in a major university, holder of an endowed chair, with savings, investments, disability insurance, a retirement pension, a beautiful house, a car, a long list of publications; still I am liable to agonies of anxiety and insomnia because, alone, at some level, I still feel so terribly vulnerable to the contingencies of an untrustworthy world.

I cling to our furniture because, in an oblique way, it saved us. All Jewish property was declared state-owned, although it was permissible to buy one's possessions back. Obviously, this was another fund-raising maneuver. Since we couldn't take more than ten German Marks (about $5.00?) each out of the country, the furniture and dental equipment were bought back and shipped in several large crates to London (a somewhat irrational step as we had no prospect then of going there). Perhaps the family could make capital out of it; perhaps we were beyond rationality. I remember wandering about disconsolately the day the packers came. A move always denotes a break and therefore has a bleak aspect, but usually this is balanced by anticipation of a new start elsewhere. We faced a blank.

We moved with a few clothes into the apartment of my uncle Robert, who had gone by taxi from prison to the airport, stopping only to pick up three suitcases, stacked one inside the other, all empty except for a large bottle of his favorite mouthwash. The customs and immigration officials at Croydon airport were perplexed by this visitor, but accepted his explanation of his bewilderment. It then fell to my father to make parcels of suits, shirts, shoes, socks, and ties to send to England. Then, one dark, foggy November day he returned from the post office with a horrendous tale: the temples were on fire, which acounted for the heavy odor of smoke. Jewish shops were being looted, and Jews made to go down on their knees to scrub the sidewalks with toothbrushes. It was hard to believe; it was Crystal Night. We escaped the roundup because we had moved. When police came to fetch us from our apartment in the Maria-Theresienstrasse, we had gone. We were at my uncle's in a house that he owned, and his janitor remained loyal to him by declaring the place "*judenrein*" (clean of Jews). We sat in the dark, glum and silent, not even daring to turn the radio on. The oppressiveness of that day is my second totally clear memory.

That was the day on which my parents, like many others, recognized that we had to try to escape illegally. Our only visa was for Liberia, which we couldn't reach because no other countries would grant us transit visas, fearing that people would jump train on the way. Among the myriad rumors circulating was one that seemed so farfetched as hardly to warrant attention: that England was prepared to admit forty Austrian dentists. So as to leave no stone unturned, my father put in his application, thinking it a very long shot.

We waited until shortly before Christmas, planning to travel under the cover of the holiday traffic. I went to school that day as usual, and said not a word to anyone. Late that night we were in a station crowded with soldiers going on leave. With minimal luggage, the three of us boarded a train going west: desperadoes in flight, without an itinerary or a destination.

Flight From Vienna

It was two days before Christmas of the year 1938. We were waiting in the large hall of Vienna's west railroad station for the train to Cologne, which was due to leave at 7 p.m. Snow had been falling all day, and we were told that the train would be delayed owing to snowdrifts along the route. We were not upset; we were in no particular hurry to get anywhere—it only meant a longer journey and probably some discomfort. Our train was due to arrive in Cologne at noon the following day. The hall was packed with people. We were jostled by the noisy, excited crowd, and we must have looked like a small island of gloom in their midst. We felt as if we were going into some darkness, some perilous adventure which was our last hope of escape to freedom. We had failed to secure an entry visa or permit anywhere in the world. We had tried hard and would have grabbed any opportunity to go anywhere and live in peace. I was willing to do any work to earn our living.

A great many German soldiers, burdened by heavy luggage and shouldering their rifles, elbowed their way through the masses of civilians. They were obviously going home to Germany for Christmas. Some were seen off

by their girlfriends. There were some civilians whose
appearance betrayed that they too were Germans. They
stood there with their wives and children and looked
disapprovingly at the soldiers' boisterous, conspicuously
loud behavior. Some of these civilians literally barricaded
themselves with suitcases and parcels as a protective
wall. They knew that they were more disliked than the
soldiers and mutely resented by the Austrians. They had
come as administrators to bring some order to the sloppily
conducted Austrian affairs and to link its economy to that
of the *Reich* (the German Empire) for their "mutual
benefit," as the official phrase went. These "brothers from
the Empire" took charge of all important government
departments. At first, they were disliked and later on,
hated passionately. They descended upon Austria like a
swarm of locusts and siphoned off all the country's assets.
The manners of the *Herrenvolk* (master nation) alienated
them from the population, even from their formerly
ardent supporters, who felt ignored and disappointed.
They belittled everything Austrian with a contemptuous
superiority; they knew everything better, and were
incredibly rude if anyone dared to oppose them. It was a
sobering awakening for many who had been looking
forward to the *Anschluss* (the joining of Austria to
Germany). The whole country was under the thumb of
these emissaries. The Austrians, including many long-
standing members of the Nazi party, didn't dare to
complain. Their old Jewish friends were the ones to whom
they could open their hearts. We had quite a number of
old friends who came to us with their laments. But it was
too late. We felt no satisfaction in hearing their troubles.
We had our own worries. We never complained to them; it
would have been useless, and possibly even dangerous.

The sweet smell of perspiration pervaded everything
in the crowded waitingroom, and it was a great relief
when we could at last get on the train. I carried a small
suitcase and a blanket; my wife held the hand of our little
daughter, who firmly clutched her most precious
possession, her schoolbag. She was the calmest among us,
watching the noisy, laughing, milling crowd. She knew

that we were leaving Vienna because we were unwanted. She had experienced the transformation of our lives, watched our worried faces, and listened to our conversations. She was too young to comprehend fully what was going on around her. She trusted her parents to make the right decisions, and she knew that the reason for all these upheavals was that we were Jewish.

When the Nazis had come to Vienna, many things in our lives had changed. We had left our apartment after sending our furniture and dental equipment to England, and by October 1938 had moved into an apartment in a building owned by my eldest brother-in-law. So we were not only protected from losing the roof over our heads, but also away from our old address where the Nazis had looked for me at the time of the Crystal Night. By that time all the members of my wife's family except us had managed to get out of Austria. Our daughter had to leave her school and transfer to another one for Jewish children. She had been to school that very morning, and had even done her homework for the next day.

When Austria was occupied, we expected our lifestyle to change for the worse. We had no illusions, having heard what had been going on in Germany. It was bad there, but despite the humiliations, it was bearable. A very slender hope still existed that things might slowly turn for the better. After the *Anschluss* things got worse there too. The storm was not blowing over, as the optimists had predicted. Wealthy people made preparations in good time and left Austria to watch from abroad what would happen. Who could blame them? Some poor Jews, who had struggled to earn a livelihood, left as well. They had only to sell their few movable possessions before emigrating. At that time the world was still open to holders of Austrian passports without the need for visas.

We had a regular "customer,"(i.e., beggar) an old Jew who had devoted his life to religious study. He usually came at the end of each month for his money. He appeared one day, not at his normal time, to put a proposition to us: we should pay him his "dues" for at least six months in advance because he was leaving Vienna to go to Paris. We agreed, and asked him what he would do there. After all, he had his regular supporters in Vienna. "What a question!" he exclaimed in surprise, "The same as here. I shall find supporters there, too." For us and the majority of doctors, lawyers, accountants, bank employees, and small businessmen, it was not so simple.

My first impulse was to go to my relatives in Hungary until the situation became clearer, but the border was closed almost instantly. It wouldn't have solved our problems in the long run, anyway. We decided to stay and wait and see. One day the eyes of the clever and cultivated Germans would be opened up; they would not and could not tolerate for too long these barbarians who would discredit the name and reputation of Germany before the civilized world. We loved living in Vienna, we loved our home, and we would not give up everything in a fit of panic.

A few days after the Nazis' entry I received a letter from the executives of the clinic where I had worked for seven years. I was dismissed forthwith because I could not fulfil the stipulations of the Nuremberg laws. The letter was signed by the president who, with his wife, had been my patient for years. In recognition for my past services I was given three months' salary. This was very decent of them, since they were not obligated to pay me anything.

In April 1938, the Austrians held a plebiscite to have the *Anschluss* approved and legalized. Needless to say, nearly 100 percent voted for it. The plebiscite also provided a means to identify the tiny minority in opposition and to arrest them as wicked enemies of the state, the government, and the people—malicious, unscrupulous, antisocial elements that had to be destroyed. A story went around that, in a small provincial town, two old ladies wrote in a vote for the Emperor Franz Josef. They were later questioned by the Gestapo. This was supposed to be a secret ballot.

In Vienna, conditions for us were deteriorating from day to day, and it was sheer luck that I was still alive and free. It became clear to us that the new regime was determined to annihilate us, systematically and ruthlessly, without mercy, at first morally and economically, and later on probably physically, too. Tragic examples demonstrated this to us daily.

The system to separate us Jews from the population was well-organized. It operated through the press, radio, and mass meetings. It was hammered into the Austrians' heads that the Jews were the root of all evil, and they were intimidated by threats into having nothing to do with us. We were, for all intents and purposes, outlaws. The police didn't dare to protect us from open insults and degrading indignities. Jews were forced to rub old election slogans off walls and sidewalks. Well-dressed Jewish men and women had to scrub sidewalks on their hands and knees, surrounded by jeering mobs. At times they were kicked and beaten. Some were taken to barracks and offices to clean the toilets. I carried a "protective" letter from the Medical Board saying that I should be exempted from "public work" as I was in the health service. All Jewish employees had to be dismissed immediately and most Jewish businesses had to be handed over to *Kommissars* (supervisors), whose only qualification was that they were members of the Nazi party. They soon sold the goods, and the former owners didn't dare to ask what had happened to their money. Many shops and warehouses were broken into, in broad daylight, and the goods whisked away. The police didn't dare to ask questions. Often uniformed men were with the plunderers. Jewish doctors and dentists were allowed at first to treat only Jewish patients, and then were altogether forbidden to practice. Some of our non-Jewish patients sent their maids to collect their dental records, fearing that it would be held against them to have patronized a Jewish practitioner.

The new military commander of Vienna, Major-General Lothar von Rendulizc, was a patient of mine, and we were on friendly terms. He explained the problems of air warfare to me. He had been retired early by the Austrian government owing to his open Nazi sympathies. This did not worry him, for he was convinced that Austria would join the German Empire, and then his time would come: he would be rehabilitated and brought back into active service. He assured me that I shouldn't be anxious about the Nazis; he would be sufficiently powerful to protect me. Sure enough, the day after the Nazis marched in, he was named commander of Vienna. He must have believed that things would turn out differently than they did with regard to the Jews. He couldn't do anything for us, even if he wanted to. He sent us an urgent message to get out, anywhere and at any cost.

Then the arrests started: first the prominent Jews, then the leading socialists, trade union officials, and all others known to be opposed to the Nazis. There were many victims of denunciation, sometimes as a form of personal vengeance. People simply disappeared, and nobody could or would give information about them. Once arrested, it was hard to get released. All the prisons were full, and many schools were used to hold the detainees. The school on Karajan Street in the district of Brigittenau was notorious, most of its prisoners were deported to the concentration camp at Dachau near Munich. The rumors about Dachau were horrifying, and turned out to be true and unexaggerated.

The political uncertainty was reflected in the bad economic situation in Austria long before the country lost its independence. Everybody tried to invest their capital in something that might keep its value: houses, diamonds, gold and silver objects, pictures, antiques, etc. We were advised to buy an apartment house. We inspected a few, but felt that this was not for us; we would have bought only worries. In the end we were right; those who owned a house had far greater difficulty in leaving the country because they were not to abandon their property. We decided to buy gold for dental use, and gradually acquired four pounds from our usual supplier for crowns and bridges. When the Nazis proclaimed their new laws and regulations, their first order was that gold had to be made available for immediate sale to the state. Dentists had to report the quantity they had used in the last three years and the amount in their present possession. We needed under a pound a year. Afraid of complications, we were glad when one of our patients offered to buy it. He had connections in the Hungarian consulate and could send it out of Austria in the diplomatic bag, or so he said. We sold it to him at a loss! We were relieved to be rid of it, and without having had to put it into Nazi hands. Murder was considered a lesser crime by the Nazis than infringing the gold and currency regulations.

A colleague of ours had been collecting "waste" gold such as old crowns and bridges for many years. He did not report it, and was denounced by his dental mechanic, who had worked for him for a long time. He was summoned to the office that dealt with this kind of offense. He was found dead on the outskirts of Vienna. He had killed himself in fear of the consequences of his "crime."

A young dentist turned up one day, introducing himself as Dr. Schlemmer. I knew his father, a respected, friendly older colleague, from dental meetings. The young man explained that he had been sent by the Nazi party to inspect our office. "What for?" I asked. "Well," he said, "there are a number of German dentists, refugees from Bukovina, whom the Party intends to resettle in Vienna." They had been expelled from their homes because they had declared themselves to be Germans, and as victims of their patriotism they deserved compensation. He was looking for suitable homes and offices. In the course of our conversation he told me that he himself had recently returned from India, where he had run his own practice. I asked him how he would have felt if an Indian dentist had come to his office and ordered him out because he was an Indian and wanted it. "You were a foreigner there, and I am an Austrian citizen. Your father, I am sure, would be ashamed of you if he knew what you were up to." I never heard anything more about this project and was not further molested by the man.

Until about June 1938 we could meet our friends in certain coffeehouses that were considered safe. We met in the Cafe Metropol on Franz Josef Quay opposite the Gestapo headquarters. We exchanged all sorts of information, partly to warn, and partly to encourage and give each other hope. Then it became too dangerous to visit public places, and we would keep in touch by telephone. If there was anything important to discuss, we arranged to meet on the Ring street. The news was mostly bad: arrests of friends, suicides, robberies, beatings, and so forth. The only good news was that some of our friends had managed to leave Austria. We envied them even if they landed in Patagonia. Nobody said goodbye, and sometimes the happy news proved to be false—the wishful rumors were just fantasies. We had to admit it: to get out as quickly as possible became our main concern. Tips circulated about how to buy visas, and about various escape routes, but on closer scrutiny they evaporated. It became clear to us that the whole world was closed to us.

A non-Jewish friend came to see us and suggested that we sell our furniture to him. He knew that we had excellent custom-made furniture. He said that he meant well by us because we would lose the things anyway. At least we would know that they were in his good hands. We were upset, and told him that we would let him know when we contemplated selling. "Don't wait too long—it might be too late," he said as he left.

Like many other people, he knew what was going on with Jewish household goods, antiques, etc. There was an organized racket with the tacit agreement of the Nazi party "legally" to rob Jews of their belongings. Two men would appear in the apartment of the prospective victims pretending to be people influential with the Nazi party, and, with more threat than persuasion, press them to sell whatever they chose of their property. Money was no object; they were prepared to pay good prices. Nobody dared to refuse such an offer; their freedom or even their life was at stake. The men paid immediately in cash and left a receipt together with a list of the objects they had bought. After a short while two uniformed Nazi officials would appear. It had come to their knowledge that a considerable sum of money was hidden in the apartment and they were authorized to search for it unless it was voluntarily handed over to them. This was, they would explain, a legal formality of safekeeping until the origin and purpose of the money could be clarified. They would

count the money and give a receipt on a clean sheet of
paper with two illegible signatures. They could not be
traced and the money would be gone. The "sold" objects
were collected the next day. Nobody dared to protest, and
it was no use going to the police—they would not or could
not take any steps.

We had a friend who owned an international moving
firm, and he advised us to send our belongings and dental
equipment abroad while it was still possible. This facility
might be blocked at any time. Before making any decision
I went to see a lawyer, Dr. Buttschädel. I knew that he
was a prominent Nazi; nevertheless, he always stressed
that he was a personal friend of ours, not merely a
patient. He was a patriotic idealist and a "selective" anti-
Semite, that is, the Jews who had lived in Austria for
generations should have the right to stay as normal
citizens; the others, who had come after 1914, mainly from
Poland, should be sent back to where they came from. I, as
a Hungarian, was acceptable. He didn't suspect that my
wife belonged to the category of those who should be
expelled; she spoke excellent German without the
slightest trace of an accent, whereas I was immediately
recognizable as a former Hungarian. According to his
point of view, we could stay. I thought he was competent to
advise me. He received me with his usual cordiality and
listened carefully to what I told him without interrupting
me. When I had finished, he answered without a
moment's hesitation: "Send everything away and follow
your things as soon as possible." He was a bitterly
disappointed man. He said that the Nazis were gangsters,
murderers, robbers, and thieves. For this kind of people
he had risked his life and existence! What a let-down! He
was a candidate for the "Blood Order" for his past
activities for the Nazi party. He used to talk about his
dream of a unified German Empire that would be
respected by the whole world. Now he had been warned
not to criticize the leading Nazis and the Party, and
threatened if he didn't follow the Party line. His parting
words to me were: "If your belongings should fall to the
bottom of the English Channel, they would still be in a

better place than in the hands of these gangsters."

It was a complicated and expensive business to get permission to send one's belongings out of the country. Accurate lists had to be made, in triplicate, with a description of every item. This list had to be submitted to a special office, and then one had to wait for approval. Bribes could speed the matter up. Our moving firm had the connections and the generosity (with our money!) to get things moved astonishingly fast. We had to pay a special tax to take out the dental equipment and instruments. A young, well-spoken man from the Office for the Protection of Valuable Objects called on us to examine our paintings. Although none was valuable, nearly all of them disappeared on the way. He apologized for the inconvenience and stamped the permission sign on the pictures, hardly looking at them. He was obviously embarrassed by this whole business. He had to do his duty so as not to get into trouble. Such decent people were closely watched, and had to be careful in order not to lose their jobs.

A committee came to check the accuracy of the lists and items. Several men watched as our things were put into large crates by the movers. The moving company arranged a reception for the customs officers: coffee, beer, drinks, sandwiches, cakes, and fruit were provided for them. Soon they were paying more attention to the refreshments than to the packing. The chief officer took a fancy to our radio and carried it away as a present, and the others were promptly rewarded too. There was no hitch, no objection, everything ran smoothly. The lists were rubber-stamped and signed, and the crates officially sealed. It was a pleasant day for everyone. The crates were loaded onto a large van. We watched from our window as they were being driven away. Were we seeing them for the last time?

Among the packers I noticed a man who was very careful not to leave behind even nails and screws. I told him we wouldn't need them, and not to bother to take them out. He looked at me and said in English, "They will make bullets out of them if you leave them." I took him

aside to repeat it in German because I couldn't
understand him. He had lived in the United States for a
few years.

Conditions during those months under the Nazi
regime can best be conveyed by some concrete anecdotal
examples.

Mr. Stollwerk was a top ranking official at City Hall,
a clean, quiet, conscientious man of about fifty, a devout
Catholic from an old patrician family. He and his wife had
been our patients for many years, in the course of which a
friendly mutual respect and trust had developed between
us, although he never talked about his work or personal
affairs. He came for his regular appointment a few days
after the Nazis took over, and we were very surprised
when he told us that he was unemployed. After thirty
years of service he had lost his job. For the first time since
we had known him, he became openly communicative, and
told us what had happened. The Nazis came into Austria
on a Saturday. The following Monday he went to his office
as usual. He found several people there, some in brown
uniforms. One asked him, "Who are you?" "This is my
office," he replied. "You must be kidding! We have been
arguing all night who is to get this job and office. One
thing is certain—it won't be you. Get out of here, and don't
show up anymore. Got it?" He left, and didn't know what
to do next. We never saw him again.

A young man came to continue his treatment. I
hardly recognized him. He was wearing a new brown
uniform with a swastika and all the paraphernalia that
belonged with his outfit. He was obviously very proud of
his appearance. He was the son of patients of ours, decent,
honest, hard-working people who had often complained
about their son and sought advice what to do with him
because he was such a good-for-nothing that he couldn't
keep any job. Now he wanted to discuss politics with me:
Who would be the new mayor of Vienna? To cut him short,
I said that I didn't care so long as there was peace in the
city. He jumped out of the chair, shouting, "But we do, and
you will soon see the changes." I was glad when he had
gone; a careless remark could have landed me in prison, or

worse.

Sometimes it was difficult to answer the tricky questions put to me. Before the ban on treating non-Jewish patients, one of them said to me, "There will be a war, it is inevitable, and we shall need doctors. What would you do if you were drafted into the army? There would be a conflict between your duty and your feelings toward Germans." I answered that I would try to the best of my ability to help suffering human beings in accordance with the oath I had taken on becoming a physician.

Early one morning two men came to see me personally. They showed me their credentials: they were plain clothes policemen. This is it, was my first thought; they will order me to go with them. "We won't keep you long," one of them said, and went on to explain that the police force intended to issue a new weekly magazine and they were recruiting subscribers. I breathed easier, and was duly enrolled as a subscriber for the next six months. Of course, I had to pay immediately, in advance. Although I never received a single copy of the magazine, I felt I had come out of it very well. The policemen may have been phonies who pocketed the money!

A number of Jews were foreign nationals. They wore small flags or brooches with the colors of their countries displayed on such prominent places as their coat lapels. It gave them some measure of protection; the Nazis wanted to avoid protests from diplomatic representatives. A Polish Jew who had been beaten up by the Gestapo went to the Polish embassy to lodge a complaint. He was asked there whether he had been beaten as a Pole or as a Jew— a thorny question. Stories went around about some of these foreign Jews. They came to Vienna and offered to smuggle out jewels, money, and valuables to England or America. They promised to deposit the things at any address, bank, or safe deposit box, in return for a certain percentage of their value. Some were honest, but the majority were swindlers who disappeared without trace.

Poland's representatives in Austria and Germany were notorious for not protecting or helping their Jewish subjects. One Jew told me how he had gone to the Polish consulate with all the relevant documents to get a Polish passport. His parents had emigrated from Poland when he was a child, and he had grown up and gone to school in Vienna. The official went through his documents and began to question him in Polish, which he didn't understand since German was spoken in his home. The Pole stood up, tore up all his documents and shouted in rage: "If you can't even speak Polish, then you aren't a Polish citizen! Get out or I'll have you thrown out!" He had lost all his precious documents: that was like a death sentence for a Jew at that time.

One of our neighbors was a well-to-do coal merchant whose wife was of Jewish descent. She agreed to divorce him so as to save his business and their two sons. They intended to remarry as soon as normal conditions were restored; they regarded their divorce as a temporary formality. No point in speculating what befell her later.

The doctors from the Jewish Rothschild Hospital were ordered one morning to line up outside the hospital in their white coats. They were given banners to carry that said, "We are dirty Jews!" They had to march through the streets for several hours, and then were dismissed. Uniformed Nazis directed this action. Two of the doctors were on their way home by tramcar when they witnessed an accident: a motorcycle with two SS men had collided with a van. The tramcar stopped, and the doctors got off and left the scene. They did not dare to give first aid for fear of being accused of having worsened the patients' condition.

There were many suicides; the ambulances automatically took them to the Jewish hospital. One unconscious man, when he came around the next day, turned out to be an SS officer who had been in civilian clothing and dead drunk.

Several thousand Polish Jews who lived in Germany were rounded up and taken to the Polish border. As the Poles did not allow them entry to their homeland, they remained in a no man's land without food or shelter. Among them were the parents of a certain young man, Mr. Grynspan. He lived in Paris, where he went to the

German Embassy to see the ambassador. The only thing
known for sure is that he shot a junior official. This
incident served as a pretext for a massive reprisal against
the whole Jewish population of Germany and Austria on
the orders of the Nazi party—the "Crystal Night" of
November 1938. Temples were burned down everywhere,
many thousands arrested by the Gestapo, and a large fine
demanded by the German government as a collective
punishment for the crime of a single desperate person.

A few days after the "Crystal Night" I met an old
school friend of mine on the street. He looked like a coal
miner, his face and hands impregnated with coal dust. He
had spent several days and nights hidden in a coal cellar.
He was a family physician in the small town of Vöslau
near Vienna. His life there was made so intolerable that
he had to move to Vienna to stay with relatives. His
papers and visa were ready for his emigration to the
United States. Unfortunately, his wife had inherited a
house for which he had to pay *Fluchtsteuer* (flight tax), a
special tax on property owners for permission to leave the
country. He couldn't sell the house. I learned many years
later that he had nevertheless managed to get out.

My wife's youngest brother, a tall, handsome man
in his twenties, was picked up on the street by the SS and
taken with some other Jewish men to a suburban house.
They had to strip, and were beaten and sexually assaulted
by a number of drunken uniformed men. After a few hours
they were released, and they considered themselves
terribly lucky.

A cousin of ours, Michael Neufeld, a wholesale
chemical dealer, told us in strict confidence what had
happened to him. He was arrested one evening and taken
to a large hall on Mariahilfer Street. People of all ages
had been assembled there, and they were forced to do
physical exercises throughout the night under the
commands of the SS. Those who collapsed were beaten
and kicked. No one knows how many died there. The
following morning those still alive were taken to police
headquarters, where they had to walk past a table,
announcing their name in a loud voice. A man at the table

would say either "Go" or "Dora." Our cousin was lucky: he was a "Go." The "Doras," as he found out later, were taken to the Dachau concentration camp.

He had another narrow escape. He went home for lunch, as was customary in Vienna. When he had finished his meal, his wife told him that two Gestapo officials had been looking for him that morning, and would come back in the afternoon. She had not wanted to tell him sooner so as not to spoil his appetite. He jumped up as if stung by a wasp, ran out, and didn't dare to go home for over a week. Eventually he managed to get away to Australia.

I was stopped on the street one day by the head of the dental clinic from which I had been dismissed. I didn't see him, and anyway I had decided not to acknowledge my non-Jewish acquaintances on the streets so as not to embarrass them. He asked me how I was, and commented that I didn't look like my old self. "You are right," I answered, "and I have plenty of reasons for it." We had not been close friends, and he wasn't the talkative type. But he tried to encourage me not to give up hope. He even told me the story of a frog who had fallen into a bowl of cream and couldn't get out. The frog kicked desperately until the cream was churned into butter so that he had a firm footing and could jump out.[1] Under other circumstances he would have made me laugh. As it was, at least I realized that there were good people, too.

Without warning, my elder sister arrived in Vienna with her husband and three children. They had lived in the provincial town of Eisenstadt in Burgenland, just on the Austrian side of the Austro-Hungarian border, where her husband was a furrier. They were the last of the town's approximately fifty Jewish families to leave. We put them up in our apartment until we could find suitable accommodation for them. They lived in Vienna for about a year before being deported to Lodz, in Poland, and subsequently to Treblinka, where they were murdered. Only the eldest son survived; he was old enough to be accepted into the Youth Alyah (the Jewish immigration organization) and went to Palestine in 1939.

The "brothers from the *Reich*" soon started to shake

up the pleasure-seeking Austrians and to solve the problem of unemployment, as they had promised. Workers had to report weekly to the employment office to collect their benefits. When they arrived they were locked into a large room and transported to Germany, where there was plenty of work to do on highway construction, fortifications on the Franco-German frontier, not to mention in munitions factories. They were not even permitted to take leave of their families, who would receive a preprinted postcard from Germany to say that they were alive and well. It made no difference what their former occupation had been—hairdresser, office worker, painter—they had to do whatever work was assigned to them.

We had an excellent shoemaker who made shoes for all the male members of our family. When he came to deliver my last pair of shoes, he was full of woes. All his best customers had left the country or were about to leave. He confessed that he had been a member of the Nazi party even when it was still illegal in Austria. "Serves me right for having been such an idiot!" Repentance came too late for the idealists; by the time they realized their mistake, they had no choice but to stick things out.

We lived near a police station from which the special vans left to take those arrested to the railroad station for deportation to Dachau. They were very busy. We could see the hands and faces of the unfortunates through the iron bars of the tiny windows. We heard gruesome accounts of these journeys. One man who was lucky enough to be released told me his experiences just before he left Austria. They were seated in small compartments of old trains, ten to a compartment. They had to put their hands on their knees and to stare into one lightbulb on the ceiling. No food or drink was given, and the use of the toilets was forbidden. They were watched from the corridor by SS men, and severe punishments were meted out for the slightest violation of these orders. Dachau, near Munich, is a long way from Vienna. Two of my friends, the antique dealer Emmerich Winter and the dental surgeon Paul Schott, protested against these inhumane regulations. When the train arrived in Dachau, they were dead.

Some families received the ashes of their relatives and had to pay the postage, too. The few who were released and had exit visas had to sign a form that they would not reveal anything of what had happened to them in the concentration camp. Despite this secrecy, conditions in the camps became common knowledge among the Jews. Dissatisfied grumblers would be silenced by the one word "Dachau."

Two of my brothers-in-law were arrested. They owned a textile business with about ten employees. A *Kommissar* was appointed to run the business, and the stock was sold to German firms. Austria was inundated with German businessmen who bought up everything at low prices. There was a shortage of consumer goods in Germany because rearmament had taken precedence over everything else. We did our utmost to get my brothers-in-law out of prison; in vain, alas! After business friends of theirs in England had secured a visa for them, a Nazi lawyer approached them. He suggested that they donate a considerable sum, voluntarily, to the Nazi Party; he would then be able to arrange for their release. They did so and were freed. They took the first available plane to England with hardly any luggage; they had no time to pack! Up to their incarceration they had firmly believed that a change for the better would come and had made no preparations to leave. They took a bitter and expensive cure. Still, they were lucky.

Aryan (non-Jewish) lawyers were overrun by the relatives of those imprisoned. They were said to have good connections. It turned out that they could do little except for those with exit visas. The lawyers must have known it. The large fees paid to them were wasted money.

We listened to the radio to get news from abroad, although this was strictly forbidden. We heard what we wanted to hear to comfort ourselves. According to the Russian radio, the Nazi regime was tottering, the Party disunited, the leaders locked into quarrels, the economy in a desperate state, and the resistance movement gaining strength: all sweet music to our ears. Unfortunately we couldn't discern the slightest sign of this decline of the Nazis.

One evening a well known jeweler came to our table in the coffeehouse to offer a beautiful antique watch for sale. He had just stolen it from his store. His business had been taken over by a *Kommissar* who granted him such a small weekly allowance that he couldn't live on it. The police were investigating a burglary at his former store, and he was asked for an inventory of what was missing. When no one was looking, he pinched the gold watch. He needed money so badly that he robbed his own business.[2]

The secretary to the mayor of Vienna, Mr. Graef, and his family, high-ranking old Catholics, were my wife's patients. He held an important and influential position; one of his sons was employed in the city administration, while the other was a judge. As a token of gratitude he arranged for us to become Viennese citizens.[3] This was in November 1937, when no Jew would have had the audacity to apply for Viennese citizenship. Mr. Graef once asked my wife this question: "Frau Doctor, I am puzzled that the women of Vienna are so crazy about him (Hitler). You as a woman can judge this better: is he really so handsome, charming, and attractive?" My wife gave him her candid opinion, with which he fully agreed.

Another of our patients, a bank manager, once arrived late for his appointment, full of apologies. He had a curious excuse. His parents already had converted from Judaism to Christianity, and he had been brought up a Christian, and so had his children. Life would be easier for them. There were many families like his in Vienna. He admitted, though, that he somehow felt most comfortable with his Jewish friends. His thirteen year old son, Tom, who had many Jewish friends, had found out about his Jewish background, had become an ardent Zionist, and insisted on becoming a Jew. The circumcision ceremony that day had taken longer than he had expected, and that was why he was late. Tom emigrated to Palestine with a youth group, and was the only member of the family to survive. Destiny plays strange tricks sometimes!

A colleague of mine at the clinic refused to supply the documents to prove that he was Aryan and not Jewish. We were all surprised, for we had never suspected that he wasn't a genuine Christian. It was of no importance to us anyway; he was a quiet, decent fellow, and a good worker. He confessed that he had been brought up by a Jewish family who had taken him in out of compassion. He was in no way related to them; he was an orphan of Christian parentage. He insisted that it was up to the authorities to prove that he was "non-Aryan." His wife and children had not the slightest inkling of his problem. His protestations were in vain; he was deported.

We heard of people who were kind and helpful to their Jewish friends at great personal risk. We ourselves benefited from such kindness on several occasions. The superintendent of our building declared to the Gestapo, who came to search for Jews, that they had all gone, although he knew that we and two other Jewish families were still living there. His son was a policeman, well aware of what was going on. Unfortunately, there were many amateur detectives who denounced Jews, either for personal gain or out of hatred. Denunciation was also regarded as a patriotic duty into which children were indoctrinated in schools and youth clubs.

One of the stories going around was that policemen were required to arrest twenty Jews per day. One policeman saw a Jewish boy of about fifteen in the tenement house where they had both lived for many years, so that he had known the boy since early childhood. "Freddy," he now said, "I have to arrest a certain number of Jews today. I hope I can make it, but if not, I'll have to take you, too." By that time the small humiliations such as cleaning the streets, and washing toilets seemed relatively harmless. And who would risk entering a park or sitting on a street bench? We were not safe either on the streets or at home. We were ordered to stay indoors on Saturday afternoons so as to make shopping easier for the Aryans.

The first step to leaving the country was to get a German passport, the Austrian one having been declared invalid. A Jew without a passport was as good as dead. There were quite a number of stateless Jews in Austria; very few of them escaped. Their Jewishness became a passport to the gas chambers.

To acquire a German passport was a complicated and thorny process. The completion of the application forms was the only easy part; after that, the calvary began. There was a sudden onrush for the necessary documents and certificates. Lines several miles long stretched in front of the offices that issued the papers; people often had to go home empty handed after waiting all day. These offices were understaffed for the task, and full of impatient, incompetent, inexperienced, and often malicious or vicious young men. The validity of each certificate was limited, and if any of them had expired before the passport could be obtained, the whole process had to be started all over again. Some of the older officials treated us with as much sympathy and humanity as they dared, but they knew they were being watched by the younger ones for any sign of softness, which could cost them their job.

One of the most vital certificates was the *Steuerunbedenklichkeitszeugnis*, which attested that all income taxes had been paid without any arrears or pending demands. My tax inspector was a morose old man who had always appeared unfriendly whenever I had had to see him in previous years. There had been no serious difficulties; however, I went to his office with some anxiety. It had to be done, but I didn't look forward to the encounter. I had the surprise of my life: I found a kindly, sympathetic man who talked to me as to an old friend, full of compassion and consideration. He was sorry about my intentions to emigrate, though not surprised given the prevailing conditions. He lamented that all his best clients were going, and issued the certificate with a much longer validity than he was supposed to. He took a personal risk to do me a favor.

The second major hurdle was a certificate from City Hall concerning the payment of the city taxes for which every householder was liable. Fortunately, the head of this department, Karl Wiesbauer, was a patient of ours. When I called him, he recognized my voice and said he would come to see me. He came the same evening, bringing all the forms and rubber stamps. He made out the forms for us immediately and without question. He knew that we were never behind in our payments. He was a great help to us.

At long last we had a passport. Some days later we were petrified by a newspaper headline: "All Jewish Passports Invalid." It was only a scare. We had to take the passport to the police, where a giant red "J" was stamped onto the front page. It was the most precious document we ever had, our lifeline. The next step was to get a visa. TO ANYWHERE. Chasing a visa was our most urgent priority in order to get out of this gigantic prison.

By the end of summer our anxiety was turning into despair. Suicides of even prominent people were no longer news. Cynics said of them, "They have improved their situation and are free of worries." Individual arrests gave way to mass arrests. Suddenly both ends of a busy street would be blocked by police cars and all the Jewish men on the street were loaded into vans and driven away. The surrounding buildings were searched, too, for fugitives.

One day I was stopped by Mr. Eisler, the *Kommissar* of my brothers-in-law's business. He wanted to have a serious talk. "Doctor, don't you see what is going on around you? Why don't you clear out? You are a strong young man, and it is inevitable that one day they will pick you up, and then no one in the world will be able to help you. Leave the country, the sooner the better." I told him that we were eager to go but short of cash. The next morning he handed me a thick envelope with a considerable sum. These were of course the firm's assets, yet it was very decent of him to help us.

Following up another rumor, I registered to be put on a list of dentists who were supposed to be admitted to England and allowed to practice there. It struck me as a fantastic fairy tale, too good to be true. As a "guarantor" I gave the name and address of an English patient of ours, Mr. Sydney Cohen, a representative of the firm Lever

Brothers, in London. It was a shot in the dark into which we didn't put much hope.

I was offered a passport to a South American country. Its consul had died recently, so I was told, and somebody had got hold of the passports and the official stamps. It would be made out in our name, and we could fly to Lisbon immediately. I didn't dare to do this, but years later I met a man who had bought such a passport and had survived the war in Lisbon. I heard too late about the possibility of getting a visa to Shanghai; when I went to the Chinese consulate, they had stopped issuing visas.

With a certificate of baptism one could enter Yugoslavia, so the rumors went; a priest could supply it for a small sum. With our religious upbringing we couldn't bring ourselves to do this. We heard later that few Jewish refugees survived there; most perished, killed either by the Germans or by the *Ustashies*, the local brand of Nazis.

Many countries deported any refugees who were smuggled in. Without the help of friends, one couldn't evade the local authorities. Some countries tolerated refugees for a while with varying degrees of restriction. They were not wanted anywhere; they created problems everywhere. Local Jews tried to help them; gradually, however, the refugees became such a liability that they couldn't cope with them. This was clear to us; we had no illusions about it, but anything was better than staying there.

It was a heyday for unscrupulous swindlers. They boasted of their connections and promised to get landing permits or visas, always demanding advance payment for expenses, bribes, and the like. They told fantastic tales which no sane person would have believed under normal circumstances. They exploited desperate people who in their dire need lost their common sense and became victims of clumsy tricks.

A colleague of mine recommended me to a man who was getting him a visa to England with a work permit too. It would be rather expensive, but worth it. I found some contradictions in his scheme which made me suspicious and cautious. I decided to wait until his case was successfully completed, although I was warned that the opportunity might not be available if I hesitated too long. The other fellow's case dragged on and on and in the end the con man disappeared. His office was closed and nobody had any information.

Another man came to see me, recommended by "somebody," he couldn't recall by whom. He wanted to sell me an invention, a rubber thumbcap for counting money, which would open the door to England for me. According to him, the British consul would issue a visa to an inventor. He was a well-spoken and well-dressed man. He urged me to act before this possibility became widely known. I asked him to accompany me immediately to the consulate—which he flatly refused to do. He left in a hurry. This is not a joke. Some people probably fell victim to this scheme.

I applied for a landing permit to Australia, enclosing a precious pound note with my application as fee. I heard of a building contractor who had also applied. He translated his profession, *Unternehmer* (entrepreneur), literally, as "undertaker."[4] He was issued a visa as a mortician. His mistake in translation saved him and his family.

We had no prospects of going to Palestine. The legal immigration quota was very small and was distributed among deserving Zionist workers. We couldn't buy a "capitalist visa" as it was far beyond our means. Illegal immigration could be arranged by traveling along the Danube by boat, then marching for some days with a backpack through uninhabited areas. Young, strong, adventurous people might make it. We couldn't seriously consider such a plan.

I was offered a "genuine" Czechoslovak passport, on which the original name would be washed out and our names and photographs substituted. This was about May 1938, before conditions became hopeless. I declined to buy it. A relative of ours, who was in mortal fear of being arrested any day, bought it and traveled to England on it with his family. They lived in England throughout the war as Czechoslovak citizens. When he applied for naturalization, he confessed. He had tried to get a Polish passport, to which he was entitled, and was informed that his documents had got lost on the way to Warsaw. In desperation he bought the false passport. Had he not done it, he explained to the British naturalization official, he and his family would be dead. He was granted British citizenship.

I bought a visitor visa to Liberia. The consul put a large impressive stamp into our passport, wrote in the date and signed it. The fee was moderate. We knew that we would never go to Liberia. No other country would have given us a transit visa for fear that we might try to stay. Such a visa was known as an "immunization visa." If people showed the police or authorities a valid visa, they were more likely to be let go since they were on the way out of the country. It was by no means foolproof, but it worked in some instances.

We never contemplated illegal entry into any country where we wanted to stay permanently. Forged documents were out of the question for us. We clearly understood the risks we were taking by sticking to our professional and ethical standards.

The whole of my wife's close family was already in England, and we ardently hoped to get there, too. Our immediate, temporary aim was to get into Holland or Belgium. We didn't want to stay there any longer than absolutely necessary, since both were too close to Germany. We feared a repetition of what was happening in Austria. We had heard from several sources that there was a reasonable chance of slipping across the border, and we had friends there. So, before resigning ourselves to a fate which didn't look as catastrophic then as it turned out to be later, we decided to try to escape illegaly.

We wanted to stay together as long as possible. We had a letter from a Jewish family in England offering a home for our daughter. They themselves had a daughter of about her age. The three of us would try to escape together. Should this fail, then my wife and I would return to Vienna and send Lilian to England to this family.

Before setting out on our journey I went to a bank for

our travel allowance in foreign currency: one and a half English pounds per person. The bank clerk knew me; he had been a patient of mine at the clinic. After entering the transaction in our passport, he handed it back and whispered to me, "Doctor, I am sorry. I haven't done anything to contribute to this state of affairs."

I had also to sign a statement that on leaving the country voluntarily, I would not return except by special permission of the government. That was an unnecessary formality.

Cologne

(LRF)

From the moment we boarded that train onward, my
memory is a more or less continuous flow with only a few
gaps, although my sense of time is sometimes unsteady. I
could not say, for instance, how many hours we were on
the train. It seemed a very long time, with delays due to
bad weather and to troop trains, which had priority. This
journey was very different from those I recall when we
were going on vacation or to Karlsbad. Then I had been
excited and exuberant, looking out of the window at every
station. I loved the *horki parki* (hot dogs) sold by vendors
from rolling carts at Czechoslovak stations; they would be
passed in through the window on a square cardboard plate
with a thick slice of dark bread and a splodge of mustard.

This time we were subdued and tried not to attract
attention. On the one occasion when I walked along the
train corridor with my father, we came upon a sight that
has remained engraved in my mind. It was a whole
carriage full of unaccompanied children, a "children's
transport," headed for England. They were seated ten to a
compartment, each with a large cardboard label bearing
name and destination hanging on a string around his or
her neck. They sat there perfectly still, unnaturally good,

and obviously miserable. Some were quite little, others bigger, but all looked already like the orphans most of them were to become. I was the only Jewish child on that train whose hand was securely gripped by a father. The children stared at him as though they wanted to grab him. And I knew that there, but for my parents' decision that we must stick together, went I. The faces of those children still haunt me, although these were the lucky ones, who did get away, and the majority of them were well received by their adoptive families.

Finally, at 1 a.m. we got off the train at Cologne, a major junction near the northwest borders of Germany, Holland, and Belgium. As we had left Vienna the previous evening, I reckon the journey took over twenty-four hours. It was very cold and damp, and I was awfully tired. We went into several hotels to find a room to rest and sleep; everywhere the answer was the same: "We are forbidden to take in Jews." We had the money to pay for the room, and we didn't look at all disreputable, just somewhat crumpled and dispirited. My father begged the clerk at one establishment to let us sit in the lobby until daybreak, but we met with the same adamant refusal. Back on the streets again, by now at 3 a.m., a man took pity on us and told us of a place willing to give us shelter. By all normal standards, our behavior in following a strange man along the back streets of an unknown city in the middle of the night, seems rash, to say the least. Who was the man, and why was he out there at that hour? We were too exhausted to ask such questions, too much in need of rest. Normal standards had gone by the board in the sheer struggle to survive. The man directed us to a modest house where the door was opened by a man in a dressing-gown, who took a quick look at us and let us in. We were given a small but clean bedroom with a large double bed, into which we all tumbled as soon as we could shed our clothes. Rarely has a bed felt so good to me.

We stayed there several days, yet I don't recall much about the place except that it didn't seem too pleasant, although we did have a wash basin and hot water—things once taken for granted, but now in our refugee existence luxuries to be prized. By day we snooped around Cologne for information about illegal frontier crossings. Banished from coffeehouses as well as from hotels, Jews had their own meeting places in dingy back rooms, where people like us would congregate to find out how to set about their venture. We heard of a loophole in the Dutch frontier and got precise instructions where to go. We left our few belongings and the rest of our money at the boarding house. No questions were asked; the less people knew of others' plans and intentions, the better. At 5 a.m. the next day we were on the train again, this time heading for Nijmegen. Many of the German workers streaming into the city from the suburbs waved to us and wished us good luck with cordial gestures. In our demoralized state, that was worth a great deal.

We didn't get into Holland. At the border station we took a taxi, as we had been instructed, and gave the driver a certain address. The driver immediately threw us a sharp look, and asked whether we had a Dutch visa. He said that route had been closed and people arrested the previous day. He advised us to get back on a train as quickly as possible before we too were picked up. That was the end of our first attempt. By mid-day we were back in Cologne and at the boarding house, where our money and things were returned to us. Under the circumstances, we were thankful for such small decencies.

Since we hadn't been able to turn up anything in Cologne, we moved on to Aachen (Aix-la-Chapelle) where we stayed in another Jewish boarding house. The atmosphere was tense. Perhaps it is a form of protective repression that I remember little about this episode or about how we returned to Cologne or where we stayed. My memory resumes at a specific scene: in a Jewish restaurant, where an elderly couple at the table next to ours struck up a conversation with us. They urged us to get out because we were young. Their children were safe in America, and nothing would happen to them, old people. Besides, he had served in the German army in the First World War, and held a medal. When my father confessed that we didn't know how to get out, they nodded to the headwaiter and told him that we wanted to leave. It sounded as though we wanted our check so as to leave the restaurant.

A little while later, a rather dour man in his early thirties joined us at our table to negotiate the deal. He could arrange to have us driven to the Belgian frontier and turned over to a Belgian, who would take us further. We were to hand him all our remaining German money, and to recruit two more adults to make it worth his while. The child could come for free. The fact that we had all the necessary papers to leave Germany made it easier. We would be collected by a car outside the cathedral at 2 p.m. the next day. No luggage.

I am still amazed at the rashness with which we purchased our lives. I can only suppose that it was a measure of our despair. The man was curt, not particularly inspiring of confidence. Yet there we were the next day at 2 p.m., outside the cathedral with two young men; Robert Pick, the son of friends from Vienna and another fellow whom he had brought. At 2 o'clock on the dot the car appeared, and we got in quickly.

It began to snow on the way, and at one point the car got stuck. Members of the Hitler Youth were at the ready with shovels to dig us out. The driver nervously told us to put our heads down so that they wouldn't recognize his cargo. My heart was in my mouth until we got moving again.

It was beginning to grow dark by the time we arrived at the frontier. Our driver recommended that I not be taken through the German border post because children were sometimes subjected to nasty body searches. Instead I was led to a nearby inn, settled in a corner with a cup of cocoa, and told to wait there until they came back to fetch me. How long did I wait? Twenty minutes? Half an hour? Longer? I have no idea. The local people glanced at me furtively, and turned aside so as not to be in any way involved in a murky affair. They knew who I was and what we were doing. It seems to have been a well frequented escape route. (In the late 1970s, at a scholarly meeting in Canada, I met an eminent Germanist who had taken the same path only two weeks earlier than us.) Left to wait alone, I was absolutely terrified: what if they didn't come back for me? I had no passport or money, and what could a seven-year-old do alone anyway? The body search, I guess, might have been even more traumatic.

By the time they returned, it was pitch dark. The driver walked us quite a way, wading through deep snow, to a railroad bridge. A dog was used, too, as I recall it, but I don't know what role it played. Our guide told us to run across the bridge when he blew a whistle; there would be a Belgian to meet us at the other end. We took the enormous risk: what if there had been no one there? I still sometimes wonder at our inexplicable trust.

There was indeed someone to meet us. He took us to his farmhouse not far away. I believe it had been arranged that he would drive me to Brussels while the adults followed by more devious means. But the weather was so bad that he thought the police patrols wouldn't be out, so he was prepared to take us all. He drove at a furious pace on winding, icy roads. I had the impression several times that we were heading straight for a tree. He stopped once, in the middle of the night, at a cottage for a hot drink. I was so worn out that I had to be carried in. At dawn he dumped us in Brussels, hardly waiting for us to shut the door before rushing away.

Cologne

We were on our way to Cologne, five people in a well-heated, comfortable compartment. Besides the three of us, there was a German officer with the rank of major, who was going home to spend Christmas with his family, as he told us later. The fifth, we surmised, might have been some sort of commercial traveler, a fat, fidgety middle-aged man in an ill-fitting suit. He soon started talking. It was a monologue about the weather and the inconvenience of arriving home later than expected; his wife would be upset, and so on. He was ignored by the officer, who was reading his newspaper, and he found no resonance in us either. Our little girl was about to fall asleep, and we only whispered to one another. He tried to make conversation with us by asking questions: what was our destination? Did we have friends or relatives in Cologne? He knew Cologne well, had many friends there, and could give us advice about where to stay and the addresses of good restaurants. We couldn't stop him with our short and reluctant answers. He commented, too, on our scanty luggage for three persons. At last he gave up and launched into a lecture on Germany and international politics. He praised the Führer to the skies, and painted the future of Germany in rosy colors—the whole world envies, fears, and respects Germany, and we will show them. He didn't say what. He obviously wanted to impress the officer, who looked bored and annoyed, and ignored his tirade.

When he left the compartment to smoke, the officer turned to us and said, "Don't take any notice of this idiot. He talks a lot of nonsense." We had no doubt that he had guessed what kind of people we were. His tone sounded friendly and sympathetic. He regarded us as inevitable victims of historic events, which take their human toll. It was an unfortunate fact. He might himself become a victim by doing his duty. None of us were masters of our fate. He told us how lucky he was in his present post on the Czechoslovak border. He lived in a beautifully furnished house, well-stocked with enough food, drink, and coal for the entire winter. It had been the house of a wealthy Jew who had been clever enough to run away in good time; his departure must have been in great haste. As he himself didn't expect a further move this winter, he intended to take his wife with him on his return. Who knew what would happen in spring? It was no use speculating. He would get his orders and carry them out without any hesitation according to the best of his ability. That was his job and his duty. He stated the facts without sounding at all apologetic. We were surprised at his frankness and friendliness. He would never have spoken like this to fellow Germans, but he must have felt he could let off some steam to these Jewish intellectuals. When the officer left later for a short time, the civilian became talkative again, making nasty remarks about these haughty officers who were at the top of the world at that time. Just wait and see—the Führer would cut them to size and put them, too, in their proper place.

On the train we saw a children's transport, a compartment full of small children with cardboard labels round their necks. Their names and the names and addresses of their recipients were clearly written on them. It was a heart-rending sight. The children, reduced to human parcels, already looked like orphans.

The train arrived twelve hours late and we were the only passengers left in the compartment. We would have loved to stay there until daylight, but had to get out. We realized how cold it was as we left the railroad station. There was hardly anyone on the streets. We walked toward the cathedral and noticed a row of hotels in a semi-circle around the "House of God." We hurried across the street into one of them, asking for a room for one night. The man at the reception desk looked at us closely, and said that he could not put us up. I assumed they were fully booked and inquired where in the neighborhood we could get a room. Nowhere, he replied; the Gestapo had forbidden them to take in Jows. He turned away and left us standing there.

We wanted to return to the railroad station for shelter when we saw a gentleman on the street. I asked him whether he could recommend a hotel. He was friendly and led us to a small hotel nearby. It was a bitterly cold night and we were exhausted after our long journey. We slept like logs.

We had two tips from friends in Vienna. One was to travel to Aachen and contact a man there at a certain address. He could arrange for us to get into Belgium. Should this fail, there was a way to enter Holland.

The next morning we set out by train for Aachen. As we could take only a small amount of money out of the country, we deposited half our funds with the hotel owner in an addressed envelope, to be sent to our poor relatives in Vienna if we had not returned within a week.

It was a sunny, cold day, and the landscape was white, covered in deep snow. There was only one hotel in Aachen that was licensed to take in Jews. All its rooms were occupied, so we were put up in a dormitory, where people slept on straw mattresses. It was a large hall, probably the ballroom of a hotel in happier times. About half the "beds" were occupied by people of all ages from babies to grey-haired persons. This motley crowd looked depressing in their crumpled suits and dresses. Some were sitting on their beds, others walking about, and a group was discussing something in a corner. Young boys and girls were playing with a ball, all in the same room. Most of them must have been "on the road" for a while, judging by the condition of their clothing. We looked comparatively civilized, but I realized that even with the utmost care we would soon look like these people. We had to make haste to get out.

Downstairs was the restaurant, full of people huddled together around tables, discussing secret plans in low voices. There were mostly men, both young and old, some with short hair, an indication that they had recently been in a concentration camp. The place looked shabby, and the air was thick with smoke, and smelly.

We set out immediately to contact our man. He lived in a suburb in a neglected house with a small front yard. An old man let us in. We gave him the present we had brought for him from Vienna, a good quality sausage. He took a smell at it and made a gesture that suggested that he was used to better things. He didn't take to us at first sight, and I must confess that the feeling was mutual. He told us his price, which was higher than we expected, yet we agreed. He showed us a large-scale map of the border region between Germany and Belgium. This map, included in the price, was to be our guide. He would explain to us the route we should take, where to stop and look around carefully, where to cross a railroad embankment. We were to rest under a railroad bridge, remain still if we heard anyone about (there could be Belgian patrols), make ourselves look respectable, then proceed to a small railroad station and buy tickets to Brussels. Altogether it would be a four- to six-hour march. He admitted that it would be difficult to find the landmarks since the ground was covered by snow. It was clear to me that with my physically delicate wife and little girl we had no chance to make it. He grew angry when I told him my doubts about his plan, and he couldn't get rid of us quickly enough. Disappointed, we returned to our dormitory.

On the hotel landing we saw a woman crying and sobbing bitterly, holding a little girl by the hand. My wife asked her what was the matter, and offered her help. The woman led her to her room and told her what had happened. She had arrived a few days before with her husband and daughter to try to cross the border into Belgium. They had exact instructions from friends who had done it successfully and were awaiting them in Brussels. After a few days of preparation they had set out that morning, but were stopped by German guards patrolling the border with dogs. She had been sent back to Aachen with the child; her husband, however, had been held there. She had just come back from the police station, where she had been told that several men, including her husband, had been transported away. They couldn't tell her more, but she knew that his destination was a concentration camp, and their horrors were common knowledge. My wife tried to console her and to give her some hope. The unforunate woman implored us not to embark on such a dangerous venture. It was heartbreaking.

We had heard sad stories how people were cheated, fleeced, and sent to their doom. They had been given promises that they would be led to Belgium by a safe route in return for a certain sum of money to be paid in advance. They were then led through woods and over hills in deep snow, shown a distant slope, and told, "There is Belgium. Just walk straight ahead and you can't miss it." Not even fit young men would take the risk.

One young couple bought tickets to Brussels and took their two small children to the train. They were three and five years old. The parents put the address of friends in the children's pockets and jumped off the train as it started to move. The children arrived safely and were in the care of their friends in Brussels. Overjoyed, they were now starting to plan their own escape.

This was nine months before the outbreak of war. In Aachen the air raid warning sounded every day at noon to get the population used to it.

The next morning we returned to Cologne. At our hotel they were not surprised to see us again. The rule there was to pay for everything, food, accommodation, etc., in advance. Some of their guests returned several times after unsuccessful attempts; others disappeared, and nobody asked or cared what had happened to them.

The following morning we set out for Cleve on the Dutch border. We had been told to take a taxi from the railroad station to the border post, not far away. As we had valid passports, we hoped the Germans would let us go. It was taken for granted that the Dutch border guards would pose no difficulties, either. We were to contact the rabbi in Nijmegen, and he would do the rest for us. The plan was so simple and straightforward that it raised our doubts. It seemed too good to be true. Still, we owed it to ourselves to try it. In desperate situations such as ours, the ardent will to succeed blurs the obvious facts and suppresses the ability to think rationally and with common sense. One is conditioned to accept miracles. Once hope is lost, all is lost.

The train stopped at Krefeld. Passengers were met by friends or relatives, and others boarded the train. Things took their normal course, but only for other people; we were no part of it. We were homeless vagrants, fugitives without having committed any crime. Did all these people not know or care what was going on in their country? We needed practical help. On our way back from Cleve, the passengers must have noticed their odd fellow travelers and had some inkling what sort of people we were. Not one sympathetic look came our way. Their faces and expressions were blank. Of course, nobody said a word to us.

At Cleve we went across the road from the railroad station to the taxi stand. When we mentioned our destination, the driver asked to see our passports. I was indignant at this request, and refused. "You are not a border or police officer," I answered. He was not offended, and he explained the situation to us: taxidrivers were under strict orders from the Gestapo not to take anyone to the border without a valid visa for entry into Holland. He would get into trouble, but that would be slight compared to the trouble we would be in. He warned us that Cleve was a very dangerous place for us, and advised us to get back into the railroad station immediately and take the

next train back to Cologne. We spent less than an hour in
Cleve.

At the hotel they handed back the envelope with our
money, and we decided to stay a few days longer to see
whether we could find any solution ourselves. Seeing so
many unsuccessful candidates walking around aimlessly,
we had no grounds for optimism. My wife remained
hopeful despite the disappointments; she felt that we had
to trust our instincts to discover a way out. We had little
support from the others at the hotel; they had "secret" tips
and sources. Somebody mentioned a suburban coffeehouse
as the center for information. I went out there to try to
find a contact. I found a dimly lit, smoky place. Not a seat
was available, and the perspiring waiters had not a
moment to answer a question. The whole atmosphere was
repulsive. Looking at the guests, I came to the conclusion
that I couldn't entrust our lives to any of them. Still, I
forced myself to walk around the tables several times,
searching for an opening. Instinctively I held my hands on
my pockets. Then I left without regret.

The meeting place for the remnants of the Jewish
population of Cologne was the community center at 22
Cecilien Street, near the ruins of a burnt-down building
that had probably once been the temple. There was a
large, clean, brightly-lit hall with a high ceiling. Waiters
were serving modest meals, coffee, and tea to well dressed
people sitting at round tables and enjoying each others'
company. This became our headquarters. The patrons
were local people who had decided to stay in Cologne. The
younger members of their families had already left. They
were friendly and soon drew us into their circle. We told
them of our recent experiences; they thought us lucky not
to have come to grief, and were not surprised at our
failures. One of the gentlemen, Mr. Beer, introduced us to
the headwaiter, Mr. Wollner, and asked him to be helpful
to us. He said that Mr. Wollner knew everybody and was
honest and reliable; he would do for us whatever he could,
and we were to trust him.

About an hour later Mr. Wollner brought a gentleman
to our table, a Mr. Levy, who could help us. Mr. Levy

assured us that his contacts were trustworthy. They were prepared to take four persons and our little girl to Belgium the following day. He mentioned a sum to be paid in advance. He would return in an hour for our answer and the payment. Discretion was essential. As he had made a good impression on us, we decided to accept his offer. There was a Viennese lad (whose parents we knew) and a friend of his who were glad to join us. The deal was on. When Mr. Levy came back, we paid him the required sum, and he gave us instructions. We were to be at a certain corner of the Eiffel Place at 2 p.m. the next day.

We were there, and exactly at the arranged time a car stopped and in no time we were in and on the move. The three of us sat on the back seat facing the two youngsters. We were separated from the driver by a glass pane. There were two men in the front, one of whom introduced himself as Mr. Müller—he was a German— while the other, "my Belgian friend," was driving the car. They were very pleased that our German passports were valid; it made their task easier. Their main worry was the steadily falling snow, which might block the road over the Eiffel mountains, through which we had to travel. Their fear was justified; near the top we got stuck. We noticed a group of young men in uniforms. When they saw us stuck, they came over to the car with their shovels, dug us out, and cleared the way. They pushed the car over the top, where the going was easier. Fortunately, we were not asked to get out, and we tried to hide our faces by bending over. We felt very relieved when it was over. After some four or five hours of travel, we stopped at a small village. Mr. Müller took Lilian to an inn, and we were directed to the German border station. A single officer was on duty, and he was not unfriendly. He examined our passports, asked how much money we had in German and foreign currency, and was satisfied with our declaration. He searched only my wife's purse, and then said, "*Meinetwegen können Sie gehen wohin Sie wollen*" ("For all I care, you can go wherever you want"), adding, "*Niemand will Sie haben!*" ("Nobody wants you!"). His voice was devoid of either hatred or sympathy; he was merely stating his view. This was our farewell message from Germany. We were not at all offended; on the contrary, we felt relieved that things had gone so smoothly.

We met Mr. Müller outside, and after we had fetched our daughter from the inn he led us through a small forest. When we came out, we saw a railroad bridge in front of us. There we had to wait. By this time it was dark; only far ahead could we see some light. The Belgian had disappeared. After about ten minutes we heard someone whistling, and Mr. Müller urged us to cross the bridge quickly. At the other end the Belgian was waiting for us. He took us to a farmhouse a couple of hundred yards away. We found ourselves in a large, well heated room, were given some hot tea, and told that we were in Belgium. Our daughter behaved very well all the time. She said, "This has been the most difficult day in our lives." She sensed it, and how right she was!

We heard the Belgian making a telephone call, and he told us that a car would soon come to take us away. We didn't ask him where. By then we had every reason to trust him; he knew what was best for us, and wouldn't let us down. Within an hour we heard a car approaching. The driver asked us to hurry; he hadn't seen any Belgian patrols on the way. Within half an hour we were at his house, and then we asked where we were: in St. Vitt. We were exhausted and hungry. His wife gave us some fresh bread, which revived us. Lilian was fast asleep. We pooled all our money and gave it to the driver to take us to Brussels. I kept just one English pound.

We carried our sleeping child from the house and set out in the unheated car for the long journey. It was freezing cold, and we huddled together for warmth. I am still astonished that none of us caught pneumonia that night. We arrived in Brussels early in the morning. The driver dropped us at the address where our friends lived and left immediately. The two young fellows went off to find the refugee committee. We waited until 8 a.m., and then rang the bell at the house. A stranger opened the door, and told us our friends had moved. Fortunately he was able to give us their new address. Our rusty French did us good service, for he understood only French.

We saw a railroad station nearby and walked there to change our English pound into Belgian francs. Now we had money for the tram which took us to Laaken, where our friends lived. They were very pleased to see us and kept us overnight. The next day we found a furnished room in the neighborhood.

We never saw the two young men again.

We were dazed and could hardly believe that we had made it.

Brussels

We were in safety, or were we? If the Belgian police spotted us, we were liable, as illegal immigrants, to be sent back to Germany and into a concentration camp. Throughout the two months we spent in Brussels, January and February 1939, we were dogged by this fear. And that first morning we were dangerously conspicuous. Our clothes, wet from our walk in the snow, had frozen into the tight wrinkles they had assumed in the car. The two young men took off on their own at once, and we never heard how they fared. It was *sauve qui peut* (each for himself). Such proverbs were among the French my parents knew.

We had one English pound note, acquired somehow in Vienna, and concealed from our driver. To change it was perilous for it meant drawing attention to ourselves, possibly having to present our passport without the requisite Belgian visa. But it had to be done. We made our way to the *bureau de change* at the railroad station as the place least likely to notice our dishevelled state—we might have come off an overnight train. With local currency we were able to board a tram to a suburb where friends from Vienna lived. They had moved. Disappointed and exhausted, we trudged on further until we found their apartment. They took us in as naturally as if we had arrived by invitation. It was a first temporary refuge.

The Sonntags had been wealthy people with money abroad so they had less difficulty in obtaining a visa as "capitalists." They had two children of about my age, Ruth and Hans, with whom I had often played. What a relief, after our hazardous wanderings, to be in a warm, comfortable home among familiar faces. A phone call was made to Vienna to my uncles' former secretary, who sent us money and clothing.

We rented a room in a working-class area where the landlady agreed not to register us with the police if we paid extra rent. The main thing I remember about the room was how cold it was; it had a small fireplace in which my father lit a fire every morning to heat water for tea. There was a bed, a campbed, a table, some chairs, and not much else. We each took a bath once a week at the Sonntags, where we spent afternoons. In the mornings we walked into the city center to the large department store, Sarma, which had the cheapest food in Brussels in its self-service cafeteria. Our main meal consisted of two portions of *pommes frites* (French fries) and one *oeuf mayonnaise* (egg mayonnaise) which was divided up between us. One day a man at a neighboring table recognized me as "Lili from the Votivpark in Vienna" and bought me a pastry. Pleased though I was at this treat, I also felt alarmed at being spotted. Our clothes were a give-away because they looked vaguely foreign. The local children wore pointed "pixie-hoods," so my mother bought a piece of cloth and sewed one for me. I was sure we were much safer for this disguise! On the way back from the Sonntags we would buy some bread and butter for supper. On this regime no wonder my father had a terrible attack of flu.

Early on during our stay in Brussels a miraculous thing happened: a letter from England that my father was among the forty Austrian dentists selected for immigration. Since he had no formal degree in dentistry, only a post graduate diploma, he would be required to study six months at a British dental school and pass the final examination of the Royal College of Dental Surgeons before being allowed to practice. The visa would be issued "shortly."

"Shortly" is one of those British bureaucratic phrases that can mean almost anything, like "as well as can be expected" to describe the condition of a patient in hospital. We optimistically took "shortly" to mean "soon." After a week my father went to the British consulate, where he was told he would be informed by letter "in due course." Another of those open-ended phrases. My father went to the consulate again, and was once more politely but firmly turned away. My uncles in London visited various offices in an attempt to speed things up. Even my mother, usually rather reserved, took the initiative of going to the consulate herself, but to no avail; she had suspected that perhaps my father hadn't spoken to the right person. "Shortly" was two months.

Meanwhile, to avoid arrest was our constant concern. We registered with the Red Cross so as to have it put on record that we were merely in transit in Belgium on the way to England. We didn't go to the popular refugees' haunts for fear of a police raid. Nor did I go to school, much to my chagrin; to enroll in school might lead to all sorts of questions, investigations, and danger. That was when I began to write, mostly letters that were never mailed and had no particular purpose other than to reach out to others. I can so well understand how Anne Frank, at the beginning of her *Diary* came to invent her friend, Kitty. The sole break in our Spartan routine was on Saturday mornings when we went to the temple, which was deliciously warm. My parents, though not assimilationists, had gone to the temple only on the major holidays, like most other Viennese Jews. Now we eagerly awaited the Sabbath for the respite it gave us from the cold.

When the visa finally arrived, we had one more major hurdle to surmount. There was no way to board the boat for Dover at Ostend without passing through the Belgian police checkpoint. The officer saw at once that we had no entry visa or stamp in our passport. It was within his power (and in accordance with Belgian law) to have us deported back to Germany. We had discussed tactics on this issue again and again without coming up with any solution other than open confession. Fortunately, at this point the Red Cross interceded in our behalf. Since England was willing to admit us, why bother to ship us back to Germany? It was simpler and more convenient for Belgium just to put us on the boat. We heaved a tremendous sigh of relief as the official handed back our passport and nodded us toward the boat. We were on our way to a new life, which was at least to restore us to a legal status, even if it did not prove either safe or free of worry for many years.

Brussels

The sense of being safe was exhilarating, and it took us several days to get used to it. We could walk the streets with less fear of being arrested, and the ringing doorbell no longer caused a palpitating heartbeat. We were in a civilized world again, although the unpleasant feeling of being uninvited guests never left us.

Forced to become flotsam, we were determined to change back into "normal" citizens as soon as we could. The euphoria of the first days gradually evaporated. We realized that Belgium was only a temporary refuge for us; we had a breathing space in which to think, plan, and make decisions about the future. It was clear to us that we would stay there for only a short time; circumstances would decide how long. We had to explore the possibilities.

This was the first time we could look back to contemplate our past life and consider the future. How could all this have happened to us? Was it our fault that we had got into this situation? We couldn't have prevented it, but should we have foreseen it in good time? No; nobody could have believed it. We were brought up to respect the laws of the land, to do our duty like every good citizen, and to rely on the protection of the authorities.

We were, of course, used to putting up with a certain
amount of anti-Semitic prejudice all our lives. It was part
of our normal life, our fate, and we didn't complain about
it. We had to work harder and be better in order to be
successful in any occupation or profession. We were a
minority often used as a scapegoat for ills for which we
were not in the least responsible. There was a Viennese
joke: *"Der Jud ist schuld. Warum? Weil's wahr ist"* ("The
Jew is to blame. Why? Because that's the way it is"). One
couldn't argue against such statements. We were satisfied
with the absence of violence. We lived in one of the most
civilized parts of the world. We refused to believe that in
the midst of the cultured and educated "nation of poets
and philosophers" (as the Germans were called), we would
not be protected from such barbarity as we had witnessed.
We believed that they would never debase themselves to
carry on a crusade against a defenseless minority. By the
time we realized our error, it was too late.

We had warnings from abroad which we took to be
wildly exaggerated. My eldest brother, who had lived in
Brazil for many years, advised us to pack up and leave
Austria, or better still, leave Europe entirely. We should
not harbor any illusions; a war was brewing and we would
be at its center. My wife didn't want to hear of it, and I
could understand her feelings. She had once had practical
experience of what it meant to be a refugee; she
remembered clearly all the difficulties and problems
attendant on being a fugitive. To give up everything that
was dear to us and all that we had achieved because of a
more or less imaginary danger? No; we would wait. Who
could blame us?

We had met a number of German Jews in the 1930s
in Karlsbad, on our annual visits there. They were
doctors, lawyers, businessmen who were living in Nazi
Germany. They summed up the situation like this:
conditions for Jews were bad and might even become
worse before things returned to normal again. They based
their judgment on solid economic facts, political pressures
from abroad, and a growing resistance to the regime
within Germany. We should not become panic-stricken

and run away. That was what we liked to hear and to believe. After their vacation they returned to Germany— with some anxiety, as we sensed, an anxiety they wanted to conceal from themselves.

Hope and self-deception, allied to fear and anxiety, paralyzed our ability to make up our minds and emigrate in good time. We didn't have enough money to live abroad for many months. So long as it was not a matter of life and death, we didn't feel that running away was justified. And where should we have gone? But now that we had got away by the skin of our teeth, we didn't want the same thing to happen to us again. We were determined to move further on as soon as possible. We had learned our lesson and had nothing more to lose.

How lucky we were to be in Belgium! The nightmare was over, and we were relatively content in our small room. It was cold, for the tiny iron stove gave off little warmth. Our windowsill served as an icebox for our scanty food supply, which was once blown away by the wind.

After about three weeks we had good news from England: I was among the forty Austrian dentists admitted to Great Britain with the prospect of practicing there. The "shot in the dark," my application for England, was a winner. It was a miracle. Since our arrival in Belgium I had often wondered what had happened to my application and so had my wife. We didn't dare to talk about it to one another. It is difficult to describe our joy. We had no means to celebrate. We could hardly believe that England was prepared to give us the chance to become proper citizens again. In a matter of days, or so we thought, our visa would be issued by the British consulate. We waited impatiently. I often inquired at the consulate; the superintendent there knew me already as a frustrated visitor until one day, after many "sorries," smiling broadly, he told me that it had at last come. It was official; it was true.

In the meantime we started to study English intensively. It was a cold winter, and our problem was to find a warm place during the day where we could sit and work. We were always on the move in order to keep warm. We were cold even in our beds. The light from the one bulb in the ceiling was weak and distant.

In the mornings we marched from Laaken to the city center. It took us nearly an hour to get to the Rue Neuf where the department stores were. They were warm and hospitable. Unfortunately, we couldn't sit down anywhere. We grew very tired. We literally dragged ourselves to Sarma, where we had lunch because it was cheap and filling. We made a slow job of it so as to get a bit of rest, too. The shops were full of exquisite goods. The fruits in the shop windows made a great impression on Lilian; she was fascinated by their beauty and variety. We would have loved to buy her some, but could only promise that we would do so as soon as Daddy earned some money. "When Daddy earns some money," she said again and again.

The question also arose as to whether we should report our presence to the Belgian police. After long deliberation our friends advised us against it. In some districts (Scarbeck, for example) the police were tolerant, in others they were very strict. They would keep the men in custody for several weeks, although generally they released them in the end. I suppose they made inquiries into their background and history. Still, to be in prison is not pleasant. As our stay in Belgium was to be temporary, it was not worth risking it. Two months before our arrival the police had rounded up a few hundred refugees and sent them back to Germany. Some were bad characters, for whose deeds many innocents had to suffer. We did report to the office of the Red Cross; we told and documented our story. We were given a card stating that we would be going to England as soon as the promised visa arrived. We could prove it with a letter from the Jewish refugee organization in London. We never made use of the card, but it made us feel that we were only semi-illegal.

We had some surprises in meeting friends and relatives with whom we had lost contact in Vienna, where the slogan was, *"Gott für alle aber jeder für sich!"* ("God for all but each for himself"). Communication was often dangerous. In Brussels we greeted each other like saved shipwrecks. We were pleased, but depressed, too, as we involuntarily compared our past standing with our present one: homeless flotsam in a strange country. Most of us were without means or occupation, without a *carte d'identité* or plans for the future. Hardly anyone complained; we were the lucky ones compared to those still in Germany.

Many people tried to move further on from Belgium, and the consulates had a busy time. With sufficient money it was not difficult to secure a visa to some South American country. Our friends, the Sonntags, could have stayed in Belgium, but they moved to Brazil. My poor relatives whom we met in Brussels couldn't get away, and perished in a Nazi concentration camp.

We also met some Belgian Jews and were astonished at their fatalistic attitude. We were a living warning to them! One of them told me at the British consulate that he was going to England to restock his business. I asked him, "Are you not worried about the possible occupation of Belgium by the Germans?" "Oh no, they got their fingers burned in Belgium in the last war; they won't run that risk again." I had been in the same frame of mind not so long ago; I couldn't blame him. In my heart I wished him better luck than we had had.

It was a strange life in Brussels. Uncertainty was in the air, but there were no signs of any kind of preparations to defend the country if it were attacked, except for what we once saw. A few soldiers were giving a demonstration in a suburban street how to extinguish an incendiary bomb. We were the only onlookers. There was an atmosphere of resignation everywhere, probably because everyone believed that it would be senseless and hopeless to resist the German army. No air raid warnings as in Aachen! There were days of quiet confidence alternating with days of near panic—all depending on the news from Germany.

A wealthy Austrian refugee tried to gatecrash into England. He flew to London with proof of his assets. He

would not be a burden to England; on the contrary, he
would open a factory and employ British workers. He was
politely told that he should explain all his plans to the
British consul in Brussels, who would then make a
decision whether to issue a visa. He had to return to
Belgium the same day.

A friend of ours, Dr. Schiller, another of the forty
Austrian dentists admitted to England, was waiting for
his visa as we were. He had been arrested in Vienna.
Fortunately, his relatives, diamond dealers in Belgium,
were able to get him a regular visa, and he had been in
Brussels for several months already. His household
belongings were sitting on the London docks, and he was
urged to remove them or make some practical
arrangement. For this purpose he wanted to go to London
for just a few days. He took all the relevant papers with
him, as well as the letter from the Refugee Committee
confirming that he would soon get his visa. The
immigration officer was very polite and understanding but
wouldn't allow him to enter England without a valid visa.
A policeman escorted him back to the boat for Ostend.

We registered with the Jewish refugee organization
in Brussels. In their office in the Rue de la Caserne they
had their hands full. Not many questions were asked, and
they helped everyone who turned to them. The amount of
money they could give us was just enough to keep body
and soul together. We were literally penniless, and we
were grateful for the support. It was heartwarming to find
that the Hebrew saying, *"Kol yisroel haverim"* ("All Jews
are brethren") was indeed true. We too had helped
German Jewish refugees in Vienna, not believing that our
fate would be the same a year later. The London Jewish
refugee organization was in full swing when we arrived,
and proved a blessing to all of us. We regarded their
financial help as a loan, and started repaying it as soon as
I began to earn. I am still a contributor![1] We tried not to
be a burden to our fellow Jews and to the countries that
gave us asylum.

There were of course exceptions—such is human
nature. Peddling all kinds of goods was not objectionable

but we heard of things that damaged our reputation. Our fate depended on the benevolent tolerance of the Belgian authorities, and it was imprudent and dangerous to strain their patience.

Two episodes come to mind as I recall the time we spent in Brussels. First, at the Red Cross office, a young man was already sitting in the waiting room when we arrived. He was very talkative and full of complaints about the hard time he was having in Brussels. He claimed that he was a German political refugee who was fighting the Nazis. It was obvious that he wanted to gain our confidence, and he started to ask a lot of questions: who we were, where we came from, where we lived, who was supporting us, how we had managed to get out of Germany and so forth. His intense curiosity made us suspicious, and we told him so. We were not prepared to answer his questions. Later we heard that there were a number of spies and informers masquerading as refugees. Our caution was justified.

On another occasion, the Sonntags introduced us to a Belgian couple. He was a man of about sixty, a retired civil servant who had worked in the Belgian Congo. She was much younger and of German origin. She spoke German fluently, but her husband spoke only French. They invited us to tea. The conversation was in both languages, though mainly in German and dominated by the wife. After a while, the husband disappeared and came back half an hour later pushing a cart with tea, cakes, sandwiches, cups, plates, spoons, and such. He wore a long apron and served the tea while his wife carried on the conversation undisturbed. It was obviously his duty, not hers. When we had finished tea, he cleared the table and left for the kitchen. The sounds from there indicated that he was busy washing up. After we left, I told my wife that I was not willing to stay in Belgium under any circumstances. We had one of our few laughs of those days.

This visit had an unexpected sequel. A few days later the wife came to our place, very upset, pale, and agitated. She told us that she had just had a message that her

husband had had an accident and had been taken to a
hospital. Our mutual friend—also a physician—was not
available, and she begged me to go to the hospital with
her. I was very anxious not to be in any way involved with
the Belgian authorities, but she implored me so
desperately that I couldn't refuse. We found her husband
in a semiconscious state, without any serious injuries. I
soon realized that the man had had a severe epileptic fit. I
was surprised that the wife was concerned above all with
searching for his wallet in his pockets. The husband
couldn't give coherent answers to her questions.
Something very important was missing; that was my
impression. I suggested that she make inquiries at the
hospital admissions office and notify the police. No, not
the police, she said. She was very distraught, and my
consoling words that her husband would soon be out of
hospital had little effect on her. She didn't seem to be
listening to me. We never met the couple again, but
gradually I found out the reason for her mysterious
behavior. Diamond smuggling from the Congo was a very
lucrative business. The man was involved in this through
his old business connections. He had gone to Antwerp that
day to collect his share of the stones. He had a seizure at
the railroad station in Brussels, and while he was
unconscious, someone stole his wallet, in which he was
carrying the contraband. It would have been hopeless to
look for the thief, and not advisable to notify the police.

Every Sabbath morning we had a very long walk to
the main temple in Brussels. It was a beautiful building
near the royal palace. Over the entrance was an
inscription in French: "Have we not been created by the
same God? Are we not all his children?"—meaningless
words for those to whom the questions were addressed.
There was a solemn service, and we thanked God for
protecting and saving us.

At last we had our precious visa stamped into our
passport. It entitled us to enter England legally for a stay
of six months. Still, we had one anxiety: the Belgian
officials at Ostend might ask us how we had entered the
country—who had helped us? what were we doing there?

and a hundred other questions. We mentally prepared our defense and had the Red Cross card handy to show them if necessary. To our great relief no questions were asked. They were frankly glad to get rid of us.

About ten years later we went back to Brussels in our own car, a Ford 10, and stayed at a hotel where we proudly presented our British passports. We visited the temple again, our only old friend in Brussels. It was the right place to say a prayer of thanksgiving.[2]

London

LRF

The crossing of the English Channel from Ostend to Dover took over four hours, and the sea was what the English call "choppy." My father walked about the deck, peering out for a glimpse of England. I stayed as still as possible beside my mother, and didn't even see the famous white cliffs of Dover. We were shaky and dizzy when we disembarked. This time, however, there was no anxiety about facing the police and immigration authorities.

Yet, on closer consideration, our status was rather ambiguous. My father had been admitted for a minimum of six months' study before the final dental exam as a preliminary to resuming his profession. Unlike some other refugees, we never had any intention (or illusion) about going back to Vienna at some later date. To my parents, the years 1928–1938 had been the closest approximation on earth to heaven. But their intuition told them that that world had gone; the extent to which it would disappear physically became apparent only gradually, especially after 1942, as word began to spread of the "Final Solution." Our move to England was, from the outset, a permanent one in our eyes. In fact, my parents could never be induced to cross the frontier into Austria again, and would shudder even to hear Austrian German spoken on our vacations in Europe after the war. While we came to England to stay, our coveted English visa, as I have it before me in our German passport with the prominent red "J" on its front page, states "SIX MONTHS ONLY. No work paid or unpaid." Since we arrived on 1 March 1939, the issue of renewal never arose because by the end of the six months the war was about to break out, and no one ever bothered to bring it up. Like the man in the story who came to dinner, we stayed in England until 1971, and my mother is buried there.

On the train from Dover to London we shared a compartment with an Englishman. My father, keen to try out his English, attempted to strike up a conversation with him. It was a chastening experience. To begin with, the man clearly had difficulty in following my father's faltering sentences and his Hungaro-German accent. Moreover, it was "not done" in England, certainly not then, casually to strike up a conversation. A lapidary comment about the weather is the most that is admissible. We were slowly to find out that a great many other things were "not done" in England, including putting one's bedding out on the windowsill in the morning to air. This caused great indignation among our neighbors, and of course, our bedding only got nastily damp. It takes a while to become initiated into these unwritten conventions of British behavior and to appreciate that curious blend of reticence and tact.

We were met in London by my uncles and taken to the house where the entire family lived. It was on Brondesbury Road, a pleasant, tree-lined street in the working-class district of Kilburn, where rents were low. I don't fully recall the living arrangements, except that it was terribly crowded, with grandparents, uncles, aunts, and cousins, three generations all on top of one another. Not one of us had a reasonable command of English, let alone a work permit or an income. One of my uncles and his wife were hawking light bulbs. We were given a room on the second floor looking out onto a small backyard. However much it left to be desired, it was a vast improvement over Brussels.

Our furniture now came in useful, though not without causing us some pain, too. We had, according to the contract, paid for transportation "from house to house." There was no mention of storage charges. To our dismay, the bill for storage amounted to £50—a fifth of the total amount we had by devious means, been able to transfer to a British bank. Two pieces, the rosewood dining room table and my father's wardrobe, were too large to go through the door of the little house, and had to be sent for auction. The exquisite table went for £5, while the wardrobe had to be scrapped. Our room was chock-full of the remaining furniture. I remember the stunned look on the face of the welfare worker who turned up one day to see where I was living. I slept on a kind of bench, since my bed had been commandeered by one of the packers in Vienna as just right for his child. Notwithstanding her amazement, the welfare worker must have concluded that I didn't look neglected or abused.

The day after we arrived I insisted on starting school; I obviously had the desire to normalize my life as quickly as possible. The local elementary school was just around the corner. I can't imagine how I was placed in any class. Not only was I unable to understand or speak a word of the language; I couldn't either, at seven-and-a-half, read or write, because I had been taught the Gothic script. Both my teachers and my schoolfellows showed extraordinary patience and kindness. To these children, some of whom were dressed almost in rags, I appeared like something out of a fairy tale or like a large doll with my many pretty dresses and matching hair ribbons. My guess is that my inability to communicate heightened the doll-like effect. They would fetch me from home and escort me back, touching the material of my dresses in real wonder, especially on my birthday when I appeared in a pink organdie dress embossed with white flowers. I was shown around the school like an exhibit from another world.

I was somewhat upset at not being able to join in any of their activities. I couldn't even knit, and implored my mother to teach me during the lunch hour of my first day. She showed me the Continental system so that I still felt

different even when I could do something with the others.
It fell to my mother, too, to teach me the alphabet and
writing and English. The school lent us a series of readers
about an old woman and her dog. My daily repetition of
the same passages got on everybody's nerves at home,
tense as they were. My schoolfellows also, taught me by a
show-and-tell method, holding up various objects and
naming them for me. They were most ingenious; one day
Colin, my special protector, turned up with a box; as he
opened it, a creature jumped out and he shouted in
triumph: "Frog!"

My father was assigned to Manchester University for
his six months' study. The policy was to distribute the
foreigners throughout the various dental schools. We saw
him rarely; he would occasionally come on a Sunday on a
cheap return ticket. Once, he brought me a small doll to
replace my Liesl, whose head had got squashed, to my
great chagrin. My younger cousins, who had arrived in
London before us, had taken possession of my table and
chairs, pulled the hair out of my toy horse, and broken
quite a few things. I was horrified. It was a case of "who is
sitting in my chair?"—which they insisted was theirs. I
think our alienation from each other in our adult lives
may have its roots in those early confrontations. I
resented too my cousin's perfectly logical question: Why
was uncle having to go back to school? Had he forgotten
how to fix teeth?

I went on looking forward to the day "when Daddy
earns some money again." It became a stock phrase, an
expression of my confidence that this was a passing phase
of our lives. We practiced the utmost frugality; a visit to
the Lyons coffeeshop on Kilburn High Street was a great
treat. I longed for what I called "a decorated ice-cream"
(an ice-cream sundae), but that cost sixpence, and I had to
make do with plain vanilla or strawberry for twopence.
Somehow I missed out on ice-cream sundaes in my life, for
by the time the money and the ingredients were available
in post-war England, I was a teenager watching my
figure. (Recently, when I had upgraded myself to first
class on a flight with my "Frequent Flyers Mileage," ice

cream with hot fudge sauce was served. I ate it with
feelings of both gratification and guilt.) Nor did I get to
see much of London during those first months. We would
set out to explore on Sundays, on foot, naturally, so as not
to spend precious pennies on bus fares. I never managed
to walk beyond Marble Arch, and it seemed an endless
trek back along Edgeware road.

Apart from English, I was acquiring another
language without realizing it. To speak German on the
streets of London in 1939 was hardly popular, so my
grandparents were advised to speak Yiddish, which
sounds somewhat like Dutch, and which has the
advantage of being a kind of international *lingua franca*
despite regional differences. I developed the belief that at
a certain age, say seventy, people switched to this
language, which I called *Altdeutsch* (Old German). More
than ten years later, when I came to study Old- and
Middle High German, I grasped the kernel of truth in my
childish misapprehension, insofar as Yiddish had indeed
evolved out of an earlier historical stage of German, which
the Jews took back to Poland in the late Middle Ages.
Polish, Russian, Hebrew, English and other elements were
added by accretion to create a highly expressive language,
which I hold in affection as my grandparents' tongue. My
early exposure to Yiddish was of considerable help when I
was faced with Middle High German.

To learn English was harder for adults than for me.
Those who learned by ear made more rapid initial
progress, but took longer to master writing. They were
also liable to make ridiculous mistakes, such as "sister-in-
lord," through mishearing. There are a host of stories
about refugee English, particularly mistakes arising from
the use of similar-sounding words, like the person who
declared, "I can become a cabbage cheaper in another
shop," on the assumption that "become" had the same
meaning as the German *bekommen* (to get). Many
refugees got into the habit of freely mixing words from
their various languages, resulting in an "emigranto"
comprehensible only to their peers. Those who followed
the slower path of learning grammar did better in the long

run. We had an ancient radio to which we listened a lot to hear the language spoken. The easiest to follow were the religious sermons, because they were enunciated slowly and emphatically. The only trouble was that their vocabulary of "redemption," "savior," and "sin" was not exactly handy in everyday usage.

I must have learned quite rapidly. At the end of the school year in July, I was at the top of my class. My schoolfellows shouted excitedly to my mother, "She's come top!" and she could only associate "top" with "mountain" and wonder what I was up to. The headmistress predicted that I might eventually get a "scholarship" to a grammar school—another term that mystified us. We asked our landlord, and gathered that a scholarship was something highly desirable.

London

The Channel was relatively calm for a mid-winter day. We felt tense but confident in facing the unknown problems that would confront us. Providence had opened our parachutes over the grey skies of England, the country of our preference. We had the promise that we could make a new home and start a new life there. We knew very little about England and its Commonwealth, on which the sun was said never to set. The cool, calm, and reserved Englishman was proverbial, and the traditional formality of English society an unwritten law. We couldn't speak the language; we were determined to learn, and to try to become worthy citizens of England. We knew it would be very difficult, but we weren't scared.

The slender figure of my wife was next to me with Lilian at her side as we watched the Prince Albert ploughing through the sea to separate us from our past and protect us from the evil emanating from Germany. We thought with heartaching compassion of those still left behind. Lilian would not move out of sight; she was always afraid of losing us. We had no plans; we didn't know what to expect. Only six weeks earlier we had not known where we might land and which language we

89

should learn: English? Spanish? Portuguese? I brushed up my rusty French, which became useful in Belgium. Lilian looked at me with admiration when she heard me speak French. As soon as our destination became certain, we had started to learn English.

I was shocked when the porters at Dover asked questions about our luggage—I couldn't understand a word. They grabbed the suitcases and we followed them. I was terribly disappointed to discover how little English I knew. We recovered a bit when we had to speak to a customs officer.

We boarded the train to London where our relatives lived. The weather was cold and grey, with a light mist lingering in the air. Some sad-looking horses were standing in a meadow, and now and then small, red brick houses were visible through the windows of the train. Nobody spoke in the compartment; it was as still as in a church. That seemed strange to us. The seats were comfortable. These were our first impressions of England. A young man opposite me was reading a newspaper. When he had finished with it, I asked him to lend it to me. He looked at me and without a word passed the paper to me. I was told later that this is not done in England. We slowly learned that many things were "not done" in England.

My wife's family had rented part of a house in Kilburn, in northwest London, where housing was not expensive. They used our furniture which had arrived long before we did. In sending the furniture to London, we were well aware that we might not see it again. Had we left it in Vienna, we would have lost it anyway. Our relatives collected our belongings from the London docks and used them. They had all left in such a hurry that they hadn't taken anything with them. Two of our crates were missing, and in their place we had one "stranger," filled with Hebrew books and two paintings of rabbis. They are fine pictures, which we still have.[1]

We received good news when we arrived in London: we were not destitute. All our savings had been deposited in a savings bank in Vienna. When we heard rumors that Jewish bank accounts would be blocked, we took the precaution of withdrawing all our money, and hid it in our apartment. This was risky, but it seemed to be the least of all evils. We had no domestic help who might have found it and denounced us. We asked an old friend, a bank manager, what to do with the money, and followed his advice. The plan was that my wife would go to the branch of the bank where he was in charge, and ask to see him personally, saying that she was Mrs. Cohen and had an appointment with him. She would bring the money with her. At the time it was still possible to buy Austrian railroad stocks which were quoted on the London Stock Exchange. He would buy those shares and send the papers to our friend, Mr. Sydney Cohen, in London. He warned us that the exchange rate would be unfavorable, but the money would be safe and abroad. When we arrived, our friend, who was also our "guarantor," handed us the sum of £255, a fortune to us. The bad news was that we had to pay £50 for expenses incurred in moving the furniture from the docks. We had believed that everything had been paid for in advance in Vienna, so this was a shock to us. We almost wished we had left the things behind.

My last activity as a dentist had been to look after my wife's teeth. One of her large molars needed a gold cap. When I removed the big old filling, there was a fair sized cavity. It occurred to me that the three-carat diamond in her ring might fit in. I tried it and found that it could be done. I fixed it in with dental cement and myself made a gold crown which covered the tooth. It would have been too dangerous to wear it on her hand or to hide it in our clothing.

On our arrival at the family "headquarters" we found a very depressing situation. The old parents were ailing and the middle generation disheartened by the long idleness and the inability to earn a living. A refugee was not permitted to accept any work "paid or unpaid," as was stamped in our passports. There was large scale unemployment in England at that time and the population would have resented it if any vacancy had been filled by a foreigner. Who could blame them for this attitude? Language difficulties, unfamiliarity with British trading habits, and lack of connections prevented my brothers-in-law from starting up their own businesses. Only one of them managed to earn his living, as a lightbulb salesman. One day Lilian said to me, "I am glad that we were not as wealthy in Vienna as my uncles. We needn't be as upset as they are about what we have lost." My sister-in-law asked us whether there was a way to be smuggled back to Vienna! It was heartbreaking to see them so despondent and demoralized. What a change! They had been hard-working, respected, self-confident, and successful business people. We, the newcomers, had to encourage them and try to lift their spirits.

Even a well-planned move to a foreign country is a big upheaval. One can prepare in advance in many ways: learn the language, study the climate, collect information about schools and the various institutions, habits, and customs of the population. We had no choice but to pick up gradually what we needed to know. Mere common sense based on former experience was not a reliable guideline. The British appeared to us at least as peculiar and incomprehensible as we were to them. We tried to learn from our blunders and to adapt to the new lifestyle as well as possible. We put milk into our tea, ate cereal for breakfast, and had our main meal in the evenings. Our staple food was herring, cheap and nutritious, although we grew tired of it after a few weeks on this diet. The children had no trouble in acclimatizing. They took to the new country and new life like fish to water. They went to the local schools, made friends, and were soon speaking excellent Cockney English.

We refugees were a very mixed crowd, people from all walks of life, from High Court judges to temple beadles. There seemed to be no systematic selection as to whom the British government allowed to enter the country. They were all in dire need and distress. On the whole, it was a fair cross section of the Jewish population of Austria. For some it was a temporary refuge until they could emigrate elsewhere. Many single young men stayed at the so-called Kitchener Camp at Sandwich in Kent. When the war broke out, those who were fit for military service volunteered for the British Army. They were admitted only to the Pioneer Corps. My youngest brother-in-law joined up too, and was later evacuated from Dunkirk with the retreating remnants of the Allied forces.

There were optimists among us who thought in terms of months before they could return "home," and pessimists who saw no hope of ever going back to Germany or Austria. Both tried to arrange their lives accordingly. We prepared ourselves mentally for a long and probably permanent stay. It was clear to us that the Austria that we had enjoyed in the 1930s was gone for ever.

We knew very little about England, mainly what we had read in its literature: Dickens, G. B. Shaw, Galsworthy, Byron, H. G. Wells, Oscar Wilde, and the Sherlock Holmes stories. We knew nothing about modern middle- or working-class England. We regarded London as the head office of the mighty and wealthy British Empire. The cool, calm, taciturn upper-class Englishman who changes into a tuxedo for dinner and is served by a butler had caught our imagination, perhaps from movies. A friend of ours bought a new tuxedo when he got his visa to England. We visited him one evening in his furnished apartment in Maida Vale. He was just having his dinner, pickled herring with bread and tea. He was not offended when I asked him why he had not changed into his tuxedo. We had a good laugh.

The language problem was a source of great worry to us. We were amazed at the fluency of some of the uneducated refugees. They picked up in a short time a few everyday expressions and a relatively small vocabulary, which they used like a juggler. They had self-confidence, and no idea of even the most elementary rules of grammar. Their writing was grotesque, their spelling phonetic, and yet they could make themselves understood in shops and markets better than we could. We felt a bit ashamed of our slow progress compared to theirs, but our ambition was to learn grammatically correct English with a wider range. My task was even more difficult, for I had to tackle medical and dental language as well. We did all

right in the long run. My wife's English had hardly any
trace of a foreign accent. I still speak all languages with a
strong Hungarian accent. The common lament of many
German refugees was: "We have lost everything we had;
why can't we lose our accent, too?"

An acquaintance of ours was noted for his
meticulously proper German. If anybody desecrated the
German language by mixing in foreign words, he grew
furious. In Vienna it was quite common for people to
introduce Yiddish, Hungarian, Czech or other terms from
foreign languages into their conversation. It was an
accepted habit and a mirror of the mixed population. This
man couldn't find his way home one evening in London.
He wandered around for quite a time until he decided to
seek help. A passing car stopped, and he asked the driver
in his best English, "Where is Brondesbury Road?" The
driver recognized his speech as that of a German refugee
and said to him in Yiddish, *Setz dach aran* (Get in), and
took him home. He told this story against himself, and
confessed that he felt ashamed of his past aversion to
Yiddish.

The Refugee Committee in Bloomsbury House and
later in Woburn House was a blessing to us. The mostly
voluntary workers did an admirable job, and no praise is
high enough in appreciation of the patient and
sympathetic way in which they dealt with us. We were not
easy customers. The variety of our problems was
incredible, all of them urgent and very fundamental.

The first person to find her feet was Lilian. The day
after our arrival I took her to the nearest primary school
in Salisbury Road, Kilburn. She was very happy there,
and soon made some friends.

My wife had her hands full, nursing her sick parents,
cooking, washing, mending, and learning English. How
she could manage all this with so little previous
experience of housekeeping is still a puzzle to me. She
wanted to earn some money, too, by doing piecework. She
sewed buttons onto cardboard, and crocheted gloves, but
the pay was so poor that she gave it up.

I went to Bloomsbury House every morning to find out what I was supposed to do in order to practice dentistry, again and to attend English courses. I learned how to pronounce "lawnmower" and the names of other gardening tools. I felt distressed on account of my poor English and slow progress.

Nobody seemed to know what the forty Austrian dentists were supposed to do to get a British dental license. After a few weeks we were at last informed; we had to spend six months at a dental hospital, and then to pass the final exams. As all of us were experienced dental surgeons, we expected this to be a formality. I admit that I was disappointed and upset, but in retrospect I can see that there were good reasons for these requirements. Though we all had medical degrees, we had no more than diplomas in dentistry, as was the norm in Austria. Six months at a British dental school would give us a better chance to integrate ourselves into the profession, to learn its customs, and to get a license like all British dentists. We were specifically asked not to use our former title of "doctor," so as to be like the British dentists. I had never before worried about exams until this one. I had family responsibilities and was in a hurry to earn our living. When my little nephew heard that I had to learn dentistry, he asked whether uncle had forgotten how to do teeth.

The forty of us were to be distributed among dental schools all over the country. Fate took me and two colleagues to Manchester.

I have here to tell of an event that very much upset me at the time. The plum places were in London dental hospitals, or at least as near to London as possible. Our families lived there, and so we could be together. It would have been cheaper, too. By the time I learned about the requirements, these places had been already been filled by colleagues who had inside information. The nearest open place was Birmingham. I happened to run into a colleague, Dr. O, who told me that he had been admitted to both Birmingham and Edinburgh. He had not decided which to accept. The matter was urgent because the next finals were just six months away. I told him that I would gladly take Birmingham if he chose Edinburgh. He promised to make his decision that day. We arranged to meet the next morning at 8 a.m. at Euston Station. Should he not turn up, I was to take the next train to Birmingham and tell them that he had given up his place to me.

He wasn't there, and I traveled to Birmingham and went straight to the dental school. I explained the situation as well as I could in my poor English. They were friendly and I had an interview with a Professor Humphrey who understood some German. I was told to come back the next morning to make concrete arrangements. I felt very satisfied. There was a temple on the way to the city center. I went in and met the rabbi, Dr. Rabinowitz, who spoke German fairly well. He invited me to his home and made several phone calls to find me accommodation for the coming six months.

The next morning I went to the dental school. The professor's secretary received me with icy coldness. She told me that Dr. O had arrived the previous day, an hour after I had left, to claim his place. He denied having made any arrangement with me (he spoke fluent English). I stood there looking like a liar and impostor. The secretary took pity on me and offered me a chair. I was shocked, and could only say that there must have been some misunderstanding. Dr. O could have cleared up the matter by saying that he had changed his mind and taken a later train. Never in my life was I in such a shameful position. I was very upset and returned to London immediately. I told my wife what had happened. She consoled me with a Hebrew saying, "*Ve gam ze letovo*" ("And this too will be for the best"). Dr. O was the only dentist among the forty Viennese whose name was later struck from the Dental Register for "unprofessional conduct." I never spoke to him again.

At the Manchester Dental Hospital the professors, students, and administrators were kind, friendly, and helpful to the three "old" foreign dentists. They didn't know what to do with us; we had no fixed duties or curriculum. Communication was very difficult, and there were some grotesque misunderstandings. Two young German refugee students, both in their final year, already fluent in English, and obviously accepted by their fellow students, acted as our interpreters. We attended lectures, which we couldn't understand, and watched the final-year students at work. I was very impressed by the quality of their workmanship. It was a good dental school with a pleasant atmosphere.

The students came from middle class families who could afford the long and costly training. Standards were high and the students had to work hard. Every one of them was known personally to the professors, and one could see them in friendly conversation. What a difference compared to my student years in Vienna! There, the professors were unapproachable demi gods. The only meeting with them was at exams; we were strangers, just numbers to them. Some of them were openly anti-Semitic; cynical, offensive remarks at the exams were not rarities.

The only bad experience for me in Manchester was to see multiple extractions under nitrous oxide general anaesthetic. Sometimes more than twenty teeth were extracted at one sitting in what was known as "a clearance." One student would give the gas, while the other did the extractions. Many teeth were broken and roots and fragments left in the jaws. It was a ghastly sight for me even when skilled experts did it, and worse when nervous students were the operators. The next days or even weeks must have been misery for the patients. It took about six months before they could be fitted for dentures. The fear of infections emanating from teeth was the reason for this treatment. The patients often wanted to get it over all at one go, so as not to fear toothache and dental treatment for the rest of their lives, or, as one student commented, "to save them from tooth-brushing." They paid a high price for small future comfort! The professor laughed when I said, "We fight the diseases and the patients are the victims." I refused to do this kind of thing in my practice. You don't cut off your toe if you have a corn, and you don't pull out a tooth because it needs a filling. I explained to my patients. The half year I spent at the Manchester dental hospital was useful; it taught me how dentistry was practiced in England.

The excellent textbook of dentistry by Collins and Sprawson frightened me. It was a voluminous book and I was determined to study it thoroughly. My initial progress was slower than that of an old, sick tortoise. I worked diligently with the help of a dictionary, looking up the many words I didn't know. I was disappointed when I pronounced them at the dental hospital and nobody could understand what I meant to say. They were patient with me and corrected my English. I persevered doggedly and slowly, and gradually reaped the benefit of my efforts.

My best English teachers were the clergymen. I listened to their sermons on the radio. They spoke clearly, slowly, and distinctly. I became more familiar with religious language than with everyday terms. My other teachers were the political speakers in Plattfields Park, the Mancunian equivalent to London's "Speaker's Corner" in Hyde Park. I was a regular listener and soon became known to speakers of all factions. I was more interested in how distinctly they spoke than in what they had to say. I tried the cinema as well, but it was more pleasant than useful, and besides, it cost money. A kind Jewish lady, an experienced English teacher, volunteered to give the refugees lessons at the temple. She asked us to put a penny in the plate for the beadle. She complained that there were less pennies than people: "Are my lessons not worth a penny?" she once asked me. She was surprised when I replied that for some of us a penny meant half a loaf of bread. We were so poor that she could hardly believe it. She also offered elocution lessons, and I told her that I had nothing to elocute yet.

My wife and daughter stayed in London during my student months. It was cheaper and she was needed there to run the household. I would have to return to London to take the exams anyway. In Manchester I turned to the Jewish community to help me to find housing, but most of them lived in North Manchester, and the Dental Hospital was on the southern side of the city. The place I was offered was so far away that I would have had to travel over half an hour each way by bus, not to mention the cost of the fares. I found a boardinghouse closer to the Hospital in Victoria Park. Mostly single young men lived there, a few students, a shoe salesman, etc. I was astonished to see a fire ready to be lit in the fireplace even in the middle of summer, but was often glad of its warmth. At 10 p.m. tea and cookies were served; I was generally too tired to wait up. We had no intention of settling in Manchester permanently; it had the reputation of having an unhealthy climate. When I bade farewell to that hospitable city at the end of the six months, I thought it was for good. I had no premonition that Providence had deposited there for us "a heap of bread," as the Hungarian saying goes. We were to spend thirty years of our lives there, and couldn't have chosen a better place in the whole of England.

War broke out in September 1939 and we were glad to be together in such critical times. There were two air raid warnings soon after the declaration of war, and London expected to be bombed. Most of the children were evacuated to country villages and towns away from industrial areas. We found a small private school in Chertsey, Surrey, for our daughter. The owner and teacher was an Oxford graduate, from whom Lilian learned excellent English. It was not far from London, but we could not visit her for three months because aliens were not allowed to travel at that time. She was happy there, and her teacher was very satisfied with her progress. When we saw her, she was reluctant to speak German, the language of the Nazis. We had some difficulty in persuading her that the language was misused by the Nazis and she should not be ashamed to speak it. Later we spoke either German or English at home. We were very strict not to mix the two languages into what we called "emigranto."

We were very worried about the fate of our relatives and friends who had to live under the Nazis. It was obvious that they would have a much harder time than the German population, but in our most pessimistic fantasies we could not have imagined what would happen to them.

I passed the exams in March 1940 and became a Licenciate in Dental Surgery of the Royal College of Surgeons of England (abbreviated to L.D.S.R.C.S., Eng.). My name was entered in the Dental Register for a fee of 15 guineas.[2] I was now entitled to practice dental surgery in the United Kingdom. It was up to me to make the best of it.

We still needed the approval of the British Home Office as to the place where we intended to settle. After a few weeks' search we decided to buy the practice of a deceased dental surgeon in Bournemouth, a beautiful seaside resort on the south coast. We saw that the equipment was outdated, but the location was very favorable and we were confident that we could revitalize the practice. We found a nice apartment not far from the office and moved in. This was in May 1940.

We invested everything we had, including the money from the sale of the diamond which I had removed from my wife's tooth in a colleague's office. We took a loan too. It was about a week before our new home was habitable, and then my wife went to bring Lilian home from Chertsey.

When they arrived back in Bournemouth the next day, I was not there to welcome them and to celebrate our reunion.

The previous day two policemen came to our apartment. They gave me just enough time to pack a small suitcase and drove me to the police station. There the whole Austrian and German male population of Bournemouth was assembled. I did not know any of them; there were about thirty of us, mainly elderly gentlemen who had retired to this pleasant place. I had hoped to see them as patients, not as fellow prisoners. It was a terrible surprise to us because we had been classified as "friendly enemy aliens."

A few days earlier the Germans had invaded Holland and Belgium, There were rumors that many "fifth columnists" had helped them. To be on the safe side, the British government ordered the police to round up all male aliens on the Channel coast opposite Europe, and all class 'A' and 'B' aliens throughout the country.

It was a bitter blow for us. Financially, we were ruined, and our hopes and expectations were wiped out. Our family was more separated than ever before.

ILLUSTRATIONS

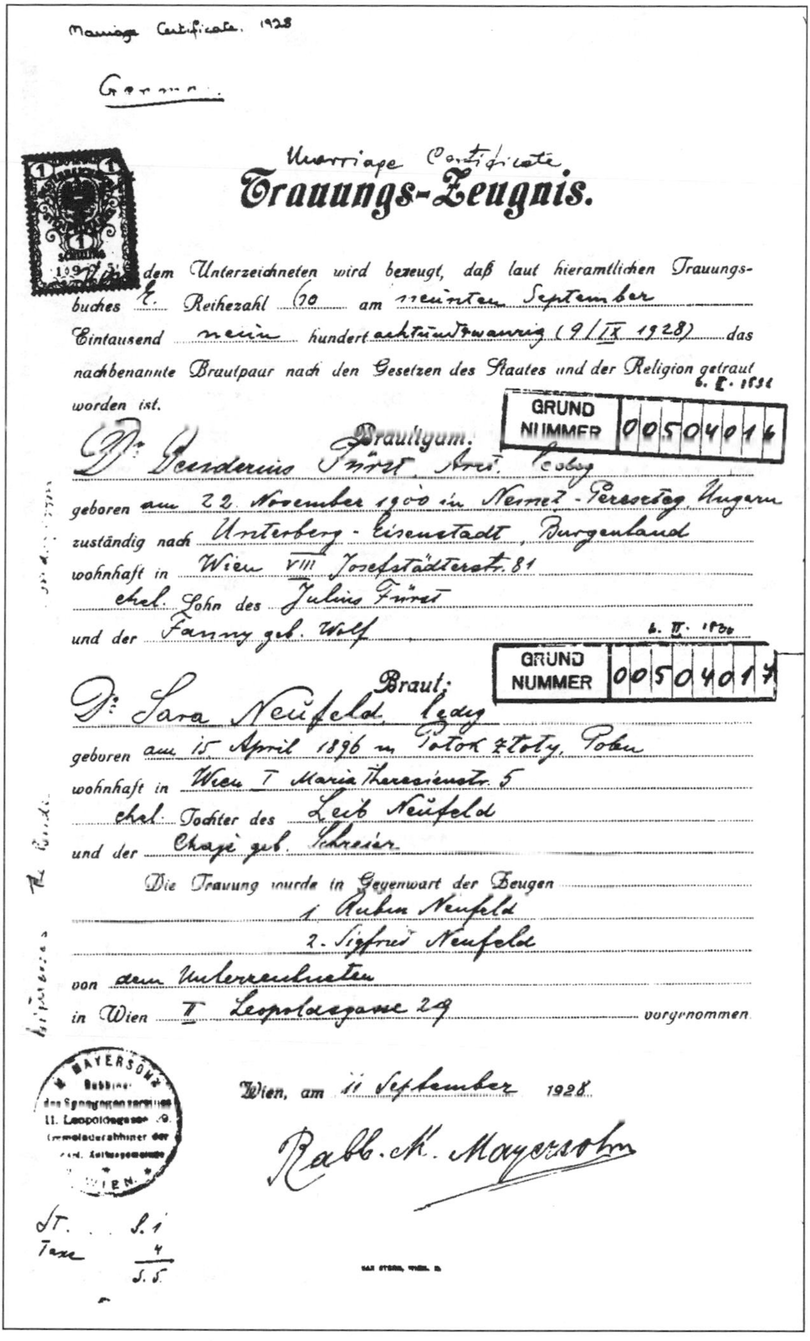

Marriage Certificate. 1928

German

Marriage Certificate

Trauungs-Zeugnis.

Von dem Unterzeichneten wird bezeugt, daß laut hieramtlichen Trauungs-buches E. Reihezahl 60 am neunten September Eintausend neun hundert achtundzwanzig (9/IX 1928) das nachbenannte Brautpaar nach den Gesetzen des Staates und der Religion getraut worden ist.

6. I. 1936

GRUND NUMMER	0	0	5	0	4	0	1	6

Bräutigam:

Dr. Desiderius Fürst Arzt ledig

geboren am 22. November 1900 in Nemet-Peresztög Ungarn

zuständig nach Unterberg-Eisenstadt, Burgenland

wohnhaft in Wien VIII Josefstädterstr. 81

ehel. Sohn des Julius Fürst

und der Fanny geb. Wolf

6. II. 1936

GRUND NUMMER	0	0	5	0	4	0	1	7

Braut:

Dr. Sara Neufeld ledig

geboren am 15 April 1896 in Potok Złoty, Polen

wohnhaft in Wien I Maria Theresienstr. 5

ehel. Tochter des Leib Neufeld

und der Chaje geb. Schreier

Die Trauung wurde in Gegenwart der Zeugen

1. Rubin Neufeld

2. Siegfried Neufeld

von dem Unterzeichneten

in Wien II Leopoldsgasse 29 vorgenommen.

Wien, am 11 September 1928

Rabb. M. Mayersohn

M. MAYERSOHN Rabbiner des Synagogenvereines II. Leopoldsgasse 29. Gemeinderabbiner der isr. Kultusgemeinde WIEN

ST. S. 1
Taxe 4
S. 5

Figure 1 Marriage Certificate, 1928

בעזה"י

______ בשבת ______ לחדש ______ שנת חמשת אלפים

ושש מאות ______ לבריאת עולם למנין שאנו מנין כאן ק"ק ______

איך מהר"ר אברהם בן מהר"ר רפאל ______ אמר לה להדא בתולתא

שרה רפואה בת מהר"ר יהודה ______ הוי לי לאנתו כדת משה

וישראל ואנא אפלח ואוקיר ואיזון ואפרנס יתיכי ליכי כהלכות גוברין יהודאין דפלחין

ומוקרין חנין ומפרנסין לנשיהון בקושטא ויהיבנא ליכי מהר בתוליכי כסף זוזי מאתן

דחזי ליכי מדאוריתא ומזוניכי כסותיכי וסיפוקיכי ומיעל לותיכי כאורח כל ארעא וצביאת

מרת שרה רפואה בתולתא דא והות ליה לאנתו ודין נדוניא דהנעלת ליה מבי אביו ______

בין בכסף בין בזהב בין בתכשיטין במאני דלבושא בשמושי דירה ובשמושא דערסא

מאה זקוקים כסף צרוף וצבי מהר"ר אברהם ______ חתן דנן

והוסיף לה מן דיליה מאה זקוקים כסף צרוף אחרים כנגדן סך הכל מאתים זקוקים כסף

צרוף וכך אמר מהר"ר אברהם ______ חתן דנן אחריות שטר כתובתא

דא נדוניא דין ותוספתא דא קבלית עלי ועל ירתי בתראי להתפרע מכל שפר ארג

נכסין וקנינין דאית לי תחות כל שמיא דקנאי ודעתיד אנא למקנא נכסין דאית להון

אחריות ודלית להון אחריות כלהון יהון אחראין וערבאין לפרוע מנהון שטר כתובתא

דא נדוניא דין ותוספתא דא ואפילו מן גלימא דעל כתפאי בחיים ובמות מן יומא דנן

ולעלם ואחריות וחומר שטר כתובתא דא נדוניא דין ותוספתא דא קבל עליו ______

מהר"ר אברהם ______ חתן דנן כחומר כל שטרי כתובות ותוספתות דנהיגין

בבנות ישראל העשויין כתקון חכמינו ז"ל דלא כאסמכתא ודלא כטופסי דשטרי

וקנינא מן מהר"ר אברהם בן מהר"ר רפאל ______ חתן

דנן למרת שרה רפואה בת מהר"ר יהודה ______

בכל מה דכתוב ומפורש לעיל במנא דכשר למקנא ביה. והכל שריר וקים:

נאום ______ ע"ד

נאום ______ ע"ד

Figure 2 Hebrew Marriage Contract

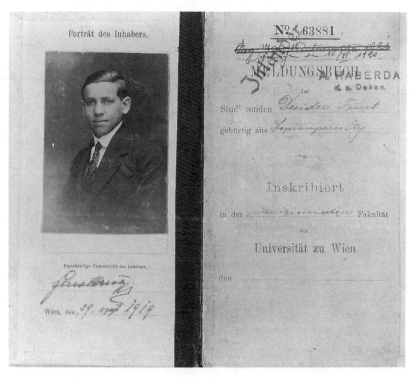

Figure 3 Desider Furst's "Registration Book" at the University of Vienna

Med. Univ.

Dr. Desider Fürst
Zahnarzt
Med. Univ.

Dr. Sári Fürst-Neufeld
Zahnärztin

Wien, IX.
Maria Theresienstraße 5

Telefon A 11-3-29

Figure 4 Visiting Card, Vienna

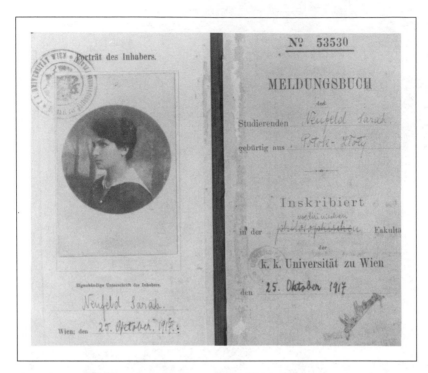

Figure 5 Sarah Neufeld's "Registration Book"
at the University of Vienna

Figure 6 Lilian Furst,
at six weeks, with her mother

Figure 7 At two years,
with her mother and Nanny

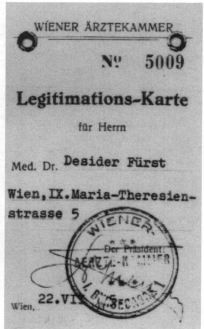

Figure 8 Physician's Identity Card, Vienna

Figure 9 Semmering
(near Vienna), 1937

Figure 10 Karlsbad, 1936

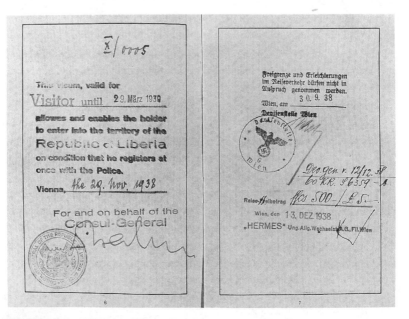

Figure 11 Liberian Visa: "Immunization Visa"
(Note top of right-hand page: "Open frontiers and easement
of travel forbidden to holders of this passport.")

Figure 12   Studio portrait of Lilian Furst in her school uniform, Manchester. The only photograph taken between 1939 and 1946; as "enemy aliens" they were not allowed to own a camera.

Figure 13   Wengen, 1950

Chertsey

$\boxed{\text{L R F}}$

In the summer of 1939, when I had just turned eight and had completed a half a year of schooling in London, I was sent for a month's vacation to a small boarding school in Chertsey, Surrey, about twenty miles southwest of London. My parents wanted me to have a break, away from the problems of the extended family commune in Kilburn. The place was recommended by the headmistress of my London school.

Before I left, I was taught how to get dressed. In Vienna this had been done by my nanny, and then my mother took over. Apparently, it had never occurred to either my parents or to me that I could manage this feat for myself. I must have been a docile child, trained to obey. Once I began, I showed quite an aptitude for buttons and laces so that I was soon ready for my first attempt at independence. Before long, during my first full winter in England, I was to extend my dressing skills by learning how to take garments off and put them on again under the bedclothes so as to avoid the bitter cold of a British bedroom.

Boarding school is perhaps too grandiose a term for the place where I went. It was a big house on a country

103

road outside the village of Chertsey, and it had a lovely
garden with a splendid lawn, flanked on both sides by a
row of lavender bushes, and surrounded by hollyhocks and
other flowers unfamiliar to me. Having always lived in a
city, with no closer contact with nature than the park
where I played, I knew nothing about trees, flowers, or
animals. At the far end of the garden there was a
vegetable patch, from which we fetched lettuce and
spinach. The owners were the Theakstones: "Granny," a
spry, cheerful woman who did the housekeeping and
cooking, and her daughter, "Aunty," a rather faded, sad
person, who had an Oxford degree and who did the
teaching. Their nephew, John, an eleven year old, stayed
with them as his parents were divorced. The other
boarders were a redhead, Eva, who must have been about
ten and who came from Czechoslovakia, and another Lilli,
a little older than I, who stayed for only a short time
before moving to America. Hardly a school, but not quite a
family, either.

Since it was summer, there were no lessons. We
played croquet on the lawn, and rode bicycles on the
paths. I was lent a small boy's bicycle that John had
outgrown, on which I wobbled about. The main thing I
learned in Chertsey was English. I knew not a word when
we landed, but had picked it up very quickly at school. By
the time I went to Chertsey, I was a fluent speaker—of
Cockney (the lower-class London accent)! I would correct
my parents, who were also learning English, and explain
that the proper pronunciation was not 'lady' and 'baby,'
but 'leidy' and 'beiby.' The genteel Theakstones must have
been horrified at the sounds I made, but they never said
anything directly, and only made me repeat each word as
it should be said. So I came to acquire a gracious,
educated, south of England accent; that was by far the
best outcome of my stay in Chertsey.

Other things did not go so well. After the initial
excitement, I was desperately homesick in an environment
very strange to me. I wrote and asked to be taken home
immediately. The Theakstones censored my letters and
made me rewrite them to say how happy I was. They told

me it would grieve my parents to receive a miserable letter when they had made sacrifices to give me a nice holiday. I could believe this, yet in retrospect I think that they also wanted to keep the £1 per week paid for my board and lodging. I felt uneasy at the deception being practiced on my parents, to which I was a partner.

The whole issue of deception proved tricky for me, and landed me in a good deal of trouble. I had been brought up always to tell the truth, however painful. So when I was asked whether Eva had gone on reading after we were supposed to be asleep, I answered "Yes." With double summertime[1] it was light so late that it was easy enough just to pull the drape back a little. Eva was told off, and in turn, took it out on me. I had no understanding at all of her anger. Eight is perhaps too young to grasp the concept of "white lies" for the protection of others. I went on being confused about this for a long time, and would catch myself telling casual lies of convenience even after I went home, having to go back to put the record straight: "No, I haven't cleaned my teeth yet."

As part of her revenge, Eva teased me without mercy. I recall with particular vividness her taunt that I would never be able to wear a skirt because I had no waist. I was rather plump, and too young to have a feminine shape. As was customary for little girls then, my skirt hung from my shoulders on a cotton "bodice," to which it was attached by buttons where the waist normally is. Eva prophesied that I would have to wear bodices all my life, a prospect that filled me with a vague terror. I am still reminded of this incident whenever I teach Carson McCullers's *A Member of the Wedding*, in which the twelve-year old heroine, Frankie, works out on the basis of her past year's growth that she will likely end up nine feet, five inches, and have to earn her living in a circus as a "freak." I also think of Eva whenever I am complimented on my small waist.

By a strange coincidence I ran into Eva once later in life when we lived in Manchester. Our neighbors were from Czechoslovakia and were distantly related to Eva who would come for short visits from time to time. When I first saw her, I didn't recognize her; I didn't *want* to know her. She, however, recognized me. We must both have been in our late teens at that time; she was an undergraduate at the London School of Economics and I was about to begin at Manchester University. To my boundless satisfaction, she was then stouter than I. Nevertheless, I made various excuses for not seeing her again.

Despite my plumpness, I was in constant trouble at Chertsey for not eating. Always rather a small and picky eater, I couldn't conform to what was expected of me, nor was I used to being pressured. I suppose Granny and Aunty felt responsible for my welfare. The food, good English home cooking, was all foreign to me, and I never have been adventurous in culinary matters. Even nowadays I find one acceptable dish at any restaurant and order it repeatedly. I liked some of the English things, especially the sticky puddings and the fruit jellos in their bright colors. There is, unquestionably, an aesthetic element in my relationship to food, which accounts in part for my predilection for fruits and salads. In Chertsey I began to drink milk and to eat fish, both white and therefore somehow "clean" to me. Aunty wrote to my parents that I had "taken to fish," which they interpreted to mean that I was going fishing. I had rejected meat since my earliest childhood, and this became a daily bone of contention. The biggest fight was over brawn (head-cheese). I couldn't stand its appearance: it was beige-grey with bits of yellowish things in it, and without knowing what was in it, I absolutely refused to touch it. I was told I would get no other food until I had at least tried it, but my revulsion was stronger than my hunger. I was resistant to the reasoning that it was another kind of the jello I liked, for to me it looked so *ugly*. I held out adamantly and stoically when it was put before me at supper, preferring to go to bed without food. By the next day the Theakstones, probably alarmed at my obstinacy, conceded this battle to me, and I was formally excused from brawn for the rest of my stay there.

I went for a month and stayed just under a year. With war imminent, all children were evacuated from London.

Rather than bring me back and have me sent to a new place, my parents decided to leave me in Chertsey, where they believed me to be happy and well-cared-for. They also consented to my going to church on Sunday mornings so that I would not be left alone in the house. In the early days of the war there was fear of a parachute attack; for several years I would be frightened to open a closet lest I found a parachutist hiding there. I rather enjoyed the Church of England service, with its cheerful hymns. I knew it wasn't the church to which I belonged, but had been told by my parents that I could pray anywhere, so I would silently say the Hebrew prayer I had been taught in infancy.

With the outbreak of war on 3 September 1939 my parents became "enemy aliens" since we were legally Germans. At least one worry was removed, insofar as our visa expiration was no longer an issue. However, my parents each had to appear before a tribunal, where a judge determined into which category they were to be placed: 'A' class aliens were interned immediately as a danger to the country; 'B' class was an intermediary, somewhat dubious group, while 'C' were "friendly enemy aliens." Quakers served as volunteer interpreters at the tribunals, for most of the newcomers still had too little English to cope with an interrogation. Like the majority of Jewish refugees, my parents were assigned to the 'C' category.

But even "friendly enemy aliens" were under certain restrictions, one of which was travel more than five miles from home. As a result, I didn't see either of my parents for several months. Very kindly, Aunty made plans to take me to the outskirts of London to a point within their five-mile radius, but before this could be arranged, my father was processed and granted permission to come and see me in Chertsey one Sunday. Needless to say, I awaited the day with eager anticipation, yet it didn't go well. My father had difficulty in following my rapid, colloquial English, and I was hardly tactful in my comment that it was peculiar for a father not to be able to understand his own child. I still understood German, although I couldn't or wouldn't speak it. My father was shocked, too, at how fat I had grown from all those puddings and that milk. Even my underwear had had to be let out.

My mother's visit, some weeks later, was much more successful. She must have been warned of my bloated appearance so that it was less of a nasty surprise to her. Also, since she had a better ear for foreign languages than my father, she could understand me pretty well. The image of her as she looked that day in 1939 is as vivid as if it had been yesterday. In her soft, black-and-white houndstooth suit, her broad-brimmed white hat with a black ribbon, her white gloves, black-and-white shoes, and a black crocodile purse, she was like an apparition from our old Viennese world, a reminder that it had indeed been our world not so long ago. She stood out like a visiting star in the homely rural surroundings of Chertsey. We went for a walk together, and I was so happy to be alone with her and away from "them." She had brought some cheese sandwiches, which she offered me; heedlessly, without realizing that this was intended as her meal on the way back, I ate them up: another memory of my world. I asked about my grandparents, of whom I was very fond. She said they were both well, but from the fleeting shadow of anxiety on her face, I suspected that something was wrong. My grandfather was dying of heart failure, and she didn't want to tell me. It was natural to wish to protect a child, yet I felt more troubled, I believe, than if she had told me the truth. It was an infringement of the total frankness that had been the rule in our threesome, a deception parallel to my own in pretending to be happy in Chertsey. In those uncertain times we were trying to make life more pleasant, or at least less unpleasant, for each other. Perhaps we did right. These were the first moral dilemmas I ever experienced. I learned the code of not "telling tales" soon enough; honesty towards my nearest and dearest was a far more problematic matter.

During the school year we must have had organized lessons, but I recall very little about them. The school was affiliated with the Girls' Public School Day Trust, conforming to its standards. The dining room doubled as a schoolroom; as to what we did there, my memory fails me utterly. The one thing that I learned was certainly not on the syllabus: my initiation into sex. One day, when the adults were busy, John drew Eva and me into the bathroom, and insisted on exhibiting his penis. Eva was intrigued; I wasn't impressed.

In the late spring of 1940, the time came for me to go home. I was wildly excited for weeks, all the more so as "home" was no longer to be the communal house in Kilburn, but our very own place in Bournemouth, an attractive resort town on the south coast, west of Southampton. We were moving there at the suggestion of the British government's Home Office after my father had passed the exams and attained the qualification to practice in Great Britain. Bournemouth was recommended because there was a shortage of dentists there, and it had a milder climate than most other places in England.

To start a practice from scratch by simply hanging out one's shingle was "not done," for it was considered a form of poaching, in effect luring other dentists' patients away. Anxious to do the right thing and conform to the customs of the country, my father bought a practice in a central location in Bournemouth from a dentist who had died. As capital, my parents used a diamond smuggled into England by my mother in a hollow tooth. They didn't get a good price for it because they sold it shortly before Holland fell to the Nazis and the value of diamonds shot up. But it sufficed to buy the practice, although it soon turned out that most of the patients, the so-called "goodwill," had long since joined the dentist in the cemetery. An apartment was rented nearby and our furniture moved from London so that we could establish a home of our own again. We all looked forward to being reunited, and thought that this would mark the end of our days as refugees.

It was not to be. My mother came to fetch me from Chertsey on 10 May 1940. On the train to Bournemouth, she began to mutter, "He won't be there." She had heard and read in the newspaper of the widespread internment of enemy aliens from the south coast following the fall of France. Fearing Quislings[2], as in Norway, the British authorities as a precaution ordered the internment of all male enemy aliens of every category from the south coast. Had we been a penny bus ride further west, in Bournemouth's twin town, Poole, which is in Dorsetshire, we would have been spared. We arrived to an empty apartment, with the drapes, which my father had been hanging, lying there desolately. From the police we learned that he had indeed been interned; we didn't know where. It was several weeks before we received a letter from Ramsey on the Isle of Man in the Irish Sea west of Liverpool. He had been herded to a school in Southampton, then moved to Huyton near Liverpool, and finally shipped to the Isle of Man, in the Irish Sea.

Meanwhile my mother and I were stranded in Bournemouth without a foreseeable source of income, and suspect as Germans. We were subject to a curfew, and had to surrender our precious radio. I was keen to go to school, but it was closed to house the soldiers evacuated from Dunkirk. With an irrepressible optimism that I wish I still had, I begged my mother to walk me to school every morning just to see whether it had reopened. The headmaster would greet us with a wan smile and say, "Maybe tomorrow." I could see his regret at having to turn away this peculiar child who was so longing to go to school. It was altogether a sad time. The shock of losing everything this second time was greater than it had been in Vienna, where the possibility of a Nazi annexation had been on the horizon for several years. Here we were in safe, hospitable England, having done all the things demanded of us, yet desperately stuck again.

We stayed about six weeks. My mother had worried that I had grown used to English food, and had got some recipes from Granny. It was a relief for both of us to go back to the simple, abstemious fare normal in our family. I lost most of my pudginess, and despite the disappointment of not being able to settle down, as we had anticipated, I was far happier than in Chertsey. My relationship with my mother was very close; I grasped intuitively that it was my function to stand by her and to help her to keep going amidst the renewed, sometimes overwhelming uncertainty about my father's fate and our future. She spoke to me mostly in German, while I replied either in English or in a curious version of German, concocted out of word-for-word translations from the English, often with distinctly comical effects: *"Ich habe einen Kalt gefangen"* ("I have caught a cold") or *"Ich habe meinen Geist geändert"* ("I have changed my mind").

We found the means to survive financially by renting our furnished apartment to Sydney and Bella Cohen from London. Mr. Cohen had been a patient of my father's in Vienna, when he worked there for a large international firm. He wanted to get his wife and child out of London, now under bombardment, while Bournemouth was a "reception area" for evacuees. Mrs. Cohen and her son moved in with us, and Mr. Cohen came at weekends. Since they were paying us rent, they treated my mother and me as their servants. The boy was a couple of years younger than I, and I was supposed to look after him, and held responsible if he lost his toys. I don't think I did a good job since I disliked him and resented their presence. What most aroused Mr. Cohen's anger (or envy?) was my English, compared to that of his son, who had the irritating Cockney habit of punctuating every sentence with "Eh?" At meals Mr. Cohen would test my spelling; after "hippopotamus" and "rhododendron," both of which I got right more by luck than knowledge, he gave up. So did we; we went back to London.

Why my mother opted to return to London at this time is not clear to me. The daily bombardment was under way in earnest so that prudence would have dictated that one avoid the city. What is more, most of her family had already moved to Manchester, where my uncles had long-standing connections in the cotton trade. My grandfather had died; he is buried in London in Streatham Cemetery, to which I still have a key. Only one of my mother's brothers was still in London. I suppose she chose to go back there partly because she already knew it, and partly because we expected that my father, on his release, would come there to join us.

We had absolutely no idea how long he might be detained—weeks? months? for the duration of the war? The uncertainty was so excruciating as seriously to undermine our morale. Letters were few, and slow to arrive due to censorship, and although he assured us that conditions at the camp were reasonable, we felt constant anxiety. We had heard enough about concentration camps in Germany to fear the very idea of such a set-up, and we couldn't be sure whether to trust his letters. With memories of my sanitized, rewritten letters from Chertsey, I couldn't help wondering whether his were similar idealizations aimed to set our minds at rest. We had a major fright when the ship, the *Arandora Star*, with a cargo of refugees bound for Canada, was torpedoed, and most of its passengers drowned. No letters came from my father for nearly a month, and we suffered agonies of apprehension lest he had been on board. Later we learned that it had been single men under forty who were shipped off. Another ship, the *Dunera*, took internees to Australia; it was a long voyage, and the sailors, mistaking the internees for "Jerries" (the British derogatory slang for Germans), treated them with such brutality that the case became notorious, resulting subsequently in questions in Parliament and an official investigation.

We rented a small second floor room, again on Brondesbury Road, across from where we had lived before. Hard though times had been for us then, we had had more hope for the future than now. The owners of this house were three elderly sisters who occupied the first floor and who were nothing like the genial Dimdor family, our previous landlords. These three were downright morose and often ill-tempered, particularly the youngest, who suffered from some strange disease, a form of elephantiasis, that had caused one of her feet and lower legs to swell to ludicrous proportions. No doubt she had good reason to be a crosspatch. I regarded all three as witches and wanted to avoid them as much as possible.

The five of us were, however, thrown into the closest proximity every night in the airraid shelter in the back yard. By the middle of 1940, London was being bombed every night without respite, and sometimes by day, too. The doleful wail of the sirens punctuated whatever we did, sending us running to the shelter. "Anderson shelters," named after the Home Minister who had instituted them, were hastily constructed in every back garden. They were small rectangular dug-outs, roughly eight feet by six, covered by corrugated iron and sandbags. They were only a few feet beneath the surface, and didn't give more than the flimsiest protection, except from flying glass. The entrance remained open. Fortunately, it was summer, so that the nights weren't too chilly, but it was damp inside and terribly cramped for four adults and a child. My mother brought down blankets and cushions in an attempt to make somewhere for me to sleep. I doubt whether sleep was possible under those circumstances, not least because of the fear we felt all the time, which no doubt exacerbated the friction between us and the three witches. Our life and limbs were in constant mortal danger, and we knew it. More than anything else it is the sheer noise that I remember as terrifying: the banging of the anti-aircraft guns, the whistle made by the bombs as they came down, and the tremendous crash as they landed. The crash was, curiously, a relief, for it meant that this one had missed you.

In the evenings we would get into our shelter clothes and walk up and down in front of the house waiting for the siren, which came as inevitably as an "amen" in church. It strikes me as rather foolish that we wore our oldest clothes for the shelter, for we would have had nothing had a bomb hit the house. Once on our walk I lost a knitting needle and was inconsolable, because of both the idleness it caused and the cost of replacing it. The incessant movement of knitting was a way to vent some of the tension. In the mornings we would crawl out to survey what else had been destroyed. Each day there were, more gaping holes, more reports of terrible damage, more rubble and injuries. Even in daylight an enemy plane would sometimes be able to sneak through without being spotted, and before the sirens went off, we could see a dogfight between two planes in the sky above us. One man in our street was said to have got so tired and confused that he went into his shelter at the "all clear," a long single note, and came out at the air raid warning, a wailing, undulating tone. Amidst the rubble signs went up: "Business as Usual" almost became a motto for the defiant Londoners.

The war was going badly for the Allies. Those men not already in the armed forces were organized into the Home Guard as a last resort defense force. Their pathetic weapons were pitchforks and other farm or household implements, there being no more guns available. This is when Churchill made his famous eloquent speech about fighting the invaders on the beaches and in the streets. It seemed a real likelihood. Morale among the refugees was very low. We had been burnt already, we underestimated the toughness of the British, and we knew we would be singled out for the Nazis' reprisal if ever they succeeded in capturing Britain. It was the nadir of our lives.

My mother and I existed in a state of limbo. Schools had been evacuated to safer areas, and the buildings were being used to house those who had been bombed out, so that there was another gap in my education. Our sole occupation was WAITING—waiting for my father to be released. Gradually the interned were being screened, and those who were deemed harmless, such as the old and the infirm, were sent home. I believe it was my idea that we should induce my father to apply for release on medical grounds. We concocted a letter asking him at length about his gallstones and expressing our concern whether he was on a suitable diet in the camp. Actually, the internees were fed a lot of herring, abundant around the Isle of Man.

The stratagem worked. One morning, on returning from the shelter, we found my father fast asleep in bed. He had been released after four months of internment, had crossed to Liverpool, and caught the train to London. The air raids disrupted all the schedules—trains halted for the duration of the raid in order to be less visible targets. He had arrived at Euston late at night, had walked back carrying his suitcase, and was so exhausted that despite all the clatter of the bombing, he had fallen into bed and gone to sleep. He was, I should add, the only good sleeper among us.

After his return, we explored other shelter possibilities so as not to have to be with the witches. One night we went into a deep underground (subway) station, all of which were open as shelters. People brought old newspapers, spread them out on the platform, and slept like sardines, almost on top of each other. The air was so stale as to be pestilential. We tried it for only one night.

Next we went into the lower basement of D. H. Evans, a large department store on Oxford Street. Like the subway, the basements of departmont stores were turned into public shelters. This was more comfortablc, and considerably less claustrophobic than our other options. I could even sleep there on a countertop. But then I was startled out of my sleep by a feeling as if I were being lifted and bounced down again. The store had had a direct hit and was on fire. Air raid wardens came to evacuate us to safety. They exhorted us to "Be British," which meant calm and stoical. There was no panic, everyone packed their things as quickly as possible, and we were led away.

The sight that met our eyes as we came out was stunning. An oil-bomb had struck John Lewis, another big store. The whole street was ablaze. I will never forget that scene, as memorable in its way as the parade when the Nazis marched into Vicnna. Glass shards a foot deep littered the street, it was as bright from the fires as in daylight, the firefighters worked frantically, searchlights roamed the sky, and the din of bombs, anti-aircraft flak, and planes made it hard to hear the instructions we were being given. Miraculoulsy, no one was seriously hurt. We were taken to the basement of Selfridge's, and though it was already full, people silently moved over to make room for us. The British at their best, and none to beat them.

After that experience we reverted to our Anderson shelter, which seemed as safe as anywhere. "If a bomb had your name on it, it would find you," was my father's fatalistic comment. Why we waited so long before leaving

London is a mystery to me. We had no reason to stay. So on our own initiative we finally evacuated ourselves.

Isle of Man

At the Bournemouth police station we were a small group; nearly everybody knew each other and the officers were acquainted with many of us. The whole atmosphere changed when we left the bus which had taken us to Southampton. We stopped in front of a large building, a school, and the bus was surrounded by young soldiers with fixed bayonets. We had become prisoners. A large hall was turned into a dormitory, and we were each issued a blanket. The room was already fairly crowded. I found a spot in a corner of the stage from which I could overlook the whole place. I couldn't see or find any friend or acquaintance; I was new to the area.

Everyone from the age of eighteen on up was liable to internment. For young people it was fun; to the old it seemed a nuisance and an inconvenience; many of the middle aged, however, felt it to be a catastrophe. We were stunned by the turn of events; we just hoped it wouldn't last long, not more than a day or two. It was an unexpected, unplanned, chaotic situation. Some sixteen year olds were included through a misunderstanding. We were fed irregularly with tea and sandwiches, and nobody bothered about us. We were not even counted. I had the feeling it was a dream or a bad joke that would end soon.

LIVERPOOL JOHN MOORES UNIVERSITY
LEARNING SERVICES

After two days we were each given a paper bag with some food and put onto a train under military escort. The episode was turning serious; we were regarded as potential enemies. We realized this during a long journey which ended in Liverpool. We were a mixed crowd of civilians, with some bearded rabbis among us. We crawled rather than marched through the streets of Liverpool in a loose, undisciplined column. Some youngsters shouted at us, "Look at the Jerries!" We were not in the mood to laugh.

We spent an uncomfortable night in the overcrowded Territorial Army Exercise Hall which looked like an antheap. The lights were kept on all night. The next morning we were moved to a suburb of Liverpool, Huyton, to a partly finished housing estate. A lieutenant who spoke Yiddish put me in charge of some invalids, and we got a house for ourselves and called it the hospital. We had beds, blankets, lightbulbs, a trestle table, and two benches, too. What luxury! One of my patients was a mentally defective man, fortunately good-natured; another was a severe diabetic, and there was a young man with tuberculosis and a pneumothorax. We had some difficulty with one man who couldn't, or wouldn't, walk. We had to wash and feed him. Was it a scheme to force his own release, or was it genuine? I didn't want to find out. He was a nice intelligent fellow. The illnesses of the others were insignificant, and they helped with feeding and caretaking. Rabbi Cohen of Berlin asked me for a lightbulb for his temple *cum* study, and I was able to get him one.

Our room with the table and benches served for a time as the meeting place for the camp organizer. Had we not had our private worries, we would have had little reason to complain about the prevailing conditions. We had no news from our families or from the outside world. We had no newspapers or radio. We were surprised to hear that the "German House" had a celebration one night: King Leopold of the Belgians had surrendered. It was our first indication that there were some real Germans among us.

I met two old friends of mine in Huyton; Dr. Josef Einleger, a chemist, and Dr. Alexander Hart, a gynecologist.[1] It was like finding lost brothers. We counted the surviving friends (there were not many), and our calamity appeared less tragic compared to the fate of the others. Some very talented and enterprising internees organized the camp with amazing speed. The officers and soldiers were very helpful. We were still waiting to be sent home, and nobody wanted to escape or make any trouble.

Two weeks later we were shipped across the Irish Sea to the Isle of Man. The "misunderstanding" was not clearing up; on the contrary, we were in deeper water. One elderly man told us that he had spent four years there during the last war, and he felt as though he were coming "home" again. This was not encouraging to us, although there was more resignation than rebellion in his voice. Our new camp already had some inhabitants, young people from the Kitchener Camp. They gave us a friendly welcome.

The camp was at the seaside resort of Ramsey. It was organized with the usual speed, keeping in mind that it would, alas, be more of a permanent place for us to stay. There were about twenty hotels facing the sea, and a promenade half a mile long. It was separated from the village by a barbed wire fence. Some elderly good-natured soldiers served as guards, symbols of authority. They never had any trouble with us. We were sorry for them. They had to walk between the two rows of wire fence all day long, carrying heavy rifles. It seemed ridiculous. The commander was an old officer, obviously recalled from retirement to take charge of the camp. He addressed us on the first day. "Gentlemen," he said, "I don't know why you are here, but I have orders to keep you here. If you play the game with me, I shall play the game with you and try to make your life as comfortable as my orders permit. Thank you." We were not familiar with the idiom "to play the game," and conferred among ourselves what game we were supposed to play at our age. A young Scottish officer, who spoke fluent German, ran the daily affairs of the camp. After the initial suspicion and mutual distrust had worn off, he became a considerate fellow. He had neither friends nor enemies among us.

We were put up in seaside hotels whose capacity was far below our requirements, thus the majority had to sleep on straw-filled mattresses, which were quite comfortable, and also had the advantage of being portable. The large rooms and halls were dormitories by night. Some fellows had to get up very early in the morning because their room was selected as a "prayer house", where the orthodox inmates gathered for the morning prayers. "This is our bedroom," some protested, while the others claimed it was their temple. Soon a satisfactory solution was found. Some of us were billeted in the servants' quarters. We were on the top floor. There was no elevator but we had proper beds.

For the first time, special letter paper was distributed, two letters per month. One could buy extra paper from those who had no one to write to. At last we had letters from home, too. My wife and daughter had left Bournemouth and gone back to London. The office was closed and our apartment rented.

The principle of the camp organizers was that every able-bodied man should contribute something to its running. There were a few exceptions. One healthy young man refused to do any kind of work. One day he found that his rations were served to him uncooked and unprepared. After that he did some kind of work. Another man stayed in bed all day. He said that he was sick, and his food had to be taken to his room. We saw him walking round the camp in the evenings. Two doctors examined him and found nothing wrong. I was asked to have a talk with him. He declared to me that he wouldn't work: he wasn't in a labor camp. I told him that he was not in a nursing home either. When the food delivery was stopped, he began to appear at meals and became a good potato peeler. Despite some shirkers, the system worked well, owing to the decency and good will of the majority. There were about twelve hundred of us distributed in several hotels, each run as a separate unit.

We had about two hundred German Protestants in one hotel. They were well looked after by their pastor. We did not mix with them. Some weeks after our arrival about a hundred Italians joined us too. Their first question was whether they could get *farina* to make pasta.

The camp was well administered by the commander and a few officers. Each house had a representative as a liaison to the administration. The food was monotonous, mainly herring, boiled, fried, etc., with potatoes and dried vegetables. Our house was fortunate to have a good cook. He knew of his importance to us and asked for some privileges—a room of his own with a proper bed. He was as touchy as a prima donna. We had no duties whatsoever except to appear at the roll calls at 8 a.m. and 6 p.m., to be counted—to see whether we had multiplied overnight, as one fellow remarked. Nobody attempted to escape; it would have been madness. One man tried to smuggle out a letter illegally and was sentenced to two days' solitary detention. They had to build a small hut for him, and he had a little rest from the crowded quarters.

We had a long promenade, and a large football field for the youngsters. No wonder that after a short while a fair number of inmates would have refused to leave the camp voluntarily. It was quite different for the majority of us. We were indignant and embittered about our unjustified detention. One is naturally egocentric. The British government was in a desperate situation; our fate was among the least their of worries. There were some engineers among us who worked in aircraft factories. They were released after two weeks because they were important to the war effort. For me it was not only a financial disaster and separation from my family; I felt I had been let down by a country in which I had faith and trust. Looking back now from a distance of many years, and with personal detachment, I can judge things differently. There were bigger mistakes in those years which cost hundreds of lives. We lived in a secluded mini-world of our own, completely cut off from what was happening outside the camp.

Paul Kery, a Hungarian writer and journalist, was my daily walking partner. He had spent some time in the Dachau concentration camp and wrote a book about it, called *Man Crucified*. He was the most sensible among us. "This is a holiday resort," he would tell us, "make the best of it. We are here by some mistake and it will be cleared up. It may take half a year or more until somebody realizes it, and then they will be glad to get rid of us. In Dachau, one never knew in the morning whether one would still be alive in the evening."

It took about two weeks until we had a well-organized camp life. After the roll call we had breakfast, and then everyone was fairly busy. The housecleaners swept the stairways and common halls. The bathrooms were cleaned. The kitchen helpers washed the dishes and helped to prepare lunch. It was about an hour's work for everyone. Around ten o'clock the language courses started; English for beginners, advanced, and literature. One could learn about eight other languages, too. English history and geography classes were well attended. Physical exercise on the playing field and laundry had also to be done. We had to watch our laundry drying because there had been some cases of theft. The big lectures came after lunch. Everyone had to bring their own chair to the lecture room and take it back afterwards. There were interesting lectures on a variety of subjects, and most had large audiences. There was a separate doctors' and dentists' group. We had lectures every afternoon, and each member was asked to speak on his chosen topic. We numbered between forty and fifty, including some world-famous experts. It was there that I heard for the first time about anticoagulants and the new treatments for pernicious anemia. I spoke about fractures of the jaw. Lively discussions followed in a friendly spirit.

We had a shoe repair workshop, and a former bank employee cut our hair, working on the street in front of his domicile. The cabaret theater was always crowded. It was called "Interndl," a take-off on the famous "Lanterndl" in Vienna.

We had a number of rabbis who held orthodox and reform services on Sabbath, which were well-attended. The Yeshiva (Jewish theological seminary) of Leeds was interned with all its teachers and students and they simply carried on as if nothing had happened.

Two doctors from the nearby village of Ramsey visited the hospital on alternate days. They were friendly, though a bit bewildered by this foreign crowd. They behaved very correctly and mostly accepted the advice of the two male nurses. A lot of bromide was prescribed as a sedative. A dentist came twice a week, and a primitive office was fitted out. I extracted a number of teeth for emergency cases in his absence.

All things considered, we were treated humanely and decently and should not have had any reason to complain. But all the distractions couldn't make us forget that we were deprived of our freedom and separated from our families at a time when we really needed each other. Basically we were unhappy, disappointed, and frustrated human beings who longed for freedom. Since we had no news of the outside world, we were dependent on rumors, and they were frighteningly bad. They were said to come from a hidden radio set. We tried not to believe them. It turned out later that they were true. Some pessimists expected German parachutists to descend one day and occupy the Isle of Man, and they wouldn't forget to bring prison uniforms for us!

There were some fellows whose humor and optimism was not affected by adverse events or news. Their influence on the spirit of the camp was very beneficial. A famous Viennese photographer pulled a wooden box around, collecting leaves and papers from the street with a sharpened stick. He was paid a shilling a day for it. It was the commander's pride to keep the camp clean and tidy. There was a palm reader, an excellent portrait painter, a preacher of some obscure philosophy, and many other eccentrics. A Polish fellow walked for hours up and down the promenade learning English from a book with the title *Polish up your English*. He made little progress and somebody told him, "You better try to English up your Polish!" He was so offended that they nearly came to blows. Some people played cards until late into the night. I took part in a chess tournament. We had some very good players. In our hotel I found some books too, and from one of them I learned the story of Guy Fawkes.[2] Camp life was not at all boring!

A new batch of internees was transferred to us from another camp and they were surprised at the beauty and cleanliness of ours. Among them I found an old friend, Dr. Marcus Lion, a prominent lawyer in Vienna, a handsome, wealthy man in his fifties over six foot tall. He was proud of having been a reserve officer in the Austrian army in an aristocratic regiment. He had comrades in all government, police, and other offices, and had the reputation of being able to work bureaucratic miracles. He and his family were patients of my wife. He took a great fancy to our daughter when she was quite little, and wanted her to marry his son!

When he arrived at our camp, he was tired and depressed. I invited him to a cup of coffee and lent him a shilling. He nearly burst into tears at such generosity. We often walked around the playing field together. He had sent his only son to Scotland in good time, and some English clients of his had managed to get him out of Austria just before the war broke out. He had refused to leave Vienna until his old comrades forced him to. He poured out his heart to me about a friend of his who had also been his family doctor. This man and his wife had both been born in Russia and were easily able to emigrate to the United States since there was no waiting list for the Russian quota. He had asked them to take a dress with them and to send it to his son from abroad. He told them that the buttons were diamonds, covered with fabric. The dress never reached his son, and it took him a long time to get a reply from his friend, who was already in the United States. He was stunned: the man had written that there must be some misunderstanding, they had never taken a dress, and had nothing to do with this mysterious business. I couldn't make out what hurt him more, the

loss of his diamonds or his disappointment in a friend who
had cheated him so shamefully.

He told me of another mishap that had befallen him
in Vienna. His bank manager had advised him, about a
year before the Nazis "invited themselves" to Austria, to
buy foreign currency as a safeguard against the economic
fluctuations. He was told to keep the money in a safe at
home, which was perfectly legal. When the Nazis came, he
decided to transfer the money to England to support his
son. The Nazis' new currency regulations closed this
possibility, and so he hoped to try a "private transfer."
It had become illegal to hold gold or foreign currency
which had to be offered for sale to the State through a
bank. He grew uneasy when he learned that his bank
manager had become an ardent Nazi, and was afraid that
he might betray him. He arranged with his wife that, if he
suspected imminent danger, he would call her from his
office and when she heard him say a certain password, she
should flush the foreign currency down the toilet. One
evening when he came home, his wife said, "I have done
it." It was his habit to call her every day at lunch, and
that day, while talking to her, he had inadvertently used
the magic word. His only consolation was that the Nazis
hadn't got the money.

The British authorities decided to give fit young men
the opportunity to volunteer for the army's Pioneer Corps.
It was announced in the camp that a medical committee
would soon come to examine candidates. A number of
them were accepted. They were allowed to go home for a
week's leave before reporting for service. They were eager
to fight the Nazis.

After a few weeks we were permitted to receive
parcels. We each had only the one set of clothing in which
we had been interned, and we badly needed underwear
and other items. The variety of boxes, cases, parcels, and
some large crates that arrived was unbelievable. They had
to be opened in the presence of an officer. Some food
parcels came too. At the beginning even sardine cans had
to be opened; later they were satisfied with less formal
inspections. The postal helpers cut the strings with razor

blades and tore off the wrapping paper; the officer gave
the contents a quick look, and the inspection was over.
The owner had to be present and to remove the mess
immediately.

One day a big fight took place at the post office. When
the strings and paper of a nicely packed parcel were
ruthlessly cut and torn, a man started to shout and
protest as if he had suddenly gone insane. His property
was being damaged. It was some time before he calmed
down. Nobody could explain his behavior; he was a quiet,
cultured man, a well-known Viennese lawyer in his mid-
fifties. I often went for walks with him, it was a pleasure
to talk to him. One day I dared to mention the affair to
him. He felt a bit embarrassed and gave me a curious
explanation. He had been brought up in a small Slovak
village, where his parents had a grocery store. The goods
arrived in boxes and parcels, and it was his task to
unwrap them carefully so that the string and wrapping
paper could be used again. Nothing was wasted. This
became his cherished passion, and even in later years
nobody dared to open any parcel either at his office or at
home. He had lost his senses when he saw those
barbarians mishandle his parcel. It was "like a stab in the
heart," he said. He felt a fool, ashamed of his behavior, but
he couldn't help it.

A great controversy broke out over the dried peas. A
religious man found some wormy ones among them, so
they were not kosher. Four old men volunteered to be "pea
selectors." They selected from piles of peas the wormy
ones, which were thrown away. It was a very boring job
but they did it willingly for the sake of their religious
convictions. One day a young man eating the peas jumped
up; he had broken one of his teeth on a small stone in
among the peas. The selectors must have overlooked it.
"Why don't you throw out the stones? Are they kosher?",
he shouted at them.

Gradually people were released for health reasons.
Suddenly all kinds of old diseases and some new ones
flared up. The doctors were lenient, especially with elderly
persons. Good connections with the nursing staff at the

hospital seemed to be an important factor. Some people were released who seemed to be in excellent health, while others who were obviously sick had to wait for weeks before their turn came.

More rumors were circulating in the camp: we were to be shipped overseas! They proved true. All men under forty were conscripted and older ones could volunteer to be included. Surprisingly, quite a number did so. The war and the Nazis were too near for their liking; the further away the better. We held meetings nearly every day to discuss the situation. We were prepared to go if our families could come with us. I was forty-one and decided to stay. The candidates were ordered to prepare their luggage, which was collected and transported away. They were to follow the next day. Some of them did not turn up at the last minute. They were found naked in their beds; they had hidden their clothing and refused to go. The transport left without them. They had lost their things, but it was worth it to them. They were not punished.

Shortly afterwards the news of the sinking of the *Arandora Star* reached us. It was one of the boats that carried internees, as well as some German sailors who were prisoners of war. The ship was torpedoed on her way to Canada and sank rapidly. We were worried about our friends. My wife was frantic with anxiety because, just at that time, she had had no letter from me for a long time. Most of the internees aboard were drowned. The German sailors fared better, having had training with lifeboats. We heard this from a survivor who was returned to our camp. His description of the disaster was frightening. He saw his friends drown. He himself had clung to a raft until he was rescued.

Some of our friends embarked for Australia on the *Dunera*, whose name became notorious. They were treated brutally, like criminals. The matter was debated in Parliament.

The Canadians and Australians were very disappointed with the transports. They had expected fierce Nazis and had prepared well guarded, fortified camps for them. The harmless civilians were herded into these camps.

They were treated with compassion. At the end of the war
the majority of them stayed in these countries for good.

Our camp at Ramsey was gradually emptying. I was
released at the beginning of September 1941. I had been
away for four months, an eternity to me. I was not allowed
to return to Bournemouth, which was still a restricted
area for us. Thus, we had lost everything. Our only asset
was my license to practice dentistry in England.

I arrived to a London in total darkness and had
difficulty in finding my way home. This was my first
experience of a real blackout. When I got to Kilburn, the
house was empty. I was tired and went to sleep. My wife
and daughter found me when they returned at daybreak
from the shelter, where they had spent the night.

London had changed a lot in the four months since I
had left. This was the period of the so-called phony war.
Still, everyone felt that war was on the threshold. The
nightly bombings were more than a nuisance; they
dislocated the normal way of life considerably, although
the population adapted to them as an inevitable
temporary inconvenience. Those who suffered losses bore
them silently, fatalistically. There were no riots or scenes
of panic. Surprisingly—to us—there was no deep hatred
against the Germans. The bomber pilots who had to bail
out of their damaged aircraft were treated to a cup of tea
until the police arrived to collect them. Everybody was
convinced that the tables would soon be turned and that
Germany would get its own medicine, and plenty of it!
That was the general mood and opinion.

We envied them their optimism and wished we could
share it. We were not defeatists, but realists. We had not
met any English people who were not convinced that
England would win the war. It was only a question of time
and endurance. "Their word in God's ear" was our prayer.
The defiant sign "Business As Usual" was painted onto
walls and windows. We remained skeptical despite our
efforts to imitate them. We felt instinctively that the fate
of England hung by a very thin thread. The expeditionary
force (the professional army) was as good as annihilated,
and we were afraid that the next blow might finish us.

There was no trained army to put up resistance, and all the heavy equipment had been lost in France. The miraculous retreat from Dunkirk was a poor consolation. The beaches were guarded by the Home Guards, elderly civilians with hunting guns. Road Signs were removed so as to make orientation more difficult for possible parachutists. The navy, the sea, and last but not least, the spirit of the British stood between England and defeat.

I talked to a soldier who had come back from France via Dunkirk. It was incredible, he said. "We inflicted very heavy casualties on them, and still they kept coming in waves. We had few reserves, and when our ammunition was spent, we had to retreat. Our planes were no match for theirs in number."

Like most people, we had our shelter outfit always at hand. We used it regularly every night. It contained two blankets, a thermos bottle filled with hot water, tea, plastic cups, and a hand towel. It made quite a bundle, fastened together with two leather straps and held by a strong handle.

We always carried a small suitcase filled with our personal documents: birth and marriage certificates, diplomas, passport, letters of recommendation, testimonials, and a few photographs from the happy old days. We were often asked what we were carrying: precious jewels? gold? or silver? People were astonished when we told them what it contained, and often laughed at us. It was probably our European attitude: without proper documents a person was a "nobody." The documents proved our identity and credentials, and could not be replaced. We never let them out of our hands; we lived or perished with them. I had once read a book by B. Traven, *The Death Ship*, about the fate of an American sailor who got left behind in Holland by his ship without his documents or any money. It was frightening what could happen to a person without credentials. Our papers were our second egos, and wherever we went, we were asked to show them. It sounds ridiculous until one tries to imagine the situation we were in, poor strangers in a foreign land.

The general opinion was that England needed time
for recovery and rearmament to meet the enemy on equal
terms. It would take a long time and would be a hard
struggle. We counted the days until the Channel would be
too stormy for an invasion of the island. Floating balloons
the size and shape of elephants prevented low-flying
attacks, but the bombing continued relentlessly every
night. Air raid warnings sounded often by day too, and
one could see on the distant sky the dogfights of the
fighter planes. Suddenly one of the planes would emit
dark smoke and fly away, obviously damaged and burning.
We hoped and prayed that it was "one of theirs."

We spent the nights in an Anderson shelter dug into
the garden. It was constructed from corrugated metal
sheets and made a room about one yard by two yards,
with a roof like a little house, covered by earth. A narrow
entrance and three steps led down into it. It was safe,
except from a direct hit, which was very unlikely to
happen. We put some thin mattresses on the floor to make
it bearable to stay there overnight. Unfortunately, we had
to share it with the three quarrelsome sisters who were
our landladies. The conditions were so crowded that we
decided to try another shelter. It was the cellar of a ladies'
clothing store on Kilburn High Street. We had the illusion
of being well sheltered, but it was a flimsy building which
would have collapsed immediately if hit by an exploding
bomb. We were squeezed into the full cellar and found
some friends there. People slept under the benches and
tables or on them, on the floor, or wherever they could.
The building was never hit or damaged.

The intensity of the bombardment increased, and we
spent a few nights on the platform of an underground
station. These were the safest shelters, and one had to be
there early to stake a claim to a sleeping space. The hard
concrete floor was far from comfortable; we had little rest
there. A friend of ours who suffered from chronic insomnia
slept there like a log on a sheet of newspaper. He enjoyed
it, and was at least temporarily cured of his complaint.

We spent the famous night of 15 September 1941[3]
in the deep cellars of the Evans store on Oxford Street.

It was a sturdy building. Most of the sheltered were regulars, but they were friendly to us newcomers. We bedded Lilian down on a table, where she soon fell asleep. The bombing started earlier than usual, and was more ferocious, too. It was around midnight when the whole building was shaken and started to tremble. It had had a direct hit. Everybody was suddenly wide awake, asking what had happened. Some air raid wardens appeared and told us, "Nothing serious; don't panic; be British!" It worked like magic. We were led a long way through passages and stairs until we found ourselves on Oxford Street. What a sight! The buildings in every direction were burning, and the fire brigade tried to isolate them. It seemed a hopeless task. The noise of the exploding bombs, guns, and the aircraft overhead was frightening. The sidewalk was full of glass splinters. Somehow we found our way to Selfridge's, where the basement was full. Room was made for us and we waited there until daybreak. We had a long walk back to Kilburn. There were no buses. A cup of tea and bed was what we urgently needed.

This was the night when the Germans lost about a hundred and eighty aircraft, and from that day on the air attacks became weaker and more sporadic. London paid a heavy price on that night, but it was one of the turning points of the war. The Nazi war machine was checked and their confidence broken for the first time since the war had begun.

All this time I was looking for a job as an assistant or locum for a dentist but I couldn't find anything. Life in London became very strenuous, and anybody who could leave did so. Friends of ours found us acommodation in Bedford.

Bedford

(LRF)

We were to go to Hereford. Indeed, parcels of our bedding had already been sent there and were retrieved only with some difficulty. Considerable confusion as to our destination reigned for a while. We were to go together with one of my mother's younger brothers and his family. To what extent they determined our choice of haven, I don't know; I was ten at the time and heard the adults' discussions with only half an ear. At any rate, it was Bedford where we landed.

Bedford was a lively little town on the river Ouse about one and a half hours by train northwest of London. Surrounded by agricultural land and with relatively little heavy industry, it was a reception area for evacuees from London, and like all such areas, already terribly overcrowded. Housing was hard to find at any price, and we were poor, our sole income being the rent from our apartment in Bournemouth. In our favor was the sympathy extended to Londoners in flight from the bombing, and the desire to help at this desperate juncture in the war. We got two rooms on Ashburnham road on the second floor of a little row house, whose first floor was occupied by an old couple. They had not had tenants upstairs before, but to give us shelter seemed to them a contribution, however indirect, to the war effort.

My uncle and his wife, because they had two small children, took the larger front room, while we had the smaller one at the back. I felt that we had been living in small back rooms for ever such a long time. This room contained a bed with two more mattresses piled on top; when these were laid out side by side at night, the whole floor was filled so that one couldn't move about at all. We slept in a row across the room, like sardines. The two families shared a stove and a kitchen sink with cold water on the landing, and further down the corridor there was a toilet. We had a tiny fireplace in which my father lit a fire first thing every morning. Sometimes he had a hard time starting it. Once the fire was lit, the kettle would be heated for our breakfast tea, and in the meanwhile the mattresses and bedding stacked away in the corner. Conditions were incredibly primitive. Once a week my mother and I went out to the public library, so that my father could wash himself in a washbasin in front of the fireplace with water heated in the kettle. You had to be quick before the water cooled off, and it was no pleasure, for that room was always chilly.

If the primary aim of our move was safety, it couldn't be deemed a complete success, for Ashburnham Road was right beside the railroad station, and on the other side of the tracks was Bedford's only munitions factory. It kept a "spotter" on the roof, who blew a siren whenever German planes flew over, to warn workers to take cover. We could clearly hear the hooter, although the sirens were not sounded so as not to alarm the population unnecessarily. Bedford was on the flight path to Coventry, which was often heavily bombed. Occasionally on the way back a surplus bomb would be dumped on Bedford. The British radio would announce that bombing had taken place at random in order not to disclose to the Germans whether they had hit their designated targets or not. They must have had some poor translators, for the German radio then frequently claimed that Random had been bombed, as if it were a town. The refugees, still struggling themselves to learn English, thought that a hilarious joke. On the whole, the damage to Bedford during the year we spent there (1941–1942) was slight.

As on our arrival in London, I was very keen to start school again as soon as possible. By the age of ten I had had precious little regular schooling, with gaps in Brussels, Bournemouth, and during our recent stay in London, not to mention the travesty in Vienna and the rather happy-go-lucky set-up in Chertsey. Where and how to find a suitable school in Bedford? My parents solved this in a speedy and original manner by consulting a policeman on patrol. It has always amused me to think that I was educated by courtesy of the police! As our clothes from Vienna still looked pretty good, he recommended the two leading schools: the Bedford Girls' High School and the Modern School. In choosing Bedford as our refuge, we had unwittingly struck it lucky with schools; the town prided itself on the excellence of its schools, supported by the Harper Trust, which financed them handsomely.

My father made appointments to see the headmistresses of both schools. He was put off by the Girl's High School because he thought it pretentious; the headmistress received him wearing her academic gown. On the other hand, he was favorably impressed by the Modern School, not least by its beautiful new building on the river bank. Considering how cramped and squalid our living quarters were, the prospect of my spending weekdays in a bright, welcoming building was an attractive one. The headmistress suggested that I start in two weeks after the half term break. "Why wait so long?" my father interjected. "Alright, let her come next Monday," the headmistress, Miss Beatrice Tonkin, was willing to compromise. "Can't she come tomorrow?" My father had the final word, and I went to school the next day, a Thursday.

I was very happy at the Modern School, which had several fine teachers. Miss Tonkin, who had herself been educated at Girton College, Cambridge, certainly had a sense of quality. The atmosphere was friendly, although the school had its rules. One of them was a prohibition on going to the cinema on weekdays, presumably to make us do our homework and go to bed at a reasonable hour. Academic standards were fairly high, but I didn't have any difficulty in keeping up. Ever since kindergarten I had loved going to school, partly because, as an only child, I wanted the company. But I also enjoyed learning in itself, satisfying my curiosity, and mastering new fields. My parents didn't press me to achieve; in fact, my father advised me that the most comfortable spot was in the middle of the class, where you didn't have to worry either about competitiveness or about failure. However, they did impress upon me the great importance of education by telling me that possessions and savings can be taken from you, but not the knowledge you have acquired. One of the sad aspects of my childhood is that I was so often thwarted by circumstances in my desire to go to school. As a result, my education is very patchy; for instance, I never learned how to do fractions. In languages, where I am gifted, I could catch up on my own what I had missed; not so in mathematics. My vita begins with my regular attendance at the Manchester High School for Girls in 1942; I maintain a discreet silence about what I did, or didn't do, before.

English was my best subject in Bedford, gymnastics my worst. I came to dread it and was terrified of the instructress, Miss de la Mare, who drilled us like an army sergeant drilled his recruits. I didn't mind doing the exercises standing up or lying on the floor and waving arms and legs about; I even mustered the courage to stand on my head. But anything involving "apparatus" petrified me. I couldn't shin up a rope. I refused point-blank to jump over a "horse" or to balance on a bar suspended three feet above the ground. Miss de la Mare would argue herself black and blue. There was a mat to land on, she stood by to catch us as we took the leap, I was perfectly well able to balance on a bar one foot off the ground, so why not at three? To no avail. I was adamant. "It's dangerous," I insisted, and despite all her pressure, I stuck to my guns. I couldn't hang upside down by my arms from bars; I have never done a handstand in my life. I was smaller than most of the class, unathletic, and disinclined to break an arm in an effort to please her. We were at daggers drawn. What made it worse was that I spoiled her class not only by preferring not to (like Bartleby!), but also by not having the regulation uniform of azure blue shorts and top. We could not afford to buy it, and used the shortage of clothing coupons as a cover for our poverty. I stuck out in every respect like the proverbial sore thumb. I think my battle with Miss de la Mare marks the beginning of my conscious nonconformism.

I managed to deal rather better with another potential source of embarrassment to me. The Modern School was quite a long walk across town from where we lived. Naturally, on the first day my father accompanied me. But he wanted to walk me there every day, carrying my schoolbag to boot. No other fathers brought their daughters (presumably they all went to work whereas mine was unemployed). I was ashamed to be escorted like a baby. First I got rid of my father at the corner of the road where the school stood; then I persuaded him to let me go on alone from the public library—it was on the way to my school, and he spent the mornings there reading the newspapers. I didn't want to hurt him by peremptorily dismissing him; his ego was bruised enough by his lack of employment. Before long he got the point, and we parted at the library, much to my relief. My first steps, literally, toward a certain independence.

No sooner had I started at the Modern School than I caught measles, which had been going around. I was very upset at having to miss school and stay in bed in that poky dark room, and afraid, too, that the spots would be permanent, notwithstanding my mother's assurances to the contrary. I had a mild case and recovered fast.

On Sunday mornings my cousins and I went to Hebrew classes at an improvised temple. Before the war Bedford had had hardly any Jewish inhabitants. With the influx of evacuees from London, communal facilities, including a kosher butcher, were temporarily instituted.

As the three of us set off every Sunday morning, our landlord and his wife would watch approvingly, and then ask to which church we were going. Our parents explained that we were Jewish and the children were going to Hebrew classes. This was met with a blank stare, and the following week the ritual would be repeated all over again. Later on in our stay in Bedford we came to understand the problem better. On explaining to our new landlady that we were Jewish, we got this response: "Oh no, that can't be. You are decent people. Jews come from London on market days and cheat you." We came up against the same disbelief at our avowal again and again.

Browsing through the newspapers in the public library, my father came on an advertisement in the local paper inserted by an elderly dentist with heart disease who was in need of a locum. My father was offered the position at a starting salary of six guineas a week. We were in seventh heaven; six guineas was more than twice as much as we had been living on. The day had come at last when Daddy was earning some money again. With his first earnings my mother bought me a cream-colored long-sleeved blouse like the other girls at school wore as part of their uniform. It is surprising how much happiness a child can derive from such a small thing.

The practice that my father took on was run down because the dentist, Mr. White, had been ailing for some time. His daughter, Joan, was his receptionist-assistant. With so many young British dentists away in the army, Mr. White had been unable to find a suitable locum before, and my guess is that he was as pleased with the arrangement as we were. The practice was strategically located on a main street just around the corner from Ashburnham Road. With the shortage of dentists, the practice soon picked up and began to prosper once more. Mr. White invited us to tea one Sunday in late autumn at his home, near a golf course on the outskirts of Bedford. This was our first foray into British social life, and it was pleasant except for the dreadful cold of the house—apart from a radius of two feet by the fireplace. Heating in British homes always consisted of a fire in one room, and I don't think that insulation had been heard of then. You got grilled on the fireplace side and frozen on the other. My father's salary rose to eight, then ten guineas a week. We were positively rich!

We had another stroke of good fortune in being offered better housing. Right next door to Mr. White's office was the office of a family practitioner, Dr. Macaskey, a charming and much beloved Scot. He used only the first floor for his office, the waiting room, and the caretaker's accommodation. The upper floor was vacant, and we moved in. It wasn't exactly ideal. There was, for instance, no kitchen, so we managed by carrying bowls of water from a rather distant bathroom and setting up some cooking facilities with an electric kettle and a gas-ring. There wasn't much food and my mother couldn't cook anyway; she was intent on medicine, and had been able to avoid cooking in Vienna by having a resident maid, as was customary in the middle class at that time. So it didn't matter that much, though it was inconvenient. In contrast to the herring of London, in Bedford we ate mainly boiled potatoes. On the positive side, we now had two rooms, a livingroom and a bedroom. Only the livingroom had a fireplace. I would go to sleep curled up on the floor in front of the fire and would be undressed there, half-asleep, by my mother, carried into the icy bedroom, and quickly put into a bed that had been warmed by a hot water bottle.

When we had been in Bedford for several months, I was suddenly asked to present myself at school one Saturday morning. I found out only after I got there that I was to take an entrance exam! I had been admitted on a temporary basis since my father had said he didn't know how long we would be staying there. But as I was still there a good many months later, I needed to go through the proper procedures. I spent the morning in school; I can't recall the exam, and never heard anymore about it. I assume that I passed.

I was happy in Bedford. We went to the movies sometimes on the weekend; I remember seeing *The Great Dictator* with Charlie Chaplin; I adored slapstick comedy. My mother didn't share my unsophisticated taste, but put

up with the farces for my sake. Once a symphony
orchestra under the great conductor, Sir Malcolm
Sargeant, came from London to play in the hall of the
Corn Exchange. Decked out in white gloves from Vienna, I
went with a school party to my first concert and heard
Handel's "Water Music." During the vacations I would go
along with my mother to do the shopping at Saintsbury's.
Everything was rationed, a certain small amount of meat,
butter, margarine, tea, sugar, and one egg weekly, while
other items such as cocoa, canned fish, and powdered eggs
were on a monthly points system. The powdered eggs from
the United States were an absolute boon; I once asked my
mother what we had eaten before they appeared in the
stores. Vegetables were in short supply, and fruit almost
nonexistent in winter. We met Miss Tonkin one day at
Saintbury's, and my mother chided me for not having
greeted (*grüssen*) her properly. I said I had greeted her
with a nice smile—I had got the hang of British manners
and proprieties before my parents did.

My cup of happiness was filled to the brim when my
father bought me a bicycle for £1 at one of the auctions at
the cattle market. It was a tall, old-fashioned, "sit-up-and-
beg" bicycle. I marvel that I managed to ride it so well. I
went all over Bedford on it. Fortunately there was
relatively little traffic, since gas for private cars was most
severely rationed. The bicycle gave me freedom of
movement and a greater measure of independence, which
I enjoyed. I went out with a young neighbor to her garden
and brought home some fresh peas and bunches of flowers
that she had grown.

The acquisition of the bicycle was one expression of
our prosperity. Another was the purchase of our first
English book, a version of the *Oxford English Dictionary*.
It cost 10 shillings and sixpence (half a guinea) and has
been worth its considerable weight in gold. Though now
badly battered and held together by tape, it is still, over
fifty years later, my primary reference work to check
spellings, meanings, etymologies of words.

Once my grandmother came from Manchester for a
visit. She brought a small amount of instant Nescafe. This

was a revelation to us, the height of gourmet consumption compared to the ghastly liquid "Camp coffee" that we had had until then. Nescafe was not rationed and therefore virtually unobtainable. My grandmother, who had experience in scrounging for her large family after World War I in Vienna, was an extraordinary shopper. That Nescafe seemed the most desirable of treats for us perhaps conveys some idea of the Spartan level of our existence. Now a confirmed coffee connoisseur myself, I can imagine what a hardship it must have been for my mother to go from the many shades of delicious coffee in Vienna to Camp coffee: an emblem of how far we had fallen in the world. But with Nescafe we had surely begun to rise again.

We also once went to London for the day. We went out by underground and bus to Streatham Cemetery to visit my grandfather's grave. It was the first time I saw it. Then we had lunch at the Lyons Corner House at Marble Arch. The "Corner Houses," though part of the Lyons chain, were quite grand, at least in my eyes. We had never before been able to afford such an outing, and I felt immensely privileged, sitting there and being waited on. In some ways, because of our long, impoverished stretch, I enjoyed the small luxuries, as they returned into our lives, more than a child who had never lost them.

While we were in Bedford, Virginia Woolf drowned herself in the Ouse. Her curiosity aroused by this news, my mother borrowed one of her novels from the public library. She was depressed at the trouble she had in reading it. She had thought her English to be reasonably good already, yet she had to give up on Virginia Woolf. She blamed her deficient knowledge of the language for this failure, not recognizing the complexities of Woolf's style and narrative techniques.

Dr. Macaskey invited us to tea at his lovely home on the Avenue, a broad road that led to a park. It was a fine summer day, so we were out in the garden. I tried to play with his daughter, Beryl, who was somewhat older than I and painfully bashful; I came across as quite brash compared to her. The Macaskeys, as tactfully as they

could, put it to my parents to have me transferred to the
High School. The Modern School was for the children of
tradespeople; the children of professionals went to the
High School. We didn't grasp these ingrained English
social distinctions. They must have thought us rather
dense, for our only answer was that I was happy at my
school.

There were a few other refugees in Bedford whom we
gradually met. I remember a young blond woman who was
a shop assistant and who later married a businessman in
Manchester. We were friends with Oskar and Edith
Hirsch for many years. Our closest friends in Bedford
were the Pacovskys from Prague. He was a dermatologist
and a fascinating raconteur, and they had two children of
about my age. Eventually they too, partly through our
agency, moved to Manchester, and later still to Pacific
Palisades in California, where my father and I visited
them when we ourselves were living in Eugene, Oregon.
The dispersal and movement, initiated by the Nazis,
propelled us onward in a restless quest. After losing our
original homes, we never struck deep roots anywhere.

I would have loved to stay in Bedford. I was not at
all pleased at my parents' decision to move to Manchester.
All my mother's family had settled there, and they urged
the move onto us, arguing that after the war Bedford
would revert to being a sleepy country town without a
Jewish community. Mr. White had offered my father a
partnership in the practice, which was flourishing. He was
very sorry to see us go. Nevertheless, in 1942, when we
had saved the sum of £100, we took another leap forward
into the unknown.

Bedford

Bedford was a small town about forty miles north of
London, and with the permission of the police we moved
there. It was a safe place, a market for farm and garden
products and a school center. We had one room, where we
slept on the floor, and access to some shared kitchen
facilities. We intended to stay there until I found a job
anywhere in England. Unfortunately we could not return
to Bournemouth, which was still a restricted area for
aliens. The invisible hand of Providence led us to Bedford;
within a month I found a job there.

I read an advertisement in the local newspaper that a
dentist urgently needed a locum, owing to illness. His
house and office were a few hundred yards from our
"home." I went to see him immediately and started to
work on the next day. We could hardly believe our good
luck. My new boss, Mr. White, found us an apartment
next door to his house. We even had a bathroom of our
own!

Mr. White was an unqualified dentist who had picked
up dentistry in the army when he was a young man. He
was a dental orderly to the army dentist and the
mechanic, too, for several years. After leaving the army,

he established himself as a dentist and built up a good practice. At that time no formal qualification was required. When I met him, he was in his sixties and had a serious heart condition. He was an uneducated, self-made man, and not at ease with me. He tried to speak very refined English, using medico-dental terms whose meaning he obviously did not understand. I let him talk without contradiction. He had some difficulty in understanding my limited English and was courteous enough not to let me feel it. He offered me six guineas a week for six days' work; Saturday, market day, was our busiest time. Gradually he became himself, his behavior grew more relaxed, and we got on very well indeed.

The practice was in bad shape when I took it over; it had been run down by a series of locums. The office was a large, spotlessly clean room, very well equipped except for the lack of an X-ray machine. As local anaesthetic Mr. White had used a cocaine solution for which I immediately substituted Novocain-adrenalin. In a hut in the yard we had a mechanic who soon became a competent help. His daughter, a well-spoken girl of about twenty, was neatly dressed as a nurse and receptionist. I had no clerical work to do. At 4 p.m. there was a half-hour tea break, and I walked across the street on the first day to tell my wife how I was getting on. She was very upset to see me so unexpectedly—she thought I had been fired!

The first thing I did when we arrived in Bedford was to see the headmistress of the High School for Girls. She received me as a distinguished visitor, a Viennese doctor, in her beautiful office, dressed in her academic gown. I was very impressed when she showed me around, but depressed too. I would have loved to send our daughter there but I knew that we couldn't afford it. She was prepared to accept Lilian as a pupil, but we could not afford to buy her the obligatory uniform, and I did not dare to ask about the fees. The girls came from the town's well-to-do families, and I was a poor refugee without means. I was embarrassed. I thanked her and left, upset and sad. In Vienna this school would have met our status. I asked a policeman where the other girls' schools were. I crossed the bridge over the river Ouse and there was the newly built Modern School for Girls. The headmistress accepted Lilian, and we agreed that she should start there rightaway the very next day. No uniform was required and no fees had to be paid. My wife bought her a school blouse from my first salary, and she was the happiest girl in the town.

We were told later that we had made a faux pas—a professional man's daughter should go to the High School. But she was happily settled at the school, and we didn't want to move her. The headmistress recognized her talent, and later, when we left Bedford, recommended her to the Manchester High School for Girls, admonishing us not to consult a policeman again.

Many Londoners evacuated their families to Bedford. The only night we had to go into a shelter was when Coventry was very heavily bombed and the German aircraft flew over us to and from their target. It was a pleasant place to live in such troubled times. We always regarded it as a temporary home. We spent a happy year in Bedford, and when we moved to Manchester, Lilian burst into tears in the middle of its "Piccadilly," and sobbed, "I don't like to live here; it's so ugly." She would have been prepared to return to Bedford at anytime with pleasure.

The news spread quickly that a Viennese dentist was practicing in Bedford, and most of the Austrian and German refugees and some of the London evacuees came to us for dental treatment. Many of them became our good friends, too.

I was very busy, and Mr. White increased my salary so that by the end of the year I was earning ten guineas per week. He offered me a partnership on very tempting terms, but we were not ready to accept it. We could not face the possibility of spending the rest of our lives there. Had it been Cambridge, only twenty miles further east, it would have been a different matter.

Mr. White had a very mixed range of patients, from leading members of the town's business and professional circles to workmen, salesmen, etc. The character of the

practice gradually changed owing to the influx of
foreigners, who were very keen to keep their teeth.
Sometimes when I suggested an extraction, they said,
"Have you become a British dentist?" With Mr. White's
patients I tried to carry on in his spirit and habits, which
sometimes caused me a conflict of conscience. In these
cases I asked for his instructions and acted accordingly.
After all, it was his practice. Patients were often referred
to us by doctors, some of whom were our patients, too.

One of the doctors nearly always requested "a
clearance," the extraction of all teeth. Often the hygienic
condition of the teeth and gums was good, sometimes even
excellent. The patients could have kept their teeth for
years without any harm to their health. I discussed this
problem with Mr. White. He saw no problem at all, "The
doctor knows best what is good for his patients and we
have to carry out his instructions. We can't afford to
oppose him and lose patients. They need dentures
afterwards, and that's good business for us." He
reluctantly agreed that I could talk to the doctor. He was a
pleasant man in his fifties, and of course he wore artificial
teeth. He was convinced that natural teeth were a great
menace to everybody's health and a source of endless
trouble, too. A toothless mouth was easy to clean and
every chance of oral infection was eliminated. The sooner
one got rid of teeth the better. Why take risks? If dentures
were provided at an early age, the patient would get used
to them more easily and remain healthier. I told him that
I respected his sincere convictions but could not agree
with them. I assured him, however, that I would carry out
his instructions.

I did so, except in one case. Patients usually did not
ask questions; this one did. She was a young woman, the
wife of a refugee trade union leader from Holland with
two children. She had recently had a miscarriage. The
doctor advised her to have all her teeth out for the sake of
her health and to prevent another miscarriage. She was
very upset and asked my opinion. The hygienic condition
of her teeth and gums was excellent. I sent her to have all
her teeth X-rayed and found that none of her teeth needed

to be extracted. I told her that if they were my teeth, I would not dream of having them out. "That is good enough for me," she said and walked out.

A poor salesgirl came twice a month to have one tooth out for the fee of half a crown (about fifty cents). She had bad teeth. Sometimes I pulled two or three adjacent teeth for the fee of one, a curious sort of charity and compassion.

I dreaded the clearances; they were messy, gory affairs. One extracted the teeth more quickly and with less caution, instinctively in a hurry, and the likelihood of breaking a tooth was greater than it should be. My anesthesiologist was an elderly doctor on whom I could not rely. Often I had to tell him to give a bit more oxygen. I was dissatisfied with and even ashamed of what I was doing. It was a poor excuse that I was under orders to do it and had no choice. I never did this in my own practice; I told the patients who requested it that I would not do this type of work.

A middle-aged man came in and wanted two teeth out. He pointed to them with his finger. I found no reason to extract them, and told him so. "I want them out, and I am paying for it," he said. I quickly consulted Mr. White. "Don't argue with the fool. Pull them out. If you don't do it, another dentist will!" I extracted them under general anesthesia. An hour later he came back. He had looked in the mirror at home and decided that he wanted the neighboring tooth out too. I didn't argue with him and pulled it out as he wished—without any additional fee.

An airforce soldier wanted a small premolar root to be extracted. He was afraid of an injection and wanted gas. Mr. White had a good day and volunteered to administer it. We were both surprised that the soldier didn't fall asleep despite the large quantity of nitrous oxide he was given. I looked at Mr. White and he winked at me to get at it. It was a very easy extraction. The patient complained that he had felt everything. When he had left, we examined the apparatus. He was right—the nitrous oxide valve was blocked, and no gas came out of the cylinder.

I had two old Czechoslovak patients, both from

Prague and close friends since childhood. They insisted on talking to me in English, which I had difficulty in understanding. I replied in German. They were intelligent people and had learned English together. They spoke English fluently to one another, or so they thought. They had literally created their own way of pronouncing the English words. Many refugees did this, including myself, but they were champions at it. They were puzzled that other people couldn't understand them. They came to me for advice about this problem. I didn't want to hurt their feelings, and told them that the Bedfordians spoke a peculiar kind of English and they should take lessons with a local teacher who would teach them the proper pronunciation. They were quite satisfied with this suggestion.

Mr. White's daughter came one Sunday morning to tell me that her father was trying to pull out one of his own teeth and was moaning in the office. Would I come across to help him? He was standing in front of a mirror and trying to extract a small front incisor, which can sometimes be tricky. It was no problem for me to take it out. He hadn't wanted to disturb me on a Sunday. I must confess that a similar thing happened to me some years later. I broke a premolar tooth of mine by biting on a breadcrust. The sharp edge of the fractured tooth was very unpleasant. I always had an emergency set of instruments at hand. I went to the bathroom, gave myself a local anesthetic, and started to take the root out. Easier said than done. It was very difficult and took me a long time to get it. I persevered only so as not to be a laughingstock among my colleagues if I had to go to one of them with a half-extracted tooth.

One of my duties was a monthly visit to a Home Office Remand School for juvenile delinquents to examine the boys' teeth and carry out the necessary treatments. There were facilities only for extractions, and Mr. White was called "the butcher." I discussed the situation with the headmaster, Mr.Crow, who did his best to be helpful to the boys. We managed to buy a used dental engine so that I could do fillings, too. Through careful handling of the reluctant patients I slowly gained their confidence, and by the end of the year there were only a few boys who still refused any treatment. There were some very intelligent boys among them. In that Remand Home they were treated well and trained for jobs with a decent future.

The year that we spent in Bedford was useful to me in my profession. It revealed to me the basic difference between patients' attitudes to dentistry in Austria and England. In Vienna we examined the hygienic condition of the teeth and gums and made suggestions as to what we intended to do. We would give an estimate of the cost of the treatment. We answered all the patients' questions. If they consented, we started the treatment immediately. Sometimes they wanted to think it over. With our regular patients this was not necessary; there was mutual trust. In Bedford most of the patients came with a firm decision, such as, "I want all my teeth out by gas." It was no use suggesting any other treatment. They asked what it would cost, including the making of dentures. They either agreed or said, "I can't afford it" and left. It was an exception for a patient to ask, "What would you advise?" or sometimes, "I am in your hands. Do whatever is best for me. Please don't hurt me if you can help it." Their unlimited confidence was flattering and I tried to live up to it.

Two major events in the war happened while we lived in Bedford: the beginning of the German-Russian war, and the attack on Pearl Harbor by the Japanese followed by the entry of the United States into the war.

Gradually, more and more evacuees flocked back to London. There were no air raids anymore. My wife longed to live near her family, who had all settled in Manchester, one of the centers of the textile industry in England. We decided to move there and to start our own practice. We had a comfortable life in Bedford and had made many friends but we were used to living in a big city. There were many excellent schools in Manchester, and the family ties were close. As soon as we could find a successor for Mr. White's practice, we set out for Manchester.

Manchester

(L R F)

I had been to Manchester once before our move. It was a brief visit in about February, perhaps at my half-term break. It was uncertain until the last minute whether I could go, because I had a horrible cold. The compromise was that I could go but should stay indoors. Manchester in winter does not have extreme cold, and snow is very rare; however, it is pervasively damp, raw, and a bleak, dark grey. Before the switch to smokeless fuel in the early 1950s, it had "pea-soup" fogs so dense that you couldn't see your hand at the end of your outstretched arm. All traffic and business would stop as people struggled to get home, abandoning their cars and either walking or getting onto one of the buses that crawled along in convoys led by a man carrying a lantern.

On that first visit I saw nothing at all of the city. We stayed in the apartment that my grandmother shared with her eldest son and her younger daughter. The apartment was in Appleby Lodge, a block completed just before the war, the first one in Manchester to have central heating. What bliss, after years of shivering, to feel really warm everywhere, even in the bathroom and toilet! Like every foreigner who lived in England then, my memories are inextricably associated with the constant sense of cold. Outdoors, cold can be combatted by extra layers of clothing and brisk movement. Indoors, it is inescapable and demoralizing. When I went to Cambridge to do my Ph.D., the Girton College instructions suggested a travel rug as a necessary piece of equipment. I was puzzled until I got there and tried to heat my room by putting shillings in the gas meter. Then I realized that the blanket was to *live in*: you wrapped yourself in it, especially for any visit to the beautiful but unheated College library.

I realize in retrospect that the purpose of our visit to Manchester was not purely social. My mother was to reconnoiter the prospects for opening a dental practice there. She made the long trip by bus to Heaton Mersey, one of Manchester's southern satellite towns, to consult Kurt Heilbronn, who had been one of my father's student interpreters at the Dental Hospital, and who was now established out there. I don't know what his advice was. I suspect that the decisive factors, certainly for my mother, were the dual lure of her family and of the central heating. She suffered more than others from the cold, partly because she was then already beginning to develop the disease that eventually killed her, and that is much aggravated by cold.

My sybaritic weekend was spoiled only by her siblings' gossip about her health, which I could hear from the next room. (I have always had exceptionally acute hearing, probably in compensation for my high degree of myopia.) I spent most of the weekend lolling on my grandmother's bed, munching the cookies that this champion shopper had rustled up for me, and reading a newspaper for the first time in my life. For a peculiar reason I was intrigued by the *Manchester Guardian* (as it was then called before its move to London when it became just the *Guardian*); its front page carried no news headlines, even in the middle of a war, but the births, engagements, marriages, deaths, and advertisements! My lazy contentment was, however deeply disturbed by the whisperings about my mother's persistent cough, which was taken as a likely sign of TB. Then already I had "the anticipatory imagination" that I have gradually learned to keep at bay, but never succeeded in totally conquering. With my mother's life endangered by TB and my father's made precarious by his recurrent gallstones, I could see myself as an orphan. It was a terribly distressing possibility not only because of my profound attachment to my parents, who had brought me to safety, but also because I couldn't envision any substitutes. My aunt was anything but maternal, and my uncle, though kindly, was a confirmed bachelor who hardly knew how to speak to a child. My best bet, I decided, would be my nurturing grandmother. The worst aspect of this secret sorrow planted in me was that I couldn't mention it to anyone. It cast a dark shadow over that first visit to Manchester, which perhaps colored my later view, too.

When we did move a little later, I disliked Manchester intensely, at least at first. Taken to Piccadilly, the city's commercial center, I burst into tears and declared I couldn't live there because it was so ugly. Beauty has never been Manchester's strong point; the buildings were black with soot, and the city was then still littered with piles of rubble, evidence of the recent bombing. I was reluctant to leave the relative security of Bedford, where I had friends and knew my way around the small town. To compound my woes, my ancient bicycle from the cattle market was a casualty of the move, and I had to start saving hard for a replacement.

But there were compensations, too. We rented an apartment in the same block as my grandmother. It was in a pleasant and convenient location, opposite a big park, Plattfields, and on a bus route, about two miles from the university and three from the city center. We had to take a large two bedroom apartment because nothing else was available. It was splendid: a living room with a balcony (the fulfillment of a childhood wish of mine) connected with sliding glass doors to the dining room, two bedrooms, kitchen, bathroom, toilet, and lots of storage closets. We would actually have preferred a smaller unit because we couldn't afford the rent, but we were willing to take risks and make sacrifices for the sake of the central heating. It wasn't as cozy as at my grandmother's because we were at the far end of the circuit and got only moderate warmth. (Tragicomically, in the bitter winter of 1947 the water in the underground central heating pipes *froze*, and so did we.) The furniture was brought from Bournemouth, and for the first time we three and all our belongings were in one place. Also for the first time since we had left the Maria-Theresienstrasse I had a room of my own, a pretty room with a view of trees. Though I didn't then know about Virginia Woolf's concept of the need for a room of one's own, I was so immensely proud of it that I dragged all visitors to see it before they went from the hall into the living room, to my parents' considerable embarrassment. But they couldn't stop me.

This time I was not to be educated by courtesy of the police. Miss Tonkin had been categoric about it; I was to be transferred to the Manchester High School for Girls, whose headmistress, Dr. Mary G. Clarke, had been at Girton College in Cambridge with her. So without ever taking an entrance exam or any other formalities, I got into the most exclusive girls' school in the area, a sister institution to the famous Manchester Grammar School for Boys. My casual admission aroused much anger and envy among the neighbors whose children had tried—and failed—to get in through the normal procedures, whereas I "sailed in," as they put it. I sailed in as they put it, in the middle of the school year and term, and had to share a desk with another girl; a chair was simply put in for me. I was supernumerary, and made to feel it. The school was operating under extremely difficult conditions. Its brand new building had been one of the casualties of the bombings, and was in total ruins. Makeshift accommodation was found in an old abandoned school building for the senior school, and in two houses for the juniors. We commuted between the buildings and met twice a week for assembly in a church hall halfway between the three locations. This arrangement, despite its inconvenience, had one enormous advantage as far as I was concerned: this school had no access to a "gym" hall so that I was liberated from "apparatus!"

Before I could start at the High School, one awkward matter had to be negotiated: we couldn't possibly afford the fee of eight guineas per term (over £25 per year) on our savings of £100. It fell to my mother to go and see Dr. Clarke, an eminent educator, and scion of a distinguished Scottish family. She cut short my mother's apologetic explanations by ruling that the school's Governing Board would be satisfied with £2 per term. Even that was quite a burden for us. Of course I again had no uniform, although I did get a school hat with the distinctive black and yellow hatband. I was glad to have an excuse not to have to wear the hideous uniform—a black tunic with elastic at the waist and a yellow badge over the chest, scratchy thick black woolen stockings and underpants, black and yellow tie and cream blouse—an unflattering outfit even for the shapeliest girl, and downright disfiguring for those less than perfect. Dr. Clarke also agreed that my mother should tutor me in Latin, which the others in my class had been learning for six months. We went at breakneck speed in daily lessons so that I caught up in six weeks.

Latin at age eleven was among the many unusual features of the Manchester High School for Girls. It offered a superb academic education which I have come to appreciate more and more over the years. Several highly gifted teachers made a deep impression on me, especially the elegant Miss Law in English and the vivacious Mrs. Herbert in French, who both later became university lecturers in education, teaching students how to teach. We began French at age twelve, and Greek and German at fourteen, in addition to the customary curriculum of English language and literature, history, geography, mathematics, and general science, which comprised biology, chemistry, and physics. In all these subjects we were repeatedly urged to "Think for yourself", the best motto for our future lives. The education was strictly academic: no typing, driving, cooking, or swimming. My mother once asked when I would learn to cook, and got the reply that I was doing Latin. She had me find out where the other girls learned to cook, and I came back with the reply, "From their mothers." The subject was never mentioned again.

My strengths obviously lay in languages, as Dr.
Clarke told my mother when I had been there for a year.
It was a great disappointment, since I had always seen
myself going to medical school. I remember the silence in
the house following this verdict, as if my parents had
heard that I was on drugs. They didn't know how to deal
with this, and were concerned primarily with the practical
question: How will she earn her living with languages? It
would mean being employed by others, and they firmly
believed that an independent profession was preferable
for Jews. The topic was shelved temporarily, for we had
more pressing problems to face.

The immediate issue was once again how to earn a
living. On our £100 we could hold out at most for three
months with the expenses of the apartment and the office.
I think my uncles had given a tacit guarantee of help if
necessary. We didn't have to make use of this offer, but
psychologically it was reassuring. Having already bought
a practice in Bournemouth, my parents felt that they had,
literally, paid their dues to the profession. In any case
they had no funds to buy again. So they took the
unconventional and risk-laden step of renting two rooms
and hanging out my father's shingle. His success in
rebuilding Mr. White's practice in Bedford must have
restored his professional self-confidence and given him the
courage to act as he did. What is more, after much
deliberation as to the choice of location, my parents
decided against a suburban practice, which would have
involved much evening and weekend work as well as the
prevalent British extractions-and-dentures routine, and
opted for the city center, as in Vienna. The office was on
St. Peter's Square, directly opposite the magnificent
municipal library, near Manchester's best hotel, The
Midland, and above a branch of Boots, the pharmacy
chain. It was a distinct advantage that one of the rooms,
unfortunately the smaller and darker of the two, already
had a washbasin. In time the washbasin was moved so
that the large corner room became the office.

The shocking enormity of our enterprise was brought
home to us when I had the obligatory school entrance

medical examination, conducted by Dr. Catherine Chisholm, the school doctor and a veritable old battle-ax. My mother had to be present to answer questions not merely about my medical history but also about our social circumstances. When my mother rather timidly told her that we were starting a dental practice in St. Peter's Square above Boots, Dr. Chisholm dropped her stethoscope, stared at her, and almost shouted: "Do you mean to say that you have taken Mr. Morley's rooms?" It was like the scene in Oscar Wilde's *The Importance of Being Earnest* when Lady Bracknell discovers that Ernest had been found in a bag on the Worthing railroad line. We, needless to say, had never heard of this Mr. Morley. It turned out that he was one of Manchester's leading surgeons who had just retired. Dr. Chisholm clearly thought us rash to the verge of insanity to try to start a practice there, and somewhat improper, too. I was more than glad when the examination was over and so was my mother, but we were chastened and quite discouraged by this response to our initiative.

My father read *Gone with the Wind* and other long books while waiting for patients. We kept hearing how hard it was to get a dental appointment because so many dentists were in the armed forces, but no one came to us. My father opened his office at 8 a.m., as in Vienna, hoping to catch early birds before their work day began, only to learn that nothing was done in England before 9 or 9.30 a.m.. He took one Saturday afternoon off to go to a soccer match and was told on Monday morning by the Boots staff that a patient had come in his absence. He must have turned pale, for they offered him a cup of tea, the British panacea for all adversities. His first patient was a Norwegian sailor. Gradually a few more came; he would have one at 9 a.m., perhaps another at 1 p.m., and with luck, a third at 5 p.m. His first receptionist stole the clock from the waiting room. My mother did the cleaning; it hurt me to see her on her hands and knees, washing the floor. I joined her during school vacations and became very good at polishing. It was embarrassing if someone came to make an appointment, for it was fairly obvious that we were not a professional cleaning crew, but the doctor's family.

To help make ends meet, my father took a part-time job, on Wednesday afternoons and evenings and most of Sunday, as assistant to a Mr. Moody. His practice was like Mr. White's in Bedford, and he needed a second person to do the clearances. It was far away in North Manchester (we lived in a southern suburb) and involved a long journey by two buses, unpleasant in the blackout. On Wednesdays my father would drag himself home late at night. Long after I had gone to bed, I would see my mother's slender figure silhouetted against the dark as she stood at the dining room window, anxiously awaiting his return. She had good reason to be anxious; he was having gallstone attacks again and was giving himself a shot of morphine before setting off for Mr. Moody's. It was a precarious existence; he couldn't afford life or health insurance, and, as he confided to me later, could rely only on my mother's brothers to care for her and me if anything happened to him.

In the context of such major worries, my parents didn't have much time or energy to put into my troubles at school. I was quite acutely unhappy at the Manchester High School for Girls. The further up the social ladder, the less hospitable my schoolfellows were, or so it seemed to me. The school, because of its excellence, had a large catchement area, so that girls lived far apart and were not likely to see each other out of school—a very different situation from the American neighborhood school. They were clever, ambitious girls who resented my intrusion into the pecking order when I came top in Latin. I didn't hit it off at all well with the mathematics teacher, who was inept at explanation. It was a revelation to me when my father demonstrated with pieces of paper that triangles, spheres, etc. were actual shapes, not just abstract formulae. I would sit weeping at breakfast that I didn't want to go to school. What increased my ostracism was that, apart from being "brainy," which was bad enough in itself, I was no good at sports: too small for netball (basketball), too myopic for tennis, too slow on my

feet for "rounders" (a mild version of baseball). I was
invariably the last to be picked when the class was
divided into teams. I could understand that I was
undesirable, yet it was painful to me. I avoided the
rougher games, hockey in winter and cricket in summer,
by absconding. It was easy to do—since the school had no
playing fields of its own, we had to go to a park, and I
simply disappeared on the way. After trying hockey and
getting hit on the shin with a stick, and catching a cricket
ball without realizing how hard it was, I privately decided
that both these games were, like acrobatics on apparatus,
dangerous, at least for me.

Two things brightened my life during those early
years in Manchester: Hebrew classes and the Girl Scouts.
The Hebrew classes were held every Sunday morning
from 10 a.m. to 1 p.m. at the nearby South Manchester
Hebrew Congregation on Wilbraham Road. I was very
keen indeed to go, but as my parents couldn't afford the
temple membership dues, they doubted whether I would
be admitted. Nor did they want to expose themselves to
the possibility of the humiliating snub of rejection if they
applied on my behalf. It wouldn't have done any good to
make our extreme poverty known. So they encouraged me
to go and ask for myself, which I did. The minister, the
Rev. L. Weiwow,[1] who was also headmaster of the Hebrew
school, was an unconventional man with a quarrelsome
wife; they didn't get on well with the congregation, and
eventually left for Nairobi. But he was a generous human
being and a superb teacher. He accepted me without a
single question about the payment of fees or dues. He was
more interested in an enthusiastic learner than in money.
He taught the senior class, to which I advanced quite
rapidly, and where I was the only girl among a group of
older boys. We read and translated various Old Testament
stories. What made it so exciting was the quality of Rev.
Weiwow's teaching; he explained to us the structure of the
Hebrew language, in which all words are reducible to a
three letter root. Once one learns the declensions, the
conjugations, and the system for the formation of nouns,
adverbs, etc., it becomes relatively easy to construe the

text, especially as most Biblical stories have a fairly limited vocabulary of recurrent words. For me this was an exhilarating initiation into the world of language, the more so as it coincided with my beginnings in Latin.

The Girl Scouts gave me a totally different kind of pleasure. I joined a nondenominational "company" and was a member of the "Daffodil Patrol." The guider, Margaret Norris, a young woman full of gusto and good cheer, found me a dark blue uniform dress and a belt with "Be Prepared" on the buckle. Perhaps I was so much happier at Guides than at school because, for once, I was dressed like everyone else. I took everything very seriously and spent my time working for various badges: "Thrift" (that was—and is—second nature to me), "Laundress," "Booklover,"and others. For the rank of "Second Class" I had to turn out and clean my room, for which I was already well-trained through office cleaning. I got my "First Class" too, and did well in fulfilling all the requirements except one: making a fire and cooking a meal in the open air. This was not a matter of electric grills or barbecues; it meant starting from scratch by neatly cutting and laying back the turf, so that it could be replaced at the end without any sign of damage. The wood had to be gathered, the fire laid and lit, and the food cooked. I am afraid that, for the one and only time in my life, I cheated just a bit. To get the fire going, my mother gave me some wax, remnants of her Friday night candles. And I took a more-or-less cooked hamburger, which needed only slight cosmetic "cooking." Yet I nearly came to grief. As the examiner came to inspect my efforts, the margarine in my pan flared up into a spectacular orange fire. Nevertheless, I passed. I also went camping one summer weekend; we slept in tents, were drenched in the almost incessant rain, and spent most of our time trying to keep our fire going with damp twigs and leaves. I have never had any desire to go camping since then, nor do I want a fire—I fill my fireplace with plants. Still, I enjoyed the Guides, and curiously could do there some of the things I bungled at school such as taking part in a three-legged race. Self-confidence was certainly involved, but also the sense of acceptance by others, which I had at Guides and lacked at school.

Since my parents were very busy and preoccupied with getting the practice started, I was left pretty much to my own devices. I had a key to the apartment, would do my homework in a trice, eat a tomato sandwich, and go out to play—sometimes with a boy of my age who lived in Appleby Lodge, more often alone with my precious tennis ball. Like everything else, tennis balls were unavailable during the war, but somehow I got one, and I cherished it as if it were solid gold, knowing it to be irreplaceable. By dint of use, all its felt covering wore off to reveal the bare black rubber underneath. The more sorry and bald it looked, the more I loved it.

There were only occasional air raids by then. I had very specific instructions what to do in the event of a raid when I was alone. I was to take a small pigskin suitcase embossed with my mother's initials out of her closet and go down to my grandmother's apartment, which was safer, being on the first floor, whereas ours was up on the top floor. I never looked into the suitcase or asked what it contained. Years later, before we emigrated to the United States, I did open it and was disappointed to find nothing but papers. Now, another twenty years later, I appreciate their value.

I carefully saved my shilling-a-week pocket money until I had enough to buy another bicycle. This one was much more modern and beautiful than the old one, with shiny chromium handlebars which I cleaned with a religious fervor. It was kept in the lobby of our building, fastened to a railing with a chain and padlock. One day it was gone. I was utterly heartbroken. To me this crisis warranted calling my father at the office, although we never otherwise disturbed him. I couldn't even speak, I just sobbed. When I finally got it out that my bicycle had been stolen, he was very relieved; he thought something had happened to my mother. It was only a bicycle. Not many weeks later he managed to get a replacement through a patient. However, this one had black handlebars, and I never loved it as passionately as the one

I had bought with my own savings. My father got himself a bicycle too, and we went out exploring on Sunday afternoons. Once we got as far as Ringway (now Manchester Airport), where paratroops were in training. My mother scolded us for going near a military installation; she feared our arrest and internment for spying activities.

I very much wanted to have music lessons like the other girls. At school, music theory was taught as part of the curriculum, but theory doesn't make much sense without playing some instrument. We had no piano; that was one of the things that had mysteriously disappeared on the way from Vienna. I could learn the violin, and the school even agreed to lend me an instrument to save the expense of buying one, which we certainly couldn't have afforded. My father was of the opinion that even the cost of the lessons was beyond our means, but my mother pleaded, and so finally I did learn for a short while. I joined the junior school orchestra, and played at Founders' Day and Speech Day. I never got beyond second violin, but I enjoyed it, and also renewed my acquaintance with the English hymns I had sung in Chertsey.

Slowly but surely my father built up his practice. He was one of several refugee dentists in Manchester to whom the other refugees flocked because they spoke German and were less hasty to pull teeth. There were even some patients from Bedford who had become so attached to him that they made the three-hour train journey once a year to be treated by him. English patients came too, attracted by the convenient location, the excellence of his work, his humorous personality, and modest fees. Neither medicine nor dentistry were money-making professions in Europe or in England as they are in the United States. My father preferred to undercharge rather than overcharge, sometimes making grotesque mistakes in the process. He told me of the strange looks he got from a rather shabby couple when he charged them a minimal amount; they turned out to be wealthy factory owners. After he had retired, he said that he might have been able to make £5,000 (about $7,000) more in his lifetime, but would it have made him any happier? We continued to live very modestly; the habit of thrift was a virtue in England, particularly in wartime and in the post-war years when the motto was "Make-do and mend." I was quite an adept needlewoman, letting out seams and lengthening dresses with pieces of white fabric as I grew out of them.

In 1944 we took our first vacation since our trip to Italy in 1937. We went for a week to the coast of North Wales, to Llandudno, an attractive small town on a promontory with a bay flanked by two hills, the Great Orme and the Little Orme. The hotels were still occupied by the American army, and our means were limited anyway. We had been recommended to a boardinghouse with the grandiose name, The Wellington, on the promenade near the pier. Since all the boardinghouses took guests from Saturday to Saturday, the trains were notoriously crowded that day. We decided to travel on Friday, trusting that we could find accommodation for one night. I was so excited that I spent most of the previous week packing and repacking my little suitcase. This was to be a fun adventure. It proved somewhat more adventure and somewhat less fun, at least at the outset, than I had anticipated. When we turned up at The Wellington on Friday afternoon, Mrs. Jones, the owner, met us with an icy stare and the declaration, "You are not due till *tomorrow* afternoon." With that she more or less slammed the door on us. Everywhere was full, of course; in fact, people were sleeping on the beaches. Finally my father remembered that one of his Austrian dental colleagues had settled in Llandudno. We managed to contact him and he let us spend the night in his waiting room. The next morning we stood in line at Woolworth's for a cup of tea. It wasn't quite the kind of vacation we had expected. Considerably chastened, we presented ourselves at the Wellington on Saturday afternoon, and were assigned a rather dark, dreary room. We were fortunate in having exceptionally fine weather that week so that we could be outdoors all day. We had to learn the mores of boardinghouse behavior. For meals, all boarders were crammed into one room at set times. If you were late, it was hard luck; the food was put down at your place whether you were there or not. One morning we set out to walk around the Great Orme, not realizing how far that was. As the one o'clock lunch hour approached, my parents pressed on relentlessly, leaving me to drag behind with sore feet. We arrived at 1.30 p.m. to cold tomato soup and disapproving glances.

That was our first and last boardinghouse. The following year we moved up to a small hotel in Southport on the Lancashire coast. It was there that we heard of the atomic bomb dropped on Hiroshima and the end of the war. The reports of the ravage wrought by the bomb had a distinctly sobering effect, dampening the joy we might have felt at the cessation of hostilities.

There was another reason for our constrained mood: the ever present threat of my father's gallstones. He proved to be something of a medical curiosity, the world's "champion gallstone maker," as he deemed himself. He had had his gallbaldder removed in 1931, but repeatedly made new stones. His attacks became more and more frequent, keeping him off work for days on end just as the practice was beginning to blossom. However loyal, patients don't like to have their appointments cancelled suddenly at short notice. I remember his disappearing when we were at a wedding ceremony and finding him on a chair in the lobby doubled over in pain and perspiring profusely. It was like a heart attack, only on the right side of the body. It took days, sometimes weeks for him to recover from the ensuing jaundice. Because of this "time-bomb in my stomach," as he called it with grim humor, we always ate abstemiously, avoiding rich, fat, or spicy foods so as not to irritate "the monster." My eating idiosyncracies were undoubtedly shaped by the lean diet to which I became accustomed.

By 1945 he was so desperately sick that a tumor was suspected. An Australian surgeon, Mr. McEvedy, who had his office in the same building as my father and who was a patient and a friend of his, performed surgery on him, removing a single small stone which had been moving up and down the bile duct. Mr. McEvedy, an outstanding surgeon, had certain pet principles, he favored local anesthesia, and one particular hospital in Manchester's worst slum, Ancoats. So while victory in Europe was being celebrated in May 1945, I was going every day for three weeks to visit my father in Ancoats Hospital. That was when I saw Manchester's nineteenth-century industrial row houses, women in shawls and clogs scrubbing the steps and whitening them with some kind of chalk block. The houses were neatly maintained with lace curtains, but the people on the ancient trolley-bus I had to take smelled awful. When emergencies occurred during his recovery, my mother would stay until late at night while I was alone at home, not knowing what had happened. It was an anxious time.

I had a fright, too, when my aunt proposed to my mother that, now that the war was over, she could go back to Vienna to resume her profession. I knew how deeply my mother suffered through the loss of her beloved profession, and how much influence her only sister wielded over her. I feared she might really go, and saw myself abandoned. My aunt's argument was that, at age fourteen, I was old enough to fend for myself, and as for my father, she thought him as good as dead with this gallstone affliction. To my immense relief, my mother didn't heed her suggestion.

We were never fully integrated into the social life of Manchester. As soon as they could, my parents became members of the South Manchester Hebrew Congregation, but my father declined invitations to serve on various of its committees; after a day at the office and the trip there and back on a crowded bus, he wanted only to stay at home and read. Although they went to friends' houses and received visitors in return, they dreaded rather than enjoyed these occasions because they involved conspicuous consumption. We much preferred to do our own things quietly; going for a daily walk even in winter; driving out to the seaside at Blackpool or Southport on Sundays; an occasional movie; opera when London's Covent Garden came to Manchester every spring and autumn; the theater at the small auditorium in the library, or at the university, or when new plays were tried out in Manchester before their London openings. It was a less glamorous but more secure life than in Vienna, especially after we became British citizens in 1947.

As "foreigners with British passports," as we were called, we remained somewhat apart. Our closest friends were also ex-refugees. No doubt our experiences had to some extent marked and bonded us. Manchester certainly had a distinctive refugee subculture. "Austria House" was the meeting place of those who intended to go back after the war. Later our otherness was a less readily perceptible but still potent social factor. The ex-refugees gravitated toward German or Austrian doctors and dentists, whose philosophy of treatment was attuned to their own. Some degree of tension also arose between the British Jews and the newcomers. The British Jews were in the majority *Ashkenazim*, who had come from Eastern Europe, with a sprinkling of *Sephardim* of Hispano-Portuguese origin. We belonged to the former category. But the years spent in Central Europe had exposed us, the ex-refugees, to a secular culture which the British Jews by and large did not share. They had had a hard economic struggle to work their way up, and seemed to be a generation behind us in education. They resented the fact that we, because of our background, were more readily accepted into good schools and by our middle-class English neighbors than they with their greater wealth and longer standing in the country. "Background" is one of those ineffable concepts that play a central, though ill-defined and often concealed role in English society.

The immediate post-war years, despite the relief from the human losses and suffering, brought other hardships. Rationing of food, fuel, and clothing not only continued, but even intensified. Bread, for instance, was rationed in Great Britain for the first time only *after* the end of the war. The terribly cold winter of 1947 marked a low point. Britain had won the war and lost the peace, it was ruefully said. There was considerable resentment at the Marshall Aid given to Germany by the United States to help rebuild its factories and economy. The defeated were being rewarded, while the victors had been bled to death.

To us refugees the post-war period brought another trauma: the lists of survivors. News of the Final Solution had percolated through, notwithstanding endeavors to keep it secret. In the early stages of the war, occasional letters would still arrive from Europe, transmitted after long delays, by the Red Cross via Switzerland. We even received, incongruously, a parcel of cookies from Hungary, crunched into crumbs on the way, on which we had to pay customs duty! That was the last sign of life we ever had from my father's family. Yet it was hard, at first, to believe what we heard. Deportations, concentration camps, forced labor and brutalities had long been known to us, but the very idea of mass murders in gas chambers was almost impossible to countenance. By 1944 the refugees were in a state of shock and mourning; everyone had left some relatives or friends behind, and we were in terror of what was happening to them. The pictures of Bergen-Belsen, released when the Allies occupied the camp, horrified the world, and none more so than us refugees, who imagined our dear ones (or ourselves but for the luck of the draw and the grace of God) in such conditions. Gradually the Red Cross began to publish lists of survivors. My mother went every week to scan them at Austria House, spending despondent hours in search of familiar names. For all her efforts she found just one, a Polish colleague of hers from medical school, Dr. Sofie Weissberg, who had survived in Vienna as a nurse to some quarter-Jews. We immediately wrote to her, sent her food and medications, and later had her come to stay with us for extended convalescent visits. Of the fate of my father's family we knew nothing for a while. Their complete disappearance had something uncanny about it. Eventually we learned that his youngest brother had survived in the Tot Work Organization; that his mother had died shortly before the deportations in 1944 and been hastily buried without any marker (a small tombstone was erected in the cemetery where she is buried in 1980 with the help of one distant cousin who had survived); his elder sister and her family perished in Treblinka at an unknown date, while his younger sister had been gassed in Auschwitz in June 1944. We, the fortunate ones, had won our lives but lost our families and our world.

As I grew into my later teens, I came to like Manchester rather better for its rich cultural resources. It was the home of the Hallé Orchestra, which underwent a great renaissance after the appointment of its new conductor, Sir John Barbirolli, in 1942. He, too, lived in Appleby Lodge. Manchester's concert hall had been bombed so that concerts were for a long time held out at Bellevue, usually the venue for circuses or boxing matches. It was not a congenial environment for a concert, but we had to "make do." Later a fine concert hall was built, not far from my father's office in St. Peter's Street. It was named the Free Trade Hall, and bore the shields of all the surrounding towns that had been active in the nineteenth-century Free Trade movement. Manchester, I learned, though it was ugly, had a glorious liberal tradition, of which it was rightly proud.

It also had a fine university, where I was an undergraduate from 1948 to 1952. My career direction had been decided for me by fate when I developed nephritis at age fifteen following a strep throat infection. Antibiotics were not then generally available in England; the treatment was bed rest. I missed almost a year of school. Under these circumstances it was clearly not possible to pursue the sciences, which demanded presence in a laboratory. But I could and did read. My schoolfellows behaved splendidly in this crisis—the British always rise to a challenge. Someone came to see me nearly every day and gave me the homework assignments so that I could keep up with my class. My teachers also visited occasionally, and the school authorities arranged for me to take the public exam for the School Certificate at home. This enforced rest intensified my apartness, but it also fostered in me at an early age habits of independent study and a certain ingenuity in coping with handicaps.

Although I went back to school for a further two years, I remained more detached than ever. The school, of course, wanted me to try for Oxford or Cambridge. I was advised against this for health reasons, because of the cold living conditions in the colleges; the central heating at home would be safer for me. I went to Manchester University quite willingly, not least because I would be following in my father's footsteps and establishing a family tradition. I took the Entrance Scholarship exams, a series of four papers in Latin, English, French, and German. I came home the first day from the Latin exam extremely disheartened; one candidate had walked out after an hour while I had barely been able to finish in the allotted three hours. In face of such brilliance I thought it futile to continue. My father consoled me by offering a quite different interpretation of the event: the other candidate had left because he could do no more and had bitten off all his nails. So I was persuaded to go back for the three other papers. On my application form I had put a very minor scholarship as my first choice, and when the competition results came, I looked for that particular one. To my disappointment, my name wasn't there, and I tossed the list away. When my mother picked it up later, she noticed that I had been awarded the premier scholarship.

I was as happy at Manchester University as I had been unhappy at school. It had a highly distinguished faculty, including the historian Sir Lewis Namier, and in my field, Eugène Vinaver as head of the department of French Studies and Ronald Peacock as head of German. Both were comparatists in their work, Vinaver in medieval studies, Peacock in modern drama. Vinaver in particular exerted a strong influence on me, both through his scholarliness and his exemplary courtesy to students. He was a humanist in the truest sense. He had been born in St. Petersburg, where his father, a lawyer, had been a member of the parliament and had, incidentally, financed the painter, Marc Chagall, to go to Paris. In 1917, at the Russian Revolution, the family emigrated to France, where Eugène was educated. He remained a French citizen throughout his life although he came to Oxford for postgraduate work, married an Englishwoman, and spent most of his life in England. As head of the department, he built probably the finest French department in Great Britain through his broad and generous vision. Long before interdisciplinary approaches came into fashion, his was a department of French Studies, comprising French history, thought, and art as well as language and literature. It was also Vinaver who founded Comparative Literary Studies at Manchester. He taught *Madame Bovary* to the freshman class, and although I was unable to understand it at age seventeen, his teaching made such an impact on me that I reread the novel ten years later, and have gone on doing so ever since. I regarded him as my intellectual father, and dedicated my first book to him. I am sure that my attraction to Comparative Literature stems in large part from his influence.

I took some part in the university's social life, though not much. My mother chased me to go to things, but I went rather reluctantly, except to concerts, lectures, and plays. The dances and socials bored and depressed me, as did the courtship rituals. A number of eligible young Jewish men, budding lawyers, doctors, and physicists, dated me at one time or another. I found them awfully dull intellectually and awkward socially, and I have no doubt that they found me awfully intellectual and rather reserved (I dressed more conservatively in my youth than I do now.). I had a far better time with one of my young instructors, who asked me to marry him, a step I wouldn't even consider because he was not Jewish. To marry out of my religion would have been to me a betrayal of the heritage for which I had been persecuted and to which I have a deep loyalty.

I often hear comments nowadays how unusual was my choice not to marry in the 1950s. I have to admit that I am not aware of ever having made a conscious choice. I was not—am not—"domesticated," though I take great pleasure in looking after my house. I was once engaged to a mathematician, an assistant professor at the University of Manchester. It was a somewhat comical business. He was among the young men I knew, but I had no particular interest in him. So when he asked me to meet him for coffee one afternoon and suddenly proposed marriage, I was quite taken aback. All I could say was that I would think about it. I was twenty-three at the time, bogged down in my dissertation at Cambridge, and uncertain of my future. Marriage was, of course, the socially accepted path, and Peter was deemed eminently suitable. He had originally come from Germany, had been brought up on a farm in England, and had made his way on scholarships. Because he had lacked close relationships in his adolescence, he was gauche and ill at ease with people, and as I discovered in the next few months, he kept feelings at bay. His only passion was research in mathematics; nothing else mattered to him. As the wedding arrangements were made, I grew increasingly miserable, often spending half the night in the kitchen with my mother, weeping and trying to explain what bothered me. Finally, six weeks before the day, I told him that I didn't want to go through with it. He couldn't understand, but I was adamant. The very next day I saw an assistant professorship in German advertised at the Queen's University of Belfast. I was lucky enough to get the position. Several weeks later people began to tell my mother that I could come back to Manchester, that the episode had been forgotten. They were surprised to hear that I had no intention of coming back. I loved my work; as soon as I started teaching, I knew that I had found my metier. After all the years of penny-pinching and insecurity, it felt good too to have a salary of my own. I was more than reluctant after that to give up my independence. I don't have any regrets.

During my years at Manchester University we enjoyed a modest prosperity and greater security than I had known since the day the Nazis arrived in Vienna. My father's gallstones were in remission, the practice was flourishing, and we seemed settled. With our brand new British passports we went back to the Continent in 1949 for a vacation in Switzerland. We crossed by boat from Dover to Calais and saw from the train window the total devastation of the French coastal region, which had been the launching area for the V2 "Flying Bombs" toward the end of the war, and had been destroyed in an attempt to stop these attacks. The "Pas de Calais," so often mentioned on the news as a target for bombing, was still deep in rubble four years after the end of the war. The next morning, breakfast at Basle station was like experiencing a transformation scene: the strong, fresh real coffee, cream, sugar, rolls, ample butter, and choice of preserves. The orderliness, cleanliness, and affluence of Switzerland was worlds away from still-struggling postwar Britain. We saw displayed in the stores many British goods not available at home, manufactured for export only—Heinz baked beans, Dundee marmalade, Wedgewood china, and cashmere sweaters.

In 1948 we got our first car after more than two years on a waiting list. My father would call once a week to ask about his prospects, and one morning he was told, "It is a good morning—your car has come. You can fetch it as soon as you like." Little did the dealer know how much consternation this news caused. My father couldn't drive, although he had a valid driver's license. He had passed the test, which was then purely theoretical, many years previously in Vienna, where he had been allowed once in a while to drive my uncle's car under the close supervision of the professional chauffeur. But we had never owned a car, which was hardly necessary where we lived in the city center. In England he had acquired a license, too, during the war, when tests had been suspended. On the way to paying the electricity bill in the town hall he had passed the driver's license office, and thought it a useful thing to have, and at five shillings a bargain, too. Now he was expected to drive away a 10 horsepower Ford with an awkwardly stiff gear change and a rather gruff temper. He persuaded one of the dealer's employees to drive the vehicle home and to show him how to work it. He spent the next few Sunday mornings driving it slowly up and down a quiet road until he felt ready to risk passengers. The car gave us a lot of pleasure; we went out on Sundays to explore the lovely countryside around Manchester in the Derbyshire hills or on the coast. Then we made a trip to the Lake District, a tour of Stratford, Oxford, Windsor,

Cambridge, and Scotland, to get to know our new homeland. During the week we continued to use the convenient public transport since parking in the city was difficult and expensive. My father taught me to drive, too. He would tease me that I should patent a system for driving a car without gas since I always came back with an empty tank—until I got stuck one day. I, for my part, would say that we shared the car: he paid for it and I used it! It was not a comfortable car, without heating, and so poorly sprung that the backseat passenger had to duck at every railroad crossing so as not to bump her head on the ceiling. Yet we loved it so dearly that we parted from it with great reluctance after it had sprung a leak in its roof over the front passenger seat. My mother had to ride in the back, and gossip began to circulate that the Fursts were on such bad terms that they wouldn't even sit next to each other in the car.

In the summer of 1949, we shipped the car across the Channel and retraced the route we had so painfully traversed in 1938: Brussels, Aachen, Cologne. Now we had British passports, now we could buy fruit, now we need fear no one. Nevertheless, we didn't stay long in Germany, where my parents felt ill-at-ease, nor did we enter Austria. We opted instead for Switzerland, France, or Italy for our vacations. We had made it, though not without some scars on our souls.

Manchester

For me it was a return to Manchester. I could now speak English fluently—of course with a strong foreign accent—and was quite hopeful though also a little anxious that I would be able to make a living there. Within a month we moved into a nice apartment in Appleby Lodge and started a practice in St. Peter's Square, one of the loveliest parts in the center of Manchester near the library and the town hall. It would have been easier to start a mass extractions and dentures ("blood and vulcanite") practice in a suburb, but I would have hated it. We decided to take a risk despite our weak financial position. The first year was difficult, but we won through.

The Manchester High School for Girls accepted Lilian, and she became very successful there, a credit to the excellent headmistress and the teaching staff.

We became normal, average citizens again, with the daily worries, pleasures, anxieties, and hopes, like any other family. We avoided speaking German outside our home, as a precaution. We lived through critical times in England, and learned to admire the population for their unbreakable spirit. Churchill's speeches gave us hope and confidence for the future. America's entry into the war

changed the whole situation. Our daily life was deeply
affected by the ups and downs of the war. The
commentaries on the radio and in the newspapers were a
daily part of our existence—Lilian asked us once what the
newspapers write about in peacetime! We were treated
with the utmost fairness by the British people and
authorities. We had the same rations in food, clothing, and
everything else. I wish that I could adequately pay
homage to the British for their generosity toward us. They
gave us a new lease on life and a home.

We had three short Red Cross messages from my
people in Hungary. Then there was complete silence for
the rest of the war. I don't know whether they received our
Red Cross letters.

When we arrived in England, we were surprised at
the complacency of the British. They did not realize with
whom they were dealing in the Nazis. At first we thought
that perhaps we had become so frightened that our
judgment was affected. Normal people could not imagine
or believe what was going on in Germany—there was not
the slightest chance of organized resistance, political or
military, against the Nazis. Once their blackmail over
Czechoslovakia had succeeded, there was no stopping
them. "Less butter and more guns" had been no empty
slogan but preparation for the coming war, which was
inevitable.

We had lived among them for nine months. We were
their first targets for annihilation. We had watched the
happenings from the inside. The slightest opposition was
ruthlessly crushed. Fear and distrust dominated
everything. Families and old friendships were broken up;
people did not dare to talk freely to one another. The
teachings of Fichte, Hegel, Treitschke, and Nietzsche were
cited as valid doctrines to justify the regime's beliefs: the
State is everything, the fate of the individual doesn't
count.

We Jews knew that beneath this officially created,
artifical mood, there was deep, mute dissatisfaction and
discontent. We were the only ones to whom they dared to
complain without any risk of denunciation or betrayal. We

listened to them and never expressed any opinion.

Frightening and incredible rumors started to circulate, and strange names were mentioned in connection with them: Auschwitz, Birkenau, Bergen-Belsen, Mauthausen, Treblinka, and others too. We knew of Dachau before we left Austria. It became gradually sure that the Germans were murdering the Jews of Europe. Their hatred was so intense that they diverted trains, which they needed badly for their army, to transport these unfortunate people to the gas chambers. Horror filled the hearts of all decent people throughout the world, and despair filled ours. To others the victims were faceless numbers; to us they were our parents, sisters, brothers, and children. In the history of mankind there was no example of such planned and systematically executed mass murders of millions of people. It cannot be made good; the shame will sit forever on the name of Germany. They made some exceptions. The young and able-bodied had to work to exhaustion before they were killed. Some of them survived through the sudden collapse of the German Empire. Among them was my youngest brother.

Our personal struggle for survival and to create a new life was overshadowed by historic world events. The whole world had misjudged Nazi Germany at the outset. It was difficult for people of normal sense to believe that this once civilized country was governed by an unscrupulous gang headed by a lunatic gangster. The German defeats at Stalingrad and El Alamein were the turning points of the war. The American landing in North Africa and the successful invasion from England to France marked the beginning of the end. On Victory Day I was in hospital recovering from serious surgery after a long bout of illhealth.

We slowly found out what had happened to our relatives. My mother died a few weeks before the Jews of Sopron were deported to Auschwitz. My younger sister and other relatives died there in the gas chambers. My elder sister with her husband and two children were murdered in Treblinka. I heard only many months later that my youngest brother had survived. Of the two thousand Jews in Sopron about one hundred and eighty survived.

When the war was over, many of our friends and patients asked us when we would be going back to Vienna. They couldn't believe that we had decided to stay in England. We had spent the best years of our lives in Vienna; we had been young, adaptable, and despite all our worries, we thought there was no better place on earth to live than there. But then we were humiliated beyond description, cheated of our human rights, degraded as citizens, and turned from dignified professional persons into homeless scum. The Nazis had failed to achieve their aims, but we could never forget how ruthlessly they had tried. We had seen our friends and acquaintances turn overnight into deadly enemies and merciless persecutors. They had suddenly discovered that we were poisoning the air and deserved to be destroyed. All this for the glory and prosperity of greater Germany. There were a few exceptions; alas, very few. Some risked their lives and existence to help us, and we remember them with admiration and respect them as heroes and saints. However, we had lost faith in Austria; we could not trust the people or live among them. Vienna was the cemetery of our dreams and hopes. Our past persecutors were walking the streets, disguised as peaceful citizens, unpunished and probably unrepentant. Our memories were still too vivid. We could not face a population that would behave as if nothing had happened. Only the parks and the trees remained the same. Where were our friends? Many were killed, or at best dispersed all over the world. We knew that the Vienna that we had left would never be the same as it had been before.

There were quite a number of refugees who dreamed together of the time when they would return to Austria and help to rebuild their "home country." They founded an "Austria House" in Manchester near the university. They regarded themselves as temporary guests in England. They made no effort to make a new start. In Austria House time stood still; they could not imagine that conditions in the old country had changed. When I visited Austria House once, I couldn't believe my ears. The people there lived in an unreal world, full of plans to return as soon as possible. This was near the end of the war. They seriously believed that the Austrians were expecting them back. I tried to reason with them, in vain. When I warned them that the Viennese would tell them on their return "You are just the people we have been waiting for" (*Nur auf Ihna ham ma gewartet*[1]), I became extremely unpopular. Needless to say, many of them had an unpleasant awakening.

There were some who had no choice but to return: lawyers who could not practice elsewhere, journalists, actors, writers, and others with special reasons. The lawyers settled down well after some initial difficulties, and some of them became prosperous and famous like Dr. Kreisky.[2]

Among the returnees were my two eldest brothers-in-law. They succeeded in regaining their large business building in the heart of the city and in reviving their formerly highly respected textile firm. They engaged some of their old trustworthy employees. Even under the adverse post-war conditions, they could earn a good living; their reputation was their biggest asset. Both in their mid-fifties, they had not been able to settle well either in England or in the United States when they became refugees. Language difficulties, lack of connections, unfamiliarity with business customs, and, last but not least, shortage of capital and credit hampered their efforts. A number of their friends returned from all corners of the world, so they had some company, as in the good old times.

Another returnee was a colleague of mine, a Roman Catholic, who had had an excellent position in a clinic in Vienna. His wife was of Jewish origin, and they had three lovely daughters. He was requested by the Nazis either to resign his position, or, if he wished to keep his job, to divorce his wife. He emigrated to England, and had the same struggle as all of us to establish himself, in Nottingham. He returned immediately after the war. All his relatives and friends still lived in Vienna. Yet his letters to a mutual friend of ours were distressing. He was very disappointed in what he found there. Even some of his close relatives, not to mention his friends, regarded him as a traitor, who had had a comfortable life abroad while they suffered the hardships of war. He was ostracized. His former position was taken, and he had a hard time to earn his living. He died after a heart attack in his early fifties.

I had a Jewish refugee patient, a clever and hardworking man, whose non-Jewish wife had emigrated to England with him and their children. After the war his mother-in-law came to visit him. She was from a small provincial town in Austria, St. Pölten. She said to me in my office, "All the stories of cruelty and persecution are pure inventions." The real sufferers, according to her, were the Austrians who had to stay and stick it out. The fate of the Austrians was shortage of food and coal and the sacrifice of lives for survival. They felt sorry for themselves and envied those who had left the country.

England's recovery after the war was very slow. The cost of victory was far beyond the country's means. In September 1947 we became British citizens. We were settled in England and made some friends. Lilian was happy at the University. We were content to live among the good people of Manchester, and we never returned to Vienna, not even for a visit.

The Silent Third Person
(LRF)

A third person, my mother, participated in these experiences. Although she often figures in both accounts, her voice remains silent because she left nothing written except for personal letters, which I still have. It seems appropriate, at this point, to fill out the picture by trying to reconstruct her life. This differs from my father's and my own accounts, which are wholly subjective, whereas this is an attempt on my part to envisage the pattern of her life and the impact of historical circumstances on it. My perceptions are, inevitably, filtered through my eyes; they are based on my intimacy with her, on what she told me about her youth and her student days, and on the reports of those who knew her. The evidence here is, admittedly, secondhand, yet the facts themselves are beyond dispute and corroborate from another angle the dislocations and adjustments that form the core of the other two narratives.

As I recall my mother almost twenty-five years after her death in 1969, I come to realize more and more just how remarkable a woman she was. Medicine was the great passion of her life; she succeeded in going to medical school in the early 1920s when such a choice was quite

181

exceptional for a young woman from an Orthodox Jewish family. Then, after ten satisfying years of private practice, she was suddenly deprived of the profession she loved through the Nazi edict in September 1938 banning Jews from all economic activity. A bizarre, unimaginable twist of history had excluded her from the field in which she excelled. While retaining her ardent interest in medicine, she never practiced again. This loss overshadowed the second half of her life; although she bore it as best she could, she found no real substitute. Nothing could ever compensate for this arbitrary forfeiture of her central desire.

Sarah Freda Neufeld, the fourth child and first daughter of Chaja and Leib Neufeld, was born on the second day of Passover, 15 April 1896 in Potok-Zloty, a village in Galicia, near the Russo-Polish frontier. The family was neither poor nor affluent; Leib made an adequate living as a toll collector. The rights to the "gate" were put up for auction every year, but he managed to hold on to them. The work suited him, for he was a quiet, contemplative man, deeply religious, yet broad-minded. Photographs, and my memories of him, show him with his head always covered, a reminder of human finiteness before God's infinity, and frequently with a prayer book in his hands. My grandmother was the energetic one who enjoyed ruling over the family, feeding them and providing for them. She, too, right up to her death at the age of ninety, was proud of her ability to read, and relished her collections of Biblical tales. In keeping with the traditions of Judaism, learning was valued by my grandparents. Their eldest son, Robert, shared a tutor with a remarkably gifted neighbor, who was to win the Nobel Prize for Literature under the pen name Agnon. Robert, a businessman by profession, continued to study throughout his life. At social gatherings in Manchester in the 1950s he would be seated next to Alexander Altmann, the scholarly Chief Rabbi of Greater Manchester, because he was one of the very few who could engage in rewarding conversation with him.

As the family grew, with three more boys and one girl born after my mother, the Neufelds moved to the town of Buczacz so that the children could received proper schooling. I don't know whether my grandfather resumed toll-collecting there or did something else. His was a gentle, calming presence in that large family, and it was he who showed the greatest understanding for my mother from her early childhood on. As the only girl for several years, and as the only child who didn't like her mother's cooking—she abhorred garlic, and didn't like meat—she was rather an outsider. At the age of three she would strip to the skin and crouch in a corner until her father came to tell her to get dressed and be nice. Significantly, it was her father, rather than her busy mother, who responded to the little girl's transparent ploy for attention. Those episodes mark the foundations of an alliance that was to be decisive in her later plans. The birth of a sister six years her junior was a tremendous joy to my mother; at last she would have a companion. She remained deeply attached to her only sister throughout her life, but reaped mainly frustration and trouble from a petulant personality whose beauty easily won her favors, but who lacked my mother's intelligence and strength of character.

The family spoke mainly Yiddish. However, my mother also had native fluency in Polish, a good command of Ukrainian, and some Russian; she was taught Hebrew at home, and later at school, German, French, Latin, and Greek. Her evident gift for languages became apparent again when we moved to England, and she acquired impeccable spoken and written English. School was, of course, gender segregated, with the boys attending in the mornings and the girls in the afternoons. My mother would set out for school armed with green apples, which were stored through the winter in an attic, primarily for her consumption. She liked the classes despite some bad teaching; for instance, as an expression of Polish nationalism, German was deliberately mistaught with distorted pronunciations. What turned school into a tribulation was the rampant anti-Semitism. Children would chant "Dirty Jews, dirty Jews! One day we'll come and cut your throats!" Since pogroms did occur sporadically, these taunts sounded like more than empty threats to my mother. I have often wondered whether her extreme cleanliness (the kitchen was maintained like an operating room, my father would say) stemmed from these early reproaches of "dirtiness." At the age of ten she missed school for quite a while owing to an attack of osteomyelitis, an infection of the bone and bone marrow, in her left leg. Before the days of antibiotics, this was a dangerous illness that could cause blood poisoning and death. After weeks of dire pain, the infection broke through to the surface in two abscesses that allowed the pus to drain, leaving two bumps and a slightly thickened limb. Still, she got off lucky, her doctor told her. It was this experience, I believe, and her admiration for the devoted, eccentric physician who cared for her, that sparked her fascination with medicine. In her geographic location, time, and social situation, to go into medicine was an outlandish ambition for a girl.

1914 brought her considerably closer to the realization of this goal in the first of two historically induced turning points that determined her life. In the face of the advancing Russian troops, the family fled to Vienna, leaving virtually everything behind. I once asked my mother when I was maybe ten or eleven, why they had gone, arguing that Buczacz was, after all, their home. "The Russians were coming," she replied; when I insisted, she repeated her phrase, adding, "If you don't understand that one runs from the Russians, you'll never understand anything." Later I surely grew to understand. Vienna was a tremendous relief to her; it meant release from the terribly harsh winters as well as from the most blatant anti-Semitism. As far as Poland was concerned, it was good riddance, and forever. She never visited her native country again, nor did she feel any warmth toward it. In her wide ranging reading in later years, Polish literature was conspicuously absent. The only time I heard her speak the language was to a group of child survivors of the concentration camps, who came to Manchester after

World War II for rehabilitation. Her attitude to Poland was in marked contrast to my father's to his homeland, for which he retained a certain affection. He frequently spoke Hungarian, and was interested in the innovative vocabulary in the contemporary fiction that he read in his eighties. He had had a far happier childhood than she, finding acceptance among his peers, who were not as infected with anti-Semitism as was the norm in Poland.

Getting a start in Vienna was difficult, especially finding an apartment for a family with six children. One subterfuge was for prospective tenants to present themselves to a landlord with a maximum of three children, saying that another three were in the cemetery. This elicited sympathy and a lease. The other three were then smuggled in; they had indeed been in the cemetery, but not dead, as the landlord assumed. The early days in Vienna were known in the family as "the egg-crate period"; eggs were then sold in long, narrow boxes, which they used as beds. My mother went to a Polish high school where she attained the "Matura" that entitled her to enter university. Her three elder brothers had to go into the Austrian army. Two of them were discharged fairly quickly for medical reasons, and went into the cotton trade, in which they prospered sufficiently to support the entire family. Their business, Brüder Neufeld (Neufeld Brothers) became a substantial and highly respected firm. The brother immediately senior to my mother, Lippe, joined an artillery regiment, and was reported missing in action in 1917 in one of World War I's major battles on the Isonzo in Northern Italy. This was a stunning blow to my mother, for Lippe was the one who also wanted to go to medical school, and they had planned to go together. Already set apart in the family, she now lost the only sibling close to her intellectually. She tried to deny his death, fantasizing for years that he might have suffered a head wound and amnesia, and still return some day. His picture hung by her bedside.

For reasons not clear to me, she first studied chemistry for a semester in Lemberg (Lvov). My guess is that this detour was provoked by difficulties in gaining

admission to the University of Vienna. While women had
been permitted to study medicine there since 1904,
considerable resistance still prevailed, the more so to a
Jewess. On the front page of her Registration Book
(*Meldungsbuch*, the equivalent of a transcript), she
initially entered "Humanities" ("philosophischen
Fakultät") as her faculty, and then amended it to
"Medicine," although that had been her aim from the
outset. In her first semester in Vienna, apart from three
courses in chemistry, and one each in physics, anatomy,
and biology, she registered for a seminar on *Faust*, which
she dropped in favor of "History of Philosophy" taught by
the eminent classicist Theodor Gumperz. The registration
book also reveals that she postponed dissection and
histology from the second to the third semester,
continuing instead with basic sciences and embryology.
Dissection was an ordeal for her, as she readily admitted,
intensifying her revulsion to meat. After that there were
no further hesitations; she took an average of six courses
per semester, and passed all the major exams with the
grade "excellent." She was a brilliant student whose
microscopic blood tests were sought after for their high
accuracy. Her achievement has to be assessed in light of
the obstacles she overcame both in school and at home.
Many professors still persisted in refusing to admit
women to their classes so that her choices were limited.
Her first name, Sarah, regarded as provocatively Jewish,
was a distinct handicap. A friend of her eldest brother,
who had connections in City Hall, offered to get it changed
to Stella so as to make her life easier. She proudly rejected
this proposition. At oral exams, she would be addressed as
"Fräulein Neufeld, Sarah" with emphasis on the latter. At
home, too, she faced continued opposition; she was
taunted for wasting her youth in libraries and hospitals,
and contrasted with her worldly younger sister who went
dancing. Her mother reproached her constantly for not yet
having married and borne children. But her father backed
her, and this was precious support for her. Despairing of
her ever getting married, her generous brother, Robert,
set her up in an enormous, splendid six-room apartment

in the best part of Vienna on the Maria-Theresienstrasse, off the Schottenring. Beautiful rosewood and walnut furniture was handcrafted for her, she was given a modest monthly allowance, and written off as a willful spinster, the idiot in the family. Her friends were other East European medical students, many of whom were ardent Zionists, who gave up their studies to become pioneer settlers in Palestine.

With her graduation in April 1925, her troubles, far from being over, merely changed in nature. For as a result of the 1919 Treaty of Versailles, which ended the First World War, the Austro-Hungarian monarchy was dissolved. My mother, designated a Polish citizen, became a foreigner in Austria. Her altered status is reflected in her registration book in an entry in October 1921 that records *"Ganze Ausländer-Taxe"* ("Full Foreigner Supplement"). These additional fees were only the beginning of a much bigger problem. As a foreigner she was debarred from medical practice in Austria. On her large, impressive Latin diploma a tiny notation is stamped in red to the effect that, "owing to lack of Austrian citizenship, the reservation is imposed that the holder has to renounce the right to practice in the Republic of Austria." Nor could she practise in Poland, even if she had so wished because she possessed an Austrian, now foreign, qualification. It was a Catch-22 situation of a mismatch between citizenship and degree. While she had derived benefit from one historical constellation (the Russian advance into Poland in 1914), she was heavily penalized by the reorganization of Europe into discrete republics. However, by a curiously obtuse reasoning, the degree was valid for unpaid hospital work. So for three years my mother was an involuntary "volunteer." Since she received an allowance from her brother, the financial aspect bothered her less than not being allowed to have her own patients. Like many women physicians at the time, she went into pediatrics, which she found absorbing. But it was also heartbreaking in those days of relatively primitive medicine. To care for a child perhaps for weeks, to come in one morning to an empty bed, then to attend the autopsy and speak to the parents, was in the long run too stressful for a very sensitive person. So she took a further qualification in dentistry, a field in which her meticulous precision and manual skill stood her in good stead. Her work was widely admired in the hospital, where she was often surrounded by students eager to learn from her. When I spent a semester in Paris in the 1950s, I met an Austrian family who had been her patients twenty-five years earlier and who insisted on opening their mouths to show me the bridges and crowns she had installed. "And they have held up!" they pointed out in a spontaneous testimony to her workmanship.

Her mother, naturally, went on urging marriage, especially as there were no prospects for private practice. There was an incessant litany of how many children her various classmates and neighbors had already had. She did not lack suitors. Though not pretty in a conventional style, to an appreciative gaze she was strikingly beautiful with her dark, soulful eyes, her high cheekbones, her thick, wavy black hair, and her wellproportioned figure. She knew how to dress, too, within the limits of her budget; she had a preference for lace collars, dainty blouses (which she laundered and ironed herself), and the simple adornment of a string of pearls. But she was extremely serious, rather reserved, and above all, enthralled by medicine. It was the fulcrum of her life.

While volunteering at the dental hospital in the early summer of 1928, she ran into my father, whom she had known by sight in medical school. He had been in a situation parallel to hers, having been deemed a Hungarian and therefore not entitled to practice. But his predicament was far worse insofar as he had no means of subsistence; he couldn't afford the "luxury" of volunteering. He got a post at a suburban dental practice, and initiated strenuous efforts to obtain Austrian citizenship, which he had just managed to get through a political connection of his late father's. He now came to the dental hospital to find a three-week summer locum at the place where he was still employed. He invited my mother to take the position, assuring her that his boss

avoided awkward questions about citizenship. She jumped
at the opportunity to experience private practice for the
first time. He would escort her home in the evenings, and
by the end of the three weeks they were engaged. She was
not without anxieties and doubts: he aspired to a
motorcycle, which terrified her, and spoke of retiring some
day to a chicken farm, an idea as repellent to her as garlic.
They were married in a small religious ceremony on 9
September 1928. Strangely, she found it hard to
remember years after whether it had been 8 or 9
September, and resolved the difficulty by reminding
herself that she had married late. He never got a
motorcycle; more than twenty years later he became the
very proud owner of a Ford 10. As for the chickens, she
persuaded him to cultivate roses instead when he retired.

By marriage my mother became an Austrian citizen.
A handwritten addendum in the lower left corner of the
diploma in red ink, signed by the *Rektor* (Provost) of the
University of Vienna, dated 13 September 1928, states
that through the acquisition of Austrian citizenship the
holder attains the right to practice medicine in Austria.
My mother's eagerness to have this precious addendum
entered as soon as possible (and her fear of some hitch)
was such that the honeymoon was abbreviated to three
days. My father moved into her apartment with two
suitcases, one full of shabby clothes, and the other
crammed with hammers, screwdrivers, nails, and wire,
his cherished tools as a natural fixer. The apartment was
so spacious that they could establish their office there,
furnishing one of the large, light front rooms as a surgery,
and letting the adjacent living room double as a waiting
room. It was a dual practice, each having their own
patients. The slave labor in the suburbs was given up in
favor of a part-time position in a bank employees' clinic
that my uncle Robert was able to obtain for my father.
This provided some income while they waited to build up
their practice. Competition was stiff in Vienna, with its
overabundance of medical personnel, but my mother had
the nucleus of a clientele from the hospital, from which
many patients followed her. She worked only afternoons,

attending in the morning to the household, although she had absolutely no idea how to cook (as she had confessed before marriage); mostly my grandmother sent her maid over with ready-cooked meals. My father used the office in the mornings and worked at the clinic in the afternoons. They would assist each other in jaw surgery and other complex procedures. In fact, on his marriage my father had been told by one of his professors that he could learn a good deal from his bride. He was sufficiently self-confident not to feel threatened. It was my mother who was prone to anxiety; she would scan the appointments book and say, "We are alright for this month and next, and January doesn't look too bad, but what will we live on in February?" The "prospects for February" became a family joke.

The decade between 1928 and 1938 was certainly the happiest phase of my mother's life. The practice prospered, not rapidly but steadily, to give a fundamental sense of financial stability as well as deep satisfaction. My father took pride in the fact that my mother's dowry, a kind of fall-back nest egg, never had to be touched. A resident maid was hired to clean, open the door to patients, and do some cooking. A professional nanny joined the household when I was born. My mother went on working right up to my birth, wearing a loose white coat. One of her elderly male patients chided her for her weight gain, and tried to convert her to vegetarianism. He was more amused than angry when he discovered the cause of her increased girth. Another seriocomic incident occurred when the mayor of Potok-Zloty, on a visit to Vienna, sought out my mother to do his teeth. They were in such a disgusting, literally stinking condition that she couldn't face him. On his return appointment, her right hand was bandaged, and he was turned over to my father.

Besides medicine, what my mother loved best was the Viennese coffeehouse. Almost every evening my parents would snatch a bite of supper, change, and bid me good-night to go off to the coffeehouse where they met friends and family. My mother dressed with immense elegance but with restraint too, eschewing high fashion for good taste. Hats, shoes, gloves, purses matched each outfit, and subtle distinctions were observed between clothes appropriate for morning, afternoon, and evening. In addition to a hierarchy of three dressmakers, she had a milliner, who refurbished hats for each season. In the early months of their marriage, my father suspected her of extravagance when two dresses and two hats were delivered on the same day. He had to learn that Viennese ways differed from those of the Hungarian provinces. Actually, my mother was thrifty by nature, although she did sometimes splurge on beautiful clothes (as I do). She looked back on that decade as "paradise": "We were driven out of paradise," she would later ruefully comment. A small shadow was cast by her sister's hasty marriage and even hastier divorce. And a menacing shadow hung over this "paradise" in the political developments in Austria's big brother, Germany. Mostly, people adopted an ostrich attitude, hoping it would blow over, while feeling a mixture of wariness, apprehension, and helplessness.

"Paradise" came to an abrupt end on the day in March 1938 when Hitler marched into Austria. My father wanted to leave everything and go to Hungary that night to await the future turn of events. But my mother doggedly opposed any return East, motivated no doubt by her wretched memories of Poland. In hindsight, both proved right. He deferred to her judgment, and when we did eventually leave, we set off, without a specific destination, in a westerly direction. Indeed, we went on moving West until my father and I reached the shores of the Pacific in 1974, and only then, looking out over the ocean, did I tell him that the time had come for us to think East again. Meanwhile, through the spring and summer of 1938, the strategy was retrenchment: the maid left, evenings were spent at home, no new clothes. They tried the conservative tactic of lying low and being inconspicuous in the desperate hope that the Nazi regime was a temporary interlude and that things would somehow right themselves without any drastic action on our part. My mother loved Vienna, our home, her professional work, and was extremely reluctant to undergo another radical upheaval if it could possibly be avoided.

That it could not be avoided became evident in
September 1938, with the promulgation of laws forbidding
Jews to practice their professions. This triggered their
resolution to leave, although it was not until Crystal
Night, in November, that the full urgency of flight was
impressed on them. With the office closed, my parents
devoted all their time and efforts to collecting information
and scrambling for the ever-increasing number of
documents required for emigration. In an attempt to
retrain, my mother took a course in nutrition with the aim
of perhaps becoming a dietitian wherever our fate would
take us. She kept those notebooks with lists of calorific
values, minerals, and vitamins for many years. Curiously,
she, who had been such an outstanding student with such
a remarkable memory and speedy grasp of issues, had the
utmost difficulty in learning the basics of nutrition partly,
I think, because she was unable to concentrate under the
load of stress, but partly also out of a perhaps
unacknowledged fear of the implications of her retraining.
For to become a dietitian meant giving up medicine,
although in some sense it still kept her within the medical
realm in an ancillary role. She became a slow learner out
of a deep-seated unwillingness to face the hidden
connotations of the step she was taking. On the other
hand, she was "quick on the uptake" in the English
lessons on which my parents also embarked in this
interval of waiting. They both knew some French, and it
seemed a wise preparation for an uncertain future to
learn some English. My recollections of this phase of our
existence are blurred; for instance, I cannot recall what
we ate, or even that or where we ate after moving to my
uncle's apartment, although our family meals in the
Maria-Theresienstrasse remain clearly in my mind. Did
my mother cook? She must have; the maid had gone, and
so had her mother. Yet, even while the details of our daily
life escape me in a self-protective amnesia, one thing is
strongly imprinted: the awareness of the staunch
partnership between my parents. My father had genuine
respect not only for her professional expertise but also for

her wisdom, her perspicacity, and the essential astuteness of her assessments and conclusions. Decisions were always made jointly, including the crucial one that we must remain together as a family. It was a shocking surprise to me to discover later that, in many marriages and working situations, women were **not** equal, for I had been used to the reciprocal regard of parity.

As our adversity grew, so it seemed did my mother's strength. In Brussels her knowledge of French, better than my father's, was invaluable in negotiating our everyday needs. Our one room afforded little scope for housekeeping; the two extra mattresses and the bedding had to be neatly stowed away on the one bed, and the kettle boiled on the open fire. That was it. My mother suffered from the enveloping cold more than we did, as well as from the insomnia to which she had been inclined even before. No doubt about it, she was a worrier by nature, but she checked and repressed her anxieties in order to spare us. It was my father who succumbed to a violent attack of flu, through which she tended him as best she could in our difficult circumstances. She encouraged me in the writing I began to do as a substitute for going to school, and had the patience to read what I wrote, as well as an understanding of its importance to me as a means of maintaining contact in my imagination with a more normal order of life. She gave me the greatest happiness of our stay in Brussels by sewing me a "pixie-hood," a scarf sewn up into a hood at the top and with long ends to tie under the chin. It was the first time I had seen her sew. More important than these tangible services to us was my mother's heightened religious belief. Both my parents came from fairly Orthodox families, but they had gone to the temple only on the High Holy Days. Now the temple beckoned us on Saturday as a haven of warmth to which we looked forward the entire week. My mother made a vow that if she ever again had a safe, warm home, she would go to temple every week. She kept that vow to her dying day, observing the Sabbath as a token of remembrance and of thanks for our deliverance from mortal danger. The faith and hope implicit in that vow sustained us all through those dark winter months.

When we got to London in March 1939, our joy at achieving relative safety and reunion with her family was marred by the state in which they lived. It was not so much the cramped quarters, with seven adults and two children—and we three in addition—squeezed into three rooms with one bathroom and kitchen and a leaking ceiling, which my father promptly tried to repair, only to bring down a mass of rubble. Total demoralization had befallen them, and the tensions they all felt spawned harsh words and quarrels at the slightest provocation, or for no good reason at all; even my grandmother had lost her gusto and moped in the kitchen. My mother, "the intellectual," "the idiot in the family," suddenly showed a capacity to take charge that surprised everyone. Her lack of experience in the practicalities of housekeeping was outweighed by her common sense, her steadfastness, and her commitment to the welfare of her family. We had lived in far worse and more precarious conditions than those we found in London, so that we were less daunted by poverty and better able to appreciate the positive aspects, above all the release from immediate danger to our lives. My mother, previously marginalized by her family, now became its central pillar; she organized a daily routine, she talked sense into her sister, she prompted my grandmother to resume her role as caregiver. She even became successfully involved in feeding us by making, in huge quanities, the most delicious pickled herring. Maybe her course in nutrition bore fruit after all, for herring is a cheap source of protein and was plentiful and fresh in London. She would cut off the heads, filet them with the precision she had learned in dissecting, and pickle them in vinegar and lemon juice with onions and apples. If the early times in Vienna were known as the "egg-crate period," this was "the herring phase." Unfortunately, however, even the herring caused unpleasantness when hers were judged to be better than those made by the wife of one of my uncles, a woman who had prided herself on her housewifery and who resented being outdone on her special turf by an intellectual.

My mother's resourcefulness during the slow and painful process of resettlement was nothing short of amazing. She took adversity in stride, and made constructive moves, while her sister still tended to sit and pine for the past. Every day she walked quite a distance to take English lessons offered by a refugee committee for the nominal fee of a penny per lesson. She made such good progress that she was soon able to teach me. She took part in a home industry scheme by crocheting gloves and sewing buttons onto cards in an attempt to contribute to the family finances, although the pay was absurdly low. It was she who took my grandfather to the hospital when he had a badly infected hand. In her nervousness she had trouble in understanding the English pronunciation of iodine (the German, *Jod Tinctur*, sounds quite different), and was humiliated when a nurse commented that she couldn't believe she was a physician if she hadn't heard of iodine. When my father was assigned to Manchester to do his six-month study in a British dental school, the stress of separation was added to her burdens. The death in April 1940 of the father who had been her ally; the shattering of our hopes and the loss of our last savings in the fiasco in Bournemouth; my father's internment on the Isle of Man; the bombing in London; the move to Bedford where we reverted to living in one room without cooking or bathroom facilities; the seemingly endless makeshift existence we led; she bore all these blows with a stoical composure. Yet there was an outward sign of her distress in her recurrent cough of fluctuating severity. It didn't seem to be an upper respiratory infection, although it was aggravated by cold. Her siblings whispered ominously about tuberculosis. With no means for medical examination, we hoped it would go away, as it did now and then. It appeared to be psychosomatic in origin, and no wonder, considering all the stress she had to undergo.

In Bedford, where my father began to earn a salary again, her adeptness at money management came to the fore. "Penny acrobatics" was the wry name of our tactics, saving the odd halfpenny wherever possible. Our life was frugal in the extreme. By the middle of the war, food was scarce; we relied largely on potatoes to fill us up, and on feast days an egg would be thrown over them to make a dish with the fancy designation, "Italian potatoes." There was no need to buy clothing as my parents still had an ample supply from Vienna. When I grew out of mine, my mother took to knitting, at which she proved quite expert. She had the capacity to produce all sorts of skills previously unknown to us to meet our changing needs.

In Manchester we lived in the same complex as all my mother's family, occupying five apartments. The warmth of the central heating, though not always very effective, at least took the edge off the chill, and was a significant improvement in our living conditions. My grandmother's apartment served as the family headquarters, a sort of substitute for the coffeehouse. Almost every evening my mother would disappear down there, sometimes coming back upset and annoyed. The Neufelds, my father once commented, couldn't live without each other or with each other. I doubt whether they were worse than most families, except in their magnetic attachment to each other, for good and for ill. By the time we arrived in Manchester, they were all more established in their line, the cotton trade, and certainly far more prosperous than we. Yet, as in London, my mother assumed the role of emotional support for all of them. Though they tended to uphold their old posture of looking down on her, when they ran into trouble they all turned to her, acknowledging, almost against their will, her wisdom, experience, and sound judgment. They were still coping with the problems of adjusting to a lifestyle very different from that to which they had grown accustomed in Vienna. Both Robert and her younger sister were subject to bouts of depression through which she was able to sustain them. She would spend umpteen hours with them at those times, incidentally arousing my jealousy, for I felt I was getting less attention. When her youngest brother's marriage ran into difficulties, it was in her that his British wife confided and from her that she chose to seek advice. As my grandmother aged, my mother became the primary caregiver. This led to sharp conflicts with her siblings, who wanted to smother the old lady with constant vigilance (which she resented), whereas my mother favored granting her the maximum safe independence. I am not sure whether, in the long run, the family did not cause her more grief than joy, but she needed them as they needed her.

It was at this time, in the middle of the war when there was an acute shortage of physicians on the home front, that my mother had the possibility of re-entering her profession. A post was available as medical officer at a general hospital in Middlewich in central Cheshire. The distance from Manchester was not immense, at least not by American standards, some forty to fifty miles. But it was an awkward journey, involving a change of trains in Chester and buses at both ends, quite an adventure in the prevailing blackout. It was the gateway to a return to her professional work, for those physicians who served in British hospitals during the war were subsequently admitted to the British Medical Register with minimal formalities. It must have been a wrenching decision for her; her English was more than adequate by then and her medical competence beyond doubt, though she had been unnerved by her bad experience over the iodine. I don't think she lacked professional self-confidence; it was more that she questioned her ability, physically, to stand the long commute. Primarily, I believe, she put the interests of her husband and child above her own; having taken on the responsibilites of marriage and motherhood, she felt the obligation to fulfill her commitment wholeheartedly. In Vienna, with domestic help, the two sides of her life had been easily compatible; in this situation, it was not so. I was barely eleven then, and my father was not only struggling to build his practice and working very late part-time as an assistant to earn our livelihood, but also having repeated gallstone attacks. She knew well enough from him how trying and exhausting it was to get home at night in the pitch dark with an erratic and scant bus service. He had to come only from the other side of town; how could she cope with trains too? Circumstances argued strongly against accepting the position. Ultimately, at this crossroad, she chose to sacrifice her profession for us. Whether she ever regretted it, I don't know; she never mentioned it subsequently, perhaps because it was too painful a subject.

She hated having to designate herself as "housewife" when she got a British passport. She also intensely disliked cooking, and even more so the entertaining that was necessary to help build the practice. The customary form of entertaining in the Manchester Jewish community was to invite people to dessert. Everything had, of course, to be homemade, and as the food supply improved after the war, the offerings became increasingly elaborate, not to say ostentatious. I remember her coming home from one such gathering muttering in horror that there had been **eight** different sorts of cake. She began by having my grandmother come and show her how to bake cookies. My grandmother was puzzled by this request; to her it was so simple—you just took some flour, water, margarine, a pinch of salt, some sugar, perhaps an egg if one was available, and that was it. My mother progressed from cookies via "wartime recipes" out of the newspapers to an Austrian cookbook that had us in fits of laughter by its demands for ten eggs and a pound of butter. Entertaining was always a tribulation and source of anxiety to her; if her baking didn't turn out well, she would start all over again. She loathed it. My father and I gave advice and consolation as best we could; he would tell her that the guests came for the privilege of her company, not for the food, and once I suggested covering a failure with a meringue. By dint of perseverance, she came to manage reasonably well, but she was always nervous. Every now and then an old Austrian friend would come over from Leeds for Sunday lunch; she would do her very best, and was mortified by his verdict, "You tried hard." Cooking was never her metier.

Medicine was, even if she did not practice and never would. Our German physician passed on to her his copies of the *British Medical Journal*, and my father subscribed to *The Lancet*. These were her weekend pleasures, and if the mail was delayed, for instance at Christmas, her weekend was spoiled. Sometimes she lamented that there was too much biochemistry, which she couldn't follow despite her extensive background in chemistry. In many of her letters to me she wrote with excitement about articles she had read. Physician friends sometimes discussed their cases with her, asking her whether she had read anything new in a particular area. Being in practice, they obviously had far less time for careful reading than she did. At parties she gravitated toward the physicians who were talking shop. She would then be summoned to "come and join the ladies," whose conversation about their charwomen, plumbers, and recipes she found deadly dull.

My mother also maintained some contact with dentistry by working as my father's secretary. The post-war Health Service and socialized medicine brought a mass of paperwork in billing and in applying for permission to carry out certain complicated procedures. Most dentists groaned under the burden of having to attend to this evenings or weekends; there were then no trained medical or dental secretaries with the necessary expertise to handle the queries. My mother went to the office three afternoons a week to work at her desk, wearing a white coat, like a professional. She was paid a salary of £200 per annum, out of which in 1967 she bought me the diamond-studded Omega watch and matching ring that I still wear. On the not-infrequent occasions when an unreliable receptionist failed to turn up, she would drop all the housework and hurry to the office in response to my father's call. But she was careful not to break the law by actually performing any dentistry, not even on my father.

The 1950s and early 1960s were a reasonably good time for her. We had again achieved a level of security and respectability that enabled us to lead pleasant lives in modest style. My mother became a British citizen in 1947 consequent to my father's naturalization—history repeating itself. In our small car we explored England and the Continent. My mother didn't learn to drive, and tended to regard my father as "wild," but mostly she held her tongue. Once we took my grandmother out into the country on a Sunday afternoon; she was disappointed when we merely sat under a tree, and asked whether there wasn't a nice coffeehouse in the vicinity. My mother took vast pride in my successes in college. Her old pleasure in reading was given renewed impetus by my growing interest in literature and my subsequent commitment to a teaching career. She was far more widely read than I in English literature, going through Dickens, Thackeray, Trollope, George Eliot, and Ford Madox Ford, as well as more recent writers. She much preferred to read than to join local ladies' groups, which offered talks on fashion, diet, and child-rearing. Though she was much too tactful to say so, her level of intelligence was far above theirs. But she liked the circle of mainly Czech ladies who met for tea in town on Thursday afternoons, and on Saturdays she looked forward to her sister's visit despite the fact that it would only too often end tempestuously. She came to visit me several times in Belfast, getting me a telephone the first time, and a lovely little bright red refrigerator on a later occasion. Once we met in Dublin, where we had a glorious time, going to the theater, roaming the shops, and eating the freshest fish we had ever had. Compared to the active professional and social life she had led in Vienna, this existence in Manchester involved a considerable lowering of expectations, especially for her. But her feelings toward Vienna held bitterness rather than nostalgia; while she never ceased to mourn for her profession, she appreciated England's fine qualities, and was thankful that we had managed to escape together as a family.

By the mid-1960s her health was deteriorating rather mysteriously. The cough had recurred, intensified now into attacks of near suffocation that were terrifying to watch. Still, repeated chest X-rays showed no abnormalities. Her doctor commented, to her extreme annoyance, that he didn't know what she was coughing **for**, and asked whether her marriage was unhappy. She also developed chronic ulcers of several fingertips that would not heal. It became extremely difficult for her to write to me, yet she persevered, often asking my father to address the envelopes. Rarely was there a word of complaint, and then always with an apology appended. She read in *The Lancet* of an experimental, highly successful treatment discovered by a researcher in Bristol, which she wanted to try. Our family doctor thought twelve cases statistically insignificant. It was then that I engaged in an act that is, by British standards, not merely assertive but positively terrorist: I called the man in Bristol, who immediately agreed to see her provided she was formally referred. The simple treatment of a couple of pills a day worked wonders, saving her fingers from amputation.

However, her tendency to fatigue easily became aggravated, as did the insomnia that had been a bane ever since the refugee days. I took her to see a specialist in London, who asked us to wait, with a cup of tea naturally, while he went to read up in the library, and then advised doing nothing, since further steps would involve "nasty tests." What he kindly didn't say was that it would get her nowhere; in retrospect I realize that he recognized her disease and the lack of any effective treatment for it. Not long after, both her hands were swollen one morning. My father thought it might be an allergy to a detergent, but she said firmly that she now knew what she had; she recalled the illustrations in her medical textbooks. So she diagnosed her own disease, a highly atypical form of a rare autoimmune disease, scleroderma, that causes a hardening of the connective tissues throughout the body. Her primary concern was whether it was hereditary. All her symptoms, including the long-standing cough, were part of the syndrome. Changes in the lungs do not show up on X-rays until an advanced stage. For a few weeks she enjoyed a kind of honeymoon on steroids, but the benefit soon wore off. Scleroderma does not, in fact, respond to steroids, and still remains an enigmatic disease. It affects every part of the body: she had difficulty in swallowing, symmetrical ulcers on both ankles, a staphylococcal infection in her elbow, and, toward the end, spells of unconsciousness. Her case was so unusual that the leading expert at the Manchester Royal Infirmary wanted her to be hospitalized for research purposes. That was where her devotion to medicine stopped; she refused, and we promised to care for her at home. Even at the end, her instinctive judgment was sound; at home, after two years of extreme pain, she died a peaceful, physician-assisted death, with our full consent. She is buried in Southern Cemetery in Manchester with her mother and several of her siblings; the adjacent grave, which had been reserved for my father, was given to her sister after our emigration to the United States.

And They Lived Happily Ever After . . .

(LRF)

My mother's death, though we had expected it and wished her relief from her suffering, was a grave blow to us. It marked the end of the symbiotic threesome that had instinctively turned inward to each other for survival and security. My father, who in forty-one years of marriage had been separated from his wife only during his internment, was hit even worse than I. It was a shock to me to see this strong, resilient man so downcast through grief: suddenly he looked almost frail, lost and stranded without any sense of direction.

My pity for him began to draw me closer in response to his need. My primary attachment had long been to my mother, not least to mitigate the sadness that beset the second half of her life. By sharing my interest in literature, I was able to provide some substitute for her exclusion from her profession. My relationship to my father had been more complex. I respected and admired him; he was not only a wizard "fixer," he also had a lot of common sense and extraordinarily astute judgment of people and situations. But I also feared him a little; he was strict, not wanting to bring up a spoiled brat. Shortly before his death he pondered aloud whether he had been too strict and made me too disciplined a person. As a small child I would watch him do household repairs and offer to hand him tools; I remember telling him to call me "Georgie" so as to play the role of son to him. Later, in my early teens, we went out on our bicycles on Sunday afternoons. Once I accompanied him to a soccer match, but I found it boring and uncongenial.

My mother's death coincided with another major change in his life, his retirement. He had become an institution in the city, especially in the Jewish refugee community, through his charismatic personality, his honesty, and his kindness. His patients loved him for his wit and wisdom, and he helped them in many ways beyond their teeth. If one of them was unemployed, he would call other patients who ran big businesses and surely needed more hands. He had many eminent patients, including the Bishop of Manchester, some members of Parliament, and several leading lawyers, as well as visitors with toothaches who were referred to him by the city's leading hotel which was near his office, or the Hallé Orchestra, whose headquarters were in the same building. So he got to know the conductor, Claudio Abbado, and the then Prime Minister of South Africa, Mr. Streydom, who strenuously denied that his party was anti-Semitic. His receptionists stayed with him happily for years, generally until marriage and motherhood. One of them, Barbara Langer, became virtually one of the family, and still offers me a home in Manchester. He was active in the establishment of the Morris Feinmann House, a retirement home for Jewish refugees in the Didsbury suburb of Manchester, built with German reparation funds. He was invited to act as a consultant to the Dental Department of the Manchester Royal Infirmary, which was dedicated to the treatment of high risk patients, such as hemophiliacs, diabetics, and those with heart disease. His medical knowledge was very useful in this setting. After his retirement in 1969, patients would still come to our home to seek advice about their teeth, and to make sure that his successor, whom he had chosen with great care, was doing the right thing.

To help him overcome his depression after my mother's death I suggested we pay a visit to the United States in April 1970. His only surviving sibling, his younger brother Imre, had left Hungary in 1956 and was living in New York. I thought it would cheer him to see Imre again. Planning the trip gave him something to look forward to through the sad winter of 1969-1970; he got books about New York and maps which he pored over with such intensity that he could have become a guide or a cabbie by the time we arrived. I was glad to see him show an interest in something new. I had professional reasons for going. After publishing *Romanticism in Perspective* in 1969, I received several letters inviting me to give lectures if I was in the United States. At first I just laughed because the whole idea seemed presposterous, but when I had three such letters, I said: "Why not?" It was exciting to fly over Scotland, the North Atlantic, Greenland, the coast of Canada and Maine into Kennedy International Airport, where we finally spotted Imre in the huge crowd. We spent a week together in New York, sightseeing and catching a brief glimpse of such novelties as expressways, tollbooths, and a campus when I gave a lecture at the State University of New York Stonybrook, on Long Island. Then I took off for Dartmouth College, in Hanover , New Hampshire, the University of Wisconsin at Madison, Wisconsin, where I stayed for ten days with the Vinavers, and the University of Illinois at Urbana, while my father remained in the city. I was to join him there for the flight back to England, but Dartmouth asked me to make a detour to discuss the possibility of an appointment, so I returned to England two days later than he, via Boston.

That trip laid the foundations for our future. Dartmouth, about to go co-ed, was looking for women faculty; it was agreed that I should come visiting for the 1971–1972 academic year. About that time I was also approached by the University of Oregon in its search for a Director of the Graduate Program in Comparative Literature. The only thing I knew about Oregon was that it was the site of a major journal in my field in which I had published an article. We went to the library to look up

"Oregon" in the *Encyclopedia Britannica*, and read about its logging industry and heavy rainfall. The prospects for developing Comparative Literary Studies in Manchester already seemed rather dim by 1970, partly because of looming economic problems, and partly owing to a lack of real commitment on the administration's part. Even the name, let alone the concept, was unfamiliar then; mail would be addressed to Contemporary Literature, Contemplative Literature, or Comparative Literacy! In trying to establish an undergraduate major, I had become aware of the degree of resistance to this upstart discipline. I had got to know some American scholars at meetings of the International Comparative Literature Association, and was impressed by their openness to innovation and enthusiasm for the field. Clearly there were more interesting professional opportunities across the Atlantic than in England, where I feared I might grow stale and worn by the fight.

So began our drift into our only voluntary emigration. It had never crossed our minds to leave Manchester which had become—sort of—home, but now we began to contemplate moving on. My father was rather more reluctant than I; he thought of staying, perhaps retiring into Feinman House. Without openly admitting it, we were both motivated by the desire to leave the home where we had been three, and where our "two-ness" was painful. It was not hard to persuade my father to come with me, initially, after all, merely for a year. His brother and I were his sole relatives, and there was no point in his staying behind. His one condition was that he be allowed to "disappear" if he became a burden to me. He used to explain later that he was "in my daughter's luggage." Among my students he was as beloved as he had been with his patients. They saw in him a living piece of European social history, and were eager to listen to his stories. When he began to be introduced as "Dr. Furst's father," he took it with much better grace than I had when I had been introduced in Manchester as "Dr. Furst's daughter"; at age sixteen, I would assertively respond that I was "Lilian Furst."

The winter of 1970-1971 was devoted to filling out forms to get our visas. From the outset we went for immigration rather than visitor visas so that we could stay if it turned out to be the right decision. I was advised to apply as a laborer, skilled or unskilled, since the professional category was for all intents and purposes, closed. My father was sponsored by his brother. By the spring we had the maiden names of our grandmothers down pat. A three-month postal strike in England caused terrible delays, almost scuttling my plans to teach Harvard Summer School. Eventually we were each summoned to the U.S. Consulate in London to be questioned about our intentions to assassinate the President and to prove our literacy. We were examined, too, for TB, VD, head lice, nail fungus, and a host of other defects that might be hazardous to the United States. Understandably, this country had no desire to import more problems.

On 29 June 1971 we flew via Dublin to Boston, clutching our chest X-rays which we traded at Logan International Airport for green cards. We came from the usual 50–60 degree Northern England summer into a heat wave for which we were totally unprepared. Just to touch our British summer clothes made us hotter still. One of our first forays was to Filene's Bargain Basement to buy lighter and looser-fitting things. Our apartment didn't have air conditioning, and we were warned not to leave the windows open overnight. We would stroll down to the Charles River at nightfall, hoping to catch a breeze, not realizing that this, too, was dangerous.

After a week on the Massachusetts Bay Transport Authority my father declared that our "Hannibal days" had to end; we had to get a car. With an advance on my summer-school salary we bought the first vehicle we were actually able to drive in this country, an ancient Mercedes. The salesman told us to fetch it between 2 and 3 p.m., the quietest time of day, so that we could get it away safely. The car was far larger than any we had had in England, the traffic terrifyingly fast, the signs confusing to us, and, of course, we were driving on the "wrong side" of the road.

The daily teaching was arduous as I wrestled with such terms as "credit hours" and "pass/fail option," but even more arduous were our outings in the car. We invariably landed in the maze of Somerville's backstreets, and had a hard time making it back to our apartment on Concord Avenue and finding a space to park. My father painted "GB" on the plastic top of a potato salad container and fixed it to the back of the car in hopes of signaling why we were such erratic drivers. Our first directed expedition was to Brandeis University, of which we had heard in England; we sat there, wondering how we were going to find our way back. Later in the summer we went out to Cape Cod to have lunch with Harry and Elena Levin at their summer home in Wellfleet. We took a wrong turning and got stranded on a sandbank; when we finally arrived two hours late, oozing sand, the immaculate Harry took one look and said, "You need the bathroom."

Once we got used to the car and its quirks, it served us well. We explored New England during the year at Dartmouth, ventured north to Montreal and Quebec in the early fall, and in spring, south to Princeton, Philadelphia, Williamsburg, Charlottesville, Gettysburg, and Atlantic City, to see something of the country where we had meanwhile decided to stay. On these travels my father and I discovered that together we made one whole person; he had sharp eyesight, but was hard of hearing, while I had acute hearing and poor vision. So we were a good combination. Our shared adventures in "Samson," as the car had been named, fostered a greater closeness between us. We were also united by our awareness of how strange we appeared to others. At Dartmouth we were known as the English people—which made my father comment wryly that he had had to come to the United States in order to become English (in Austria he had been the Hungarian, and in England the Austrian). It was he, the elderly gentleman with the European accent, who was taken for the visiting professor. I was told that it couldn't be me because I was a *woman*. My first paycheck was made out to William Furst! I was constantly asked what the problems of a woman were at Dartmouth, and since I was used to mixed classes, I finally replied in some exasperation, "The lack of a good lady's hair-cutter in Hanover." Three days later I had a note from the President's wife recommending her Canadian haircutter in the neighboring town.

Looking back, I am amazed and frankly horrified at our rashness in coming to the United States. With a knowledge of America derived from books and movies, we were incredibly, dangerously ignorant of the most elementary facts. We were surprised, for instance, by the large measure of independence of each state which necessitated a driver's license, automobile registration, and insurance, not to mention taxes, wherever one was resident. We were also stunned by the sheer distances and by the extremes of hot and cold. Our worst risk was my father's lack of hospital insurance during the first five years. And we were repeatedly reminded of what he called "the timebomb in my stomach" by gallstone attacks which laid him low for days. We always carried cream of wheat and other diet foods, and sometimes we had to wait in a motel for him to recover sufficiently to move on. "Worrier" that I am, I still blanch now when I think back to what we did; that we got away with it was due more to good luck than to foresight.

Only our ignorance enabled us to set out for Oregon, 3,750 miles away, in a Samson so heavily laden that not another pencil could be squeezed in, according to my father. He was the master loader, working out scientifically how to cram the most into the vehicle by measuring its dimensions and those of our cases and boxes, and fitting things together like the pieces in a jigsaw puzzle. At the end, "orphan objects" awkward to pack, such as the telephone and the skillet, would be rammed in. Once an alarm clock went missing for a whole year because it stayed hidden in a nook not to be discovered until the next move. We had a stack of maps from the AAA as well as advice from an experienced friend, and we pretended to be very cool as we set out early one Sunday morning on the Massachusetts Turnpike West. By midday the car had broken down twice—a

radiator leak and a loose muffler. We limped along the
New York Thruway, chased off periodically by the
Highway Patrol, which ordered us to get the vehicle fixed.
No one in Utica or Amsterdam would touch a foreign car
on a Sunday. My father begged a piece of wire to hold the
muffler, and by evening we got to Syracuse. The
dealership there was willing to repair the car and started
work immediately. But by then I had grave doubts about
crossing the vast empty stretches of South Dakota and
Wyoming in that old thing, which clearly didn't want to
leave the East coast. Roaming about the lot while waiting,
I spotted a much newer used car for which we traded our
antique at a good price. Money was wired from the
Dartmouth Savings Bank, luggage switched, and we were
off in a roadworthy automobile. Only that evening in
Niagara did I realize that all our capital in the United
States had been sunk into that car. When we completed
the journey from the Atlantic to the Pacific by reaching
the spectacular Oregon coast, we felt a sense of
achievement.

That was the beginning of our "Wanderjahre," our
years of wandering and of apprenticeship in the American
educational system. We spent two years in Oregon before
going back east on an ACLS (American Council of Learned
Societies) fellowship. Then, for eleven years, we were
based in Texas at a new branch of the University of Texas,
which   was   designed   to   be   comparative   and
interdisciplinary, but didn't quite work out as planned. By
then I was wary of a hasty move, knowing that I had
much to learn. We learned the distinction between a
public and a private institution and the problems peculiar
to each. I was slowly initiated into the organization of the
profession by attending the conventions of the Modern
Language Association and the American Comparative
Literature Association. Having never been to a meeting
with multiple concurrent sessions, I was at first totally
bewildered. I held a series of visiting appointments: at
Case Western Reserve University in Cleveland 1978-1979,
at Stanford 1981-1983, at Harvard 1983-1984, and at the
College of William and Mary 1985-1986. I became very

restless, developing a kind of geographic curiosity that increased as we saw some of the wonders of this continent—Lake Louise in the Canadian Rockies, the Huntingdon Library and its grounds, as well as the Niagara Falls and the Grand Canyon. We enjoyed all the visiting positions once we got established; the planning and transitions, however, were fraught with anxieties: to find housing at our destination, to make adequate provision for the care of our home, to locate the post office, a physician and a dentist, to renew our drivers' license and automobile registration on time (we remained Texas residents), to make sure all insurances were paid and nothing vital lost in the mail, to continue supervision of my graduate students, and on our return to repair the house. Yet it was worth all the worry and effort, for it decisively broadened our horizons. These voluntary adventures were very different from the enforced ones of 1938-1945. But I wondered whether I would ever settle down, putting the washed winter sweaters away in a drawer rather than stowing them into a box for the next move.

My father really was a good sport about our peripatetic existence, although he would have preferred to stay put and cultivate his garden. He would joke in German that he had *"einen sehr bewegten Ruhestand"* ("a very mobile retirement"[1]). He said that if a soothsayer had foretold, as he lay in his cradle in a Hungarian village, that he would spend his old age jaunting about the New World in an old Mercedes, he would have laughed in disbelief. When I was invited to Case Western Reserve University in 1978, he looked up the distance from Dallas to Cleveland on the map and announced, "Twelve hundred miles. Three days. We can go."

I came more and more to appreciate not only his practical ingenuity but also his wisdom and support. In several of the places that we rented, the plumbing was left in better shape because he dismantled pipes and cleaned them out. A master at improvisation, he made collapsing furniture usable, at least temporarily, with a few nails, a backing of an old shirt, or simply by shoving a piece of luggage under a sagging chair. Above all, I could count on him for sound advice, although ultimately he left me to make my own decisions. I remember, for instance, how discouraged I was when we arrived in Cleveland and were unable to find housing. Warnings of the danger of mugging and vandalism demoralized me to such an extent that I was tempted to turn tail. It was my father who insisted that we stay, who calmed me down, and who taught me not abandon things in midstream. We had one of our happiest and most fruitful years there, although we did live in a weird place, a once-elegant old hotel that had become a retirement home for Christian Scientists—our rent included transport to church twice a week. I am afraid we desecrated the place by affixing a *mezzuzah* on the door of our apartment and by bringing in wine (We were careful to smuggle the empty bottles out discreetly.). Mostly we negotiated and compromised. I took care not to infantilize and dominate him as he grew older. The only absolute rule I ever forced on him was not to climb a ladder in my absence. When he wanted to fix the automatic garage door, I argued pragmatically that it would be more expensive and troublesome if he fell and cracked his skull than if we called a repairman. He saw the point.

Through our multiple moves, in addition to our status as strangers in the land, we formed an island of otherness wherever we went. Held together by the bond of interdependence, we learned to tolerate each other's idiosyncracies and to live happily side by side, although we were quite different in personality and interests. We came to complement each other well. But when I was down and he tried to restore my courage by telling me that I exaggerated problems, I would reply bitterly that he was "hitting me on the head with the hammer of his realism." Yet I too, would see his point, and be grateful for his ability to redress the inbalance by giving me a better sense of proportion.

Our relationship entered a new phase after he came close to dying in Dallas in 1981. This time the gallstone attacks would not subside. He could indeed claim a spot in the *Guinness Book of Records* as the world's champion gallstone maker, as he joked when it was discovered that he had made another "crop" of fifty or more stones wedged in the bile duct. Attempts to dislodge them by endoscopy resulted only in scepticemia. The surgery was deemed "no risk" since he would surely die without it, and might just survive with it. When I brought a wizened, dazed old man home from the hospital nine weeks later, I was told casually that he had become senile as a result of the shock of the infection. He was like a large, unwieldly baby that had to be washed and dressed. He didn't know what to do with his underpants, for instance, and when I told him to put one leg in one opening and the other in the other, his response was, "You can't teach an old dog new tricks." I argued that they were his old tricks. I grew alarmed when he informed me that he was 106 and a radish, thinking that perhaps he was demented. Yet he got my age right, and when he asserted a week later that he was 96, I began to grasp that he was speaking figuratively. His recovery was a long haul. When I found him one day holding a hose and watering the grass, I knew he had turned the corner. Another big milestone came when he picked up the *New York Times*, which had been beyond him for a while.

We had four very good years after that; two at Stanford, one at Harvard, and one back in Dallas. Endowed with a robust constitution, my father regained most of his strength within a few months. He decided to stop driving because he thought his reactions were slowing, but maintained his driver's license in case of an emergency. He used his privilege primarily to back the car out of the garage when it rained to get it washed. As his strength returned, the alleged senility disappeared. He read history and biography, and extensively in Holocaust studies. He would also poke his head into the literary theory I was then reading; however, he didn't care for it, maintaining that I could more readily learn and teach Japanese than this stuff. When we returned to Dallas in 1984 after an absence of three years, our house was literally falling apart. Through my dear friend, the late

Sally Ramsey, we found a professional handyman who became my father's pal. How these two communicated remains a mystery, for Chester spoke a broad Southern Black English, while my father's version was Austro-Hungarian-British. They used all sorts of sign language, and it worked well. I have a happy mental picture of my father smiling from ear to ear as he set off in Chester's pickup truck for the wholesale building supplies store. That was his idea of a treat. On Sundays we sometimes went out to a mammoth hardware store, as other people might go to a museum. My father would browse up and down the aisles, seeking advice from the salesmen. Despite his protest about not being able to teach an old dog new tricks, he became expert at adjusting our sprinkler system. I, in turn, learned to be less impatient; if he left drawers open or lights on, I would set things right without saying anything. He had become my child, as I was his. He once spoke to me, not long before his death, of the great sense of responsibility that had descended on him the day I was born and had never left him since.

His death was much more sudden than my mother's. There was some decline and a sort of sadness during his last winter. He sensed his approaching end, though with equanimity; he feared the process of dying, but not death, which he imagined as "a dreamless sleep." He suggested getting a dog as a companion for me to replace him. I had a really hard time persuading him to let me buy him a pair of shoes and some clothes. He didn't want them; he didn't need them. I persisted in ignoring these signals; I knew how tough he was, and I believed he would bounce back once summer came and we were in the easy climate of California, or "the Promised Land," as he called it.

Almost as soon as we got out to Stanford, he was hospitalized with a rare type of pneumonia, traced to bacteria from the bile duct. He was in and out of the hospital for five weeks before his death in mid-July 1985. In the end the gallstones got him. He is buried on a hillside south of San Francisco beneath a cedar and a palm tree, overlooking a flower patch. My burial plot is close to his.

I woke up the morning after his death gasping for breath as if I were drowning. In some ways, curiously, I was relieved; what I had long feared had now happened, and all I had to do was to continue to survive. It was a relief, too, not to have to worry about him. I caught myself glancing at my watch all the time, and now it was no longer necessary. No one was waiting for me. Friends openly or obliquely congratulated me on my freedom. I was frankly astonished, for I had never felt constrained. My father was singularly considerate, always urging me to go out with friends, and willing to eat his dinner whenever it suited me or to get his own. I would come back to find a light lit in the hall and him fast asleep in bed with his glasses on his nose and an open book in his hands. As I removed the book and glasses, he would wake briefly and say, "I waited for you, and I am glad you are back. Did you have a good time?" Now no one was waiting for me, and no one would notice if I never came back. This wonderful freedom is frightening.

I was directing a National Endowment for the Humanities summer seminar at the time of his death. My obligations to the twelve participants and the meetings that structured my days were welcome to me, although there were large blanks in which I was at a loss what to do with myself. I couldn't read; I xeroxed precious materials in the library for later use. I didn't know what to do in the morning when I got up; I wept because there was no one for whom to get breakfast. I lived like a recovering alcoholic, from hour to hour, from day to day.

I reached my nadir at the end of the summer when I flew back to Dallas. I was to spend 1985-1986 at William and Mary while a graduate student of mine and her husband housesat for us—no; I have to learn to say "me," not "us," for I am now in the singular. It was a shock to see our—my—house. Our furniture had been crammed into my bedroom to make way for a mass of alien objects: a huge television; a bird in a cage; a monstrous, garish sofa of the kind my father used to call "an elephant." I had lost not only my sole relative, but also my home. I had nowhere of my own. I felt that I had become one of the children I had seen on the train between Vienna and Cologne.

At William and Mary I lived in a large old house, graceful in its proportions but badly in need of repair. Fortunately, I was not responsible for maintenance; I had merely to call the Buildings Office whenever something leaked. In all that space I rattled loosely like the proverbial pea in a pod. People were extremely kind and hospitable to me, especially when they heard my English accent, which counteracted the suspect Texas license plates on my car. My father had told me that I would have to be more with other people, once he was gone, so I accepted every invitation. But I would sit in these strangers' houses and listen to their conversations and wonder what I was doing there, and why I wasn't quietly at home, as I used to be. The answer was that I had no home. On a visit to Boston, I developed an acute sinus infection. I sat on the plane back to New York with tears streaming down my face, to my neighbor's embarrassment. I wanted so much to crawl home, and I didn't know where it was—not the house with the bird in Dallas, and not that in Williamsburg.

At Christmas I drove over to North Carolina to visit a friend who had a well established home. Sitting by the fire in his cozy study, I was again seized by the desire for a home of my very own. When, shortly afterwards, I was offered a position at the University of North Carolina at Chapel Hill, I quickly bought a townhouse, almost on impulse, because I could visualize living in it. Constructed on an open plan design with cathedral ceilings and a greenhouse roof in the livingroom, it struck me as spacious enough to accommodate my Viennese furniture, yet sufficiently intimate not to overwhelm one person alone. The summer of 1986 was one of ingathering: things from Williamsburg, things from Dallas, and finally, shipped from England, the three big pieces of furniture which I hadn't seen for fifteen years. Just to see and smell them conjures up my past, back into my childhood. This home, the first I created entirely on my own, is the center of my life. It is the only place where I can read and write, and sometimes sleep, with a measure of tranquility. It is a haven, an enclave of the culture from which I come; the pictures, the rugs, the linens, the remnants of china and glass, and, of course, the books make a world that is mine.

Yet home is also nowhere, nonexistent, and ultimately unattainable except in this microcosm. The "southern corner of Heaven," as Chapel Hill proudly calls itself, is after seven years still quite foreign to me. My neighbors play golf and bridge, and walk their dogs, and talk with passion about "the game." I don't understand what matters to them any more than they understand what matters to me. Every time I go into the spa where I swim, it is like an anthroplogical expedition into an exotic land as I hear the talk of the State Fair and Halloween costumes in the locker room (Did you know that you can dye your hair orange with Koolaid?). In the great melting pot that this country is said to be, I have somehow not melted; on the contrary, I have become more myself, and thereby more other. I am not in exile from anywhere; the worlds I knew have gone, and I mourn their disappearance as I do that of the family I would have had. A student with bright red curly hair and glasses had a curious fascination for me, and it was some weeks before I realized that she reminded me of the cousin I last saw when I was six and she eight; she vanished in Treblinka.

Home is where my things are. Home is nowhere. Maybe home is beyond the grave; maybe in that yonder realm there will be release from otherness. I have dear friends, former students and colleagues, who form some tie to this world, especially when they need me. The telephone is indeed a lifeline. I float on the periphery, at home yet not truly so in Europe, Great Britain, or the United States. My geographical roots are shallow; only those created by the brand mark of the red "J" run deep into my being.

As My Father Used To Say

LIFE'S WISDOM

Anyone who tries to grab too much ends with nothing.

Anyone who has been bitten by a snake is afraid of a worm.

On worry: Leave it to the horse; he has a bigger head.

Cheap meat makes thin gravy.

A bashful beggar has an empty bowl.

Behaupten kann man alles. (Anything can be **maintained**).

Alles "zu" ist schlecht. (Everything "too," i.e., excessive, is bad.)

When you have something good, don't look for anything better.

Friendships need to be cherished and nurtured.

What to pack for a trip? "Half." **"Which** half?" "It doesn't matter; you can buy socks anywhere."

The easiest phrase to roll off one's tongue is "If I were you ..."

A poor sleeper always has an excuse for not being able to sleep—it's too hot; the bed is too hard; there's too much noise. — a good sleeper can sleep anywhere.

On thin women: you only get scratched on their bones.

A house gives you pleasure twice: the day you buy it, and the day you sell it. In between it's all trouble.

It's better to occupy the attic room in the best hotel than the best room in a minor establishment.

It's nice to grow old, but not so nice to be old.

Definition of being old: I don't even know **how** a computer works.

Economics-there are only two principles:
     a) The higher the interest rate, the higher the risk.
     b) Don't be greedy.

I once complained that I really didn't understand economics. "Neither do they," he answered.

Surgery is a last resort.

Minor surgery is surgery performed on someone else.

Fortunate indeed is the person who gets through life speaking just one language.

On his linguistic abilities: I stammer several languages fluently, and they all sound like Hungarian.

Writing a book is like distilling an ounce of uranium from wagonloads of pitch.

Irony (on which I was writing a book—LRF) is scratching your left ear with your right hand.

On deconstruction (in literary criticism): "Rape! Rape of the text!"

If I had been a German in 1942, what would I have done? Could I have risked the lives of my wife and child in order to help a Jew? Isn't that too much to expect of anyone?

It is foolish to speak of "Germans," "Arabs," "Jews," or "French." There are good and bad individuals everywhere.

Beware of fundamentalists and fanatics of any party or religion; they are dangerous.

No religion is intrinsically better than any other. They have different rituals, but they are all basically the same; their essence is humane behavior to others.

I live with two women who know today what I will be thinking in the middle of next week.

On our many moves: It's a pity God put down our bread in so many little piles in so many different places.

My father liked eating sweet things, and I once chided him for eating chocolate on the grounds that it was unhealthy. His answer was "It's Hershey's chocolate, and that is made up mostly of soybeans, so it's a vegetable, and healthy."

My father always told me to be willing to try new things at least once before deciding whether to accept or reject them. If you don't try new things, you find yourself left behind. His example was that if he hadn't tried new things, he would still have been making dentures of vulcanite, the only material available when he graduated from dental school in 1926. The vulcanite dentures became a family joke.

CENTRAL EUROPEAN WISDOM

A wine-producer, on his deathbed, summons his three sons to confide in them a great secret: wine can **also** be made of grapes.

A man is given an infallible recipe for turning stones into gold. It's very simple; all you have to do is to close your eyes, rub the stone between your fingers, and say 'Abacadabra.' But you musn't think of a crocodile while you are doing it, or else everything is spoiled. When he meets the man who has given him the instructions, he is asked how he got on. He said he couldn't stop thinking of crocodiles.

A man challenges his rival to a duel. It is duly and properly arranged, with seconds and pistols, for 6 a.m. the next day. The challenged man doesn't show up. He sends a cable: "Am delayed. You go ahead and shoot."

A teacher is demonstrating to a class that there is no life without oxygen. He puts a mouse under a bell-jar, and tries to extract the oxygen with a pump. To his embarrassment, the mouse keeps on running around. The teacher goes red in the face, turns to the class, and says, "This experiment will have to be repeated next time; this mouse is no good."

A frog falls into a bowl of cream and thinks he is about to drown. Panic-striken, he begins to lash about with his arms and legs. Before long, he realizes that he has some firm ground under his feet. He jumps onto the pat of butter he has made, surveys the scene, and after a rest to get his breath back, he takes a big leap over the moat of buttermilk to jump to safety.

The wealthy and famous Count Esterhaszy is seen on his estate wearing a terribly battered old hat. "Aren't you ashamed, you, Count Esterhaszy, to wear such a hat?" "No, it doesn't matter; everyone here knows who I am." Some weeks later he is seen in the fashionable spa, Karlsbad, wearing the same old hat. "How can you do this, you, Count Esterhaszy?" "It doesn't matter; no one here knows who I am."

A Hungarian count wants to have his dog taught to speak, and is willing to pay a high fee to anyone able to accomplish this feat. Everyone turns it down as an impossibility until a little Jew comes along who says he will undertake the task. He says it will take at least two years, and pockets the fee. His friends all think him crazy to take on the assignment. He himself is not worried; in two years, he argues, either the dog or the count might die.

To please his demanding mistress, a count wants to get her a bulldog with green spots. He will spare no expense to fulfil her wishes. Everyone refuses the deal until the same little Jew comes along, and agrees to supply the desired dog within a year. He needs a large advance, of course. His first step is to ask a friend: "what is a bulldog?"

A peasant has Communism explained to him. If you had fifty cows, he is asked, wouldn't you give twenty-five to your poor neighbor. "Yes," he replies. And if you had twenty cows, wouldn't you give him ten. Again, he says, "yes." And if you had ten cows, wouldn't you give him five? "Yes." And if you had two cows, wouldn't you give him one? "No, I have two cows."

A peasant receives a bill on which the word "ditto" appears several times. Neither he nor his wife understands the term. He makes a trip to town to find out its meaning. When he comes back, he tells his wife: "I am an idiot, and you are ditto."

A peasant was annoyed at the amount of hay his horse ate, and wanted to get it to work on less. So gradually he reduced the horse's rations a little every day, still managing to get the same work out of it. But just as he had accustomed the horse to working without hay, the wretched animal went and died!

A sign outside a shoe repair shop reads: "Shoe Repair: Laughing Gas." When the cobbler is asked what this means, he says that he had seen a sign: "Dentist: Laughing Gas." He liked the phrase, and so had it added to his own sign.

A circus act consists of two dogs, a big one who stands up and sings, and a little one who accompanies him on the piano. When someone tells the impressario it's amazing, and asks how were the dogs trained, he says: "It's even more amazing than you realize: the little dog is doing it all; he's a ventriquolist." (My father would say, when we traveled and moved, that I was the little dog in the family, and he the big one).

A man was very bothered by bedbugs that were biting him horribly. He went to a drugstore to find some remedy against them. The assistant recommended a powder and instructed him in its use. "You catch the bug, turn it over in your hand so that it is lying on its back, then you tickle its stomach and it will laugh. That's when you put the poison into its open mouth." The man pondered this advice and asked whether he couldn't squash or discard the bug once he had caught it. "Well, of course, if you insist on doing things the simple way..."

A middle-class Viennese father boasts of his daughter that she is so clever that she speaks only "per-verse." (Applies to contemporary literary criticism).

When he had been in medical school for several years and came home one summer for a vacation, his mother was asked by a neighbor what he was able to do by then. "Little things is what they start with," she replied, adding: "he can treat small children."

A medical student is asked in an oral exam to explain the mechanisms and processes of bone growth. After a long, embarrassed silence, he finally mutters that he has forgotten. The examining professor exclaims: "What a misfortune! The only person in the whole world who knew about the processes and mechanisms of bone growth, and he has **forgotten!**"

A medical student is asked in an exam in pharmacology what he would prescribe for a patient with a certain disease. When he has finished his list of medications, the professor shouts: "You unfortunate man! The patient has died, and you are in prison!"

When he was a medical student, my father went to visit a friend of his, a young engineering student, who was in hospital with a stomach ulcer. He found him running up and down stairs with a rucksack on his back. He had been told that this was part of the treatment for the ulcer.

JEWISH WISDOM

Jews don't have family trees, only bushes, because they don't stay anywhere long enough to grow deep roots.

When does a Jew eat an apple? When the apple or the Jew is rotting.

Don't forget: a Jew has a consulate in every city of the world.

An orthodox Jew goes to the rabbi for advice about the lack of space in the house for his ever growing family. The rabbi tells him to take the chickens into the house too. The man returns the following week to complain that it's like bedlam with the chickens running about amongst the children. The rabbi tells him next to take the goat in too. The man comes back almost in despair: the smell is unbearable. The rabbi then tells him to take the horse in as well, and though the man protests that this is impossible, the rabbi insists. Since he is the wise rabbi, the man takes the horse in, and the next week he is at the end of his tether—life can't go on like this. So the rabbi tells him to put the horse out again. The following week the man's face is wreathed in smiles as he exclaims, "The horse is out, it's wonderful!"

A marriage broker is looking for a wife for a very wealthy, rather elderly and extremely choosy bachelor. At long last he seems to be interested in a young woman, who is beautiful, gracious, intelligent (but not too much so), and submissive. The marriage broker, after a while, asks the man: "Well?" (in Yiddish: "Nu?") He answers, yes, he quite fancies her, but he wants one further condition fulfilled before proposing: he wants to see her in the nude. The marriage broker faces a delicate task in putting this to her parents: he argues that the man would indeed be a brilliant match, and it will all be totally proper, with the mother present. The parents are eventually persuaded, the mother conveys it to her daughter, and the viewing duly takes place. The marriage broker can hardly wait to get back to the bachelor, and again asks: "Nu?" The response is: "I don't really care for the shape of her nose." (This was told to me by way of consolation for my repeated failure for years to find a good position; in effect it is an allegory of the academic search process.)

In Austria in the 1930s the difference between a converted Jew and one who has not converted: when the converted Jew hears someone say: "dirty Jew," he turns round to see to whom the comment refers, and is surprised when he sees no one there but himself; the unconverted Jew doesn't need to turn round for he knows it refers to him.

A man writes a letter home from a concentration camp: "The accommodation is nice, the food good, the work light, and the guards friendly. My friend, Fischer, thought otherwise; his funeral took place yesterday."

An Israeli asks a Texan how big his estate is. The Texan thinks for a while, and then says: "If I get into my car early in the morning and drive all day, I still won't have reached the furthest limits of my estate by sunset." To which the Israeli replies: "What a lousy car you must have!"

A man emigrates to Israel at a time when there was a terrible shortage of consumer goods. As an immigrant he is allowed to bring in his personal property without import tax. He brings five refrigerators. The customs officials naturally ask him why he needs **five**. He answers that, keeping kosher, he has to have one for meat, one for milk, one for meat on Passover, one for milk on Passover—and the fifth is in case he ever wants to eat "trefe" (non-kosher—LRF).

On the beach in Tel-Aviv, a child sneezes. Its mother says "Bless you!" He sneezes again, and again she says: "Bless you!" He sneezes a third time. She exclaims, "Drat you! you have caught cold again."

A group of students from a very orthodox seminary are taken for a walk along the beach in Tel-Aviv, and they are astonished to see the young women lying there half-naked, sunning themselves. They ask their teacher what they are doing, and he tells them that they are "baking" themselves. "And unbaked they are no good?" they inquire.

In order to become a U.S. citizen I had to swear an oath of allegiance, which included the declaration that I was forswearing allegiance to all other states. I balked at doing this because I have a deep sense of gratitude and loyalty to Great Britain, which took us in, treated us well throughout the war despite the fact that we were technically Germans, and, above all, gave me an excellent education virtually for free. My father and I debated the issue half the night. His arguments were that I could remain loyal in my heart; that there would never be a war between Great Britain and the United States; that no one would want me, with my athletic abilities, to fight on their side, and so forth. None of this convinced me. Finally he said, "Whatever piece of paper you carry, you'll always be a Jewish refugee." I went and took the oath.

ANGLO-AMERICAN WISDOM

During the war in England a crate of sardines is sold on the black market from one dealer to another, each of whom makes a nice profit. Eventually they are bought by the owner of a restaurant, who opens one can after another, and finds them all gone bad. He makes an angry protest to the man who had sold them to him; he expresses amazement that anyone had actually thought of **eating** the sardines: "they are for making a profit with!" (This applies to scholarly books, which are not fit to be read, and serve only to get tenure).

Mr. Smith dies and goes to heaven. At the pearly gates he is told that he isn't expected, his dossier hasn't arrived. After a long search, he is directed to hell, but his dossier isn't there either, and he is sent back to heaven. Much puzzlement, until someone asks him whether by any chance he was a patient of Dr. X. He says, "yes." "That explains it: Dr. X has this habit of dispatching his patients before they are due."

A young doctor pays a house call to a family where both small children have fallen sick. He spends quite some time examining them before he comes to speak to their mother: "They both have a fever; they both have a sore throat; they both have spots;   they both have the same."

A firm wants to recruit a salesman to sell computers in South America. The qualifications are: knowledge of Spanish and Portuguese, experience of salesmanship, and familiarity with computers. Several candidates are interviewed, and all are found wanting. Finally, another one comes along. "Do you know Spanish and Portuguese?" "No." "Have you experience of salesmanship?" "No." "Familiarity with computers?" "No." He is given the job: he is the ideal person because he has "an open mind." He also happens to be the nephew of the chairman of the company.

On the climate of the United States: You either get frozen or fried, and in some places, both.

A South African lady, whom we met through friends, invited my father to come for tea to meet her mother, who was on a visit to this country. Although never at all shy, he was curiously reluctant to go, and kept putting it off. Finally, he declared that he really didn't want to go. I couldn't understand why. "She wants to marry my green card," he blurted out.

One of my students in Dallas was the wife of the senior minister of the largest and wealthiest church there. She did all she could to win favor. When I went away to Europe for two weeks, she sent one of the eleven junior ministers to visit my father. The young minister apparently tried to convert my father to Christianity, but (according to my father's account) after an hour he beat a hasty retreat for fear that he himself would end up by being converted to Judaism.

In the summer of 1976 we rented a condominium in Vail, Colorado. We went for a long walk every morning, resting for a while on a shady bench by the golf course. Ex-President Ford used to come by to play golf, preceded by two secret service men. They became very suspicious of us (I was reading Dostoyevsky's *Brothers Karamazov*), even more so after we had told them, in response to their questioning, that we came from Dallas. And we obviously had foreign accents. One day they took a photograph of us, which greatly amused my father: "Now we have an FBI file!" he said, though we were still nameless to them. Finally, Ford jumped from his golf-cart and came over to us, held out his hand, and said: "Hi, I'm Gerry Ford. Who are you?" I gave what I thought would be an appropriate answer: "I am the newest American citizen, and haven't voted yet." My father stood there proclaiming: "I am British. Wonce British, always British"—in his strongest Hungarian accent.

NOTES

COMING TO VIENNA (DF)

1. The universities had open admission for anyone who had passed the school leaving examination, and then operated by a process of selection of the fittest. LRF

2. The numerus clausus was the law limiting the enrollment of Jewish students in Hungarian universities to certain small quota.

3. With the break-up of the Austro-Hungarian Empire after 1918 and the creation of separate states, my parents became Hungarian and Polish citizens respectively. As such, they were not entitled to practice in Austria, nor in Hungary or Poland, where their qualifications had become "foreign." My father's hometown of Sopron was near the border and had a plebiscite to decide whether to join Hungary or Austria. In this secret plebiscite the voting papers for Hungary were of cardboard, those for Austria of the thinnest cigarette paper! My father discovered later that under the Treaty of Versailles he would have been entitled to opt for Austrian citizenship

within the first two years, but by the time he heard of this, the option had expired. On both my parents' large, impressive Latin medical diplomas there is a clause stamped in red saying that under the new law they were debarred from practicing in Austria. LRF

4. "A Superfluous Man" was the title my father gave to his autobiography. LRF

5. Dentistry was a special field of medicine in Austria for which one qualified by postgraduate training after obtaining the M.D.

6. It was at that time preferable but not requisite to hold a diploma in dental surgery before setting up a practice so that these two could begin with minimal training. LRF

7. A "cutaway" is the colloquial British term for the top (jacket) part of formal men's "morning dress." The "tails" at the back were cut away to turn it into a jacket.

VIENNA (LRF)

1. See my essay "Born to Compare" in *Building a Profession: Autobiographical Perspectives on the Beginnings of Comparative Literature in the United States*. Ed. Lionel Gossman and Mihai Spariosu. Albany: SUNY Press, 1994.

FLIGHT FROM VIENNA (DF)

1. This story was passed on to me by my father when I felt despondent about the progress of my research. I always tell it to my graduate students and colleagues. It has quite caught on in my circle. Indeed, I have a collection of ten frogs of different kinds given to me by those with

whom I shared the story to remind me of the need to keep going. LRF

2. I still have two gold watches bought at that time. One of my father's patients, Mr. Upprimi, told him that the Nazis were about to take over his business. He still had two gold watches for sale. Since we couldn't take money out of the country, my father bought them as movable goods. So I became the proud owner of a delicate little Omega watch, which I wear to this day, over fifty years later. When spare parts were no longer available, I had it retorfitted to a quartz battery mechanism because I couldn't bear to part with it. My father's Movado pocket watch sits in my safe deposit box: relics of a former existence. LRF

3. When my father became an Austrian, he was designated a citizen of Burgenland, one of Austria's southern provinces. To be a Viennese citizen was a distinction in that society so dichotomized between the prestigious capital and the rather despised redneck "provinces." LRF

4. "Undertaker" is the English term for mortician. LRF

BRUSSELS

1. So am I. Now called the Association of Jewish Refugees in Great Britain, it runs pleasant retirement homes and offers social services to the former refugees in their old age. The homes were built with German reparations funds and are now maintained by individual contributions. LRF

2. We also bought some gorgeous peaches at the store that I had admired so much my parents were almost afraid that I might press in its display window. LRF

LONDON (DF)

1. Indeed, I still have them in a place of honor in my living room. We called them our "adopted ancestors" and on our year-long visits to various universities in the United States, they were always among the few personal possessions we took along: symbols of our stormy past and, in a sense, homage to those who had not come into the present. LRF

2. A "guinea" was one pound and one shilling. Fancy stores and fancy physicians charged in guineas rather than pounds. LRF

CHERTSEY (LRF)

1. In Britain during War time, clocks were moved doubly to save electricity. So we had "summer time" in winter and "double summertime" in summer.

2. A traitor who serves as the puppet of the enemy occupying the country. After Vidkung Quisling (1887-1945), head of the State Council of Norway during the German occupation (1940-1945).

ISLE OF MAN (DF)

1. The man to whose scent I had objected as a small child in Vienna. LRF

2. Guy Fawkes is still celebrated in England on 5 November with effigies that are burned in bonfires. Children collect "A penny for the guy" for weeks beforehand. It is roughly the equivalent of Halloween in the United States. The historical origins, in an alleged plot to blow up Parliament in the seventeenth century, have largely been forgotten. LRF

3. The worst night in the bombing of London.

MANCHESTER(LRF)

1. In Britain, only Jewish clerics with special qualifications were granted the title "Rabbi"; others were simply referred to as "ministers" and addressed as "Rev."

MANCHESTER(DF)

1. Austrian ironic saying in dialect. LRF

2. Chancellor of Austria. LRF

AND THEY LIVED HAPPILY EVER AFTER (LRF)

1. The phrase works better in German: *Ruhestand* (retirement) means, literally, "state of rest." Thus the paradox of a very "mobile state of rest."